BREAKING CYCLES OF VIOLENCE

CONFLICT PREVENTION IN INTRASTATE CRISES

Janie Leatherman, William DeMars
Patrick D. Gaffney, and Raimo Väyrynen

KUMARIAN
PRESS

Breaking Cycles of Violence: Conflict Prevention in Intrastate Crises

Published 1999 in the United States of America by Kumarian Press, Inc.,
14 Oakwood Avenue, West Hartford, Connecticut 06119-2127 USA.

Production and design by The Sarov Press, Stratford, Connecticut.
Index by Linda Webster.
The text of this book is set in Adobe Garamond.

Printed in Canada on acid-free paper by
Transcontinental Printing and Graphics, Inc.
Text printed with vegetable oil-based ink.

∞" The paper used in this publication meets the minimum requirements
of the American National Standard for Information Sciences—Permanence of
Paper for Printed Library Materials, ANSI Z39.48–1984.

Library of Congress Cataloging-in-Publication Data
Breaking cycles of violence : conflict prevention in intrastate crises
/ Janie Leatherman . . . [et al.]
p.   cm.
Includes bibliographical references and index.
ISBN 1–56549–092–4 (cloth : alk. paper). — ISBN 1–56549–091–6
(pbk. : alk. paper)
1. Political violence—Prevention. 2. Conflict management.
3. Ethnic relations. I. Leatherman, Janie, 1959–.
JC328.6.B725   1999
303.6'9—dc21   98–52833

03   02   01   00   99   5   4   3   2   1   First Printing 1999

CONTENTS

LIST OF TABLES

PREFACE

RETOOLING EARLY WARNING AND PREVENTIVE DIPLOMACY TO MANAGE INTRA-state conflicts has become the focus of policy debates in the 1990s. These conflicts are often inter-communal and highly emotionally charged. Structural and cultural factors, accompanied by crises of governance, and in the worst cases the collapse of the state, fuel their escalation. The objective of this study is to develop analytical tools and strategies on how the international community (governments and international organizations, NGOs), local leaders, and national elites can thwart the outbreak of violence.

This project began as a collaborative endeavor between Catholic Relief Services–USCC and the Joan B. Kroc Institute for International Peace Studies, the University of Notre Dame, supported by a grant from the United States Institute of Peace. Dr. Nick Mills, former Director of Policy and Planning for Catholic Relief Services (CRS), along with Dr. Joseph G. Bock, former Director of Development Education for CRS, with the support of Professor George Lopez, former Acting Director of the Kroc Institute, spearheaded the development of the project. In the early 1990s, like many other relief and development NGOs, Catholic Relief Services began raising questions about how it might restrategize its involvement in crisis situations to better serve its core mission, while also increasing its awareness of, and possibly, strategies for, preventing and mitigating conflict, should such additional tasks prove compatible. Thus, the enhancement of training for preventive action was also a central objective motivating the project.

The Kroc Institute assembled a four-member research team, which draws on expertise in cultural anthropology, conflict resolution, multilateral diplomacy and policymaking (including in the NGO community), as well as European and African regional area studies. Professors Raimo Väyrynen, Regan Director of the Kroc Institute, and expert in European security and regional conflict resolution, has overseen the project from the outset, along with Janie Leatherman, specialist in conflict resolution, multilateral diplomacy and conflict prevention in the European context, who has handled the organizational work. She has liaised with Catholic Relief Services and had the main responsibilities editing and preparing the manuscript for publication. While Väyrynen and Leatherman's joint efforts produced the conceptual framework of the study, Professor Patrick Gaffney and Dr. William DeMars' critical reading of earlier drafts proved invaluable for strengthening the conceptual foundations and policy relevance of the study. Indeed, the integration of the whole book has been greatly facilitated by regular and frank discussions, as well as critical comments also on the empirical and policy implications of the study by all team members.

The conceptual framework is laid out in Part I of the book. Leatherman authored Chapter 1 and Väyrynen Chapter 2. They lay out the main conceptual issues and approaches to early warning and preventive action. Väyrynen is the lead author of Chapter 3, to which Leatherman also contributed. This Chapter presents an analysis of the background causes of intrastate conflict. Leatherman authored Chapter 4, which assesses the impact of background causes on the dynamics of escalation, and the implications for the early warning of conflict. Väyrynen is the author of Chapter 5, which evaluates the effectiveness of different instruments of preventive diplomacy, including military, economic, and political tools.

Part II of the book presents two empirical case studies, Burundi (Chapter 6) and Macedonia (Chapter 7), which test and integrate the conceptual aspects of the study. Rev. Patrick Gaffney, CSC, associate professor of anthropology and a Middle East and African specialist, wrote the Burundi case, while Leatherman did the Macedonia case. Part III of the book presents the policy recommendations which emerge from the conceptual framework and the findings of the case studies. Dr. William DeMars, specialist in policymaking and information flows in the NGO community, and on NGO intervention in Africa, develops these in Chapter 8.

The two case studies on Burundi and Macedonia were chosen by the research team in consultation with Catholic Relief Services. These two cases presented an opportunity to evaluate the involvement of NGOs (including CRS) in early warning and conflict prevention as part of a larger international diplomatic effort. These cases also represent two of the most prominent examples of contemporary efforts at preventive diplomacy—though the efforts in Burundi are more accurately characterized as "post-conflict" preventive action. The two case studies illuminate the problems and possibilities of their particular conflict setting, while also providing a window on the kinds of challenges the international community faces in general to achieve good results through early warning and preventive action.

The case studies were buttressed by the researchers' field work in the country and neighboring region, thus permitting extensive contacts with the conflicting parties, nonparticipant civilians, as well as local and international NGOs, government officials, and international diplomats. In addition to two years residence while teaching in Jinja, Uganda, during 1992–94—which familiarized Patrick Gaffney with the Great Lakes region of Africa—he also made a visit to Burundi and Kigali, Rwanda, in March 1995 to prepare the case study. He was hosted in Burundi by the local office of Catholic Relief Services, directed by Country Representative James O'Connor. He had discussions with leading figures in local church organizations, human rights organizations, university scholars and students, journalists, political and ecclesiastical leaders, international NGOs, and officials of various organs of the United Nations operating in Burundi. Professor Gaffney also visited two provincial centers, Bururi and Gitega in the interior. In Kigali, Rwanda, his consultations included meetings with CRS personnel, various UN representatives, and church leaders. He made two additional trips to the region, including in the summer 1995, visiting several of the Rwandan and Burundian refugee camps, including those supervised by UNHCR (United Nations High Commissioner on Refugees) in western Tanzania where both Rwandans and Burundians are lodged. He also participated in a UN-sponsored delegation to Burundi in April–May 1996, to assist with on-site investigations of human rights violations and prepare for further measures leading to possible international intervention.

Leatherman's field work on the Macedonian case involved two research trips to the South Balkans region during 1995. These visits permitted extensive contacts with the members of the various ethnic communities in Macedonia, government officials, diplomats from European organizations, the United Nations, and NGOs, among others. Catholic Relief Services, under the direction of Country Representative Julie Chen, provided valuable logistical support for her visit to Macedonia in March 1995. Before arriving in Skopje, she met with officials of the Office of the High Commissioner on National Minorities, of the Organization for Security and Cooperation in Europe, and the Director of the Foundation for Inter-Ethnic Relations, in The Hague. During December 1995, Professor Leatherman made a second visit to the South Balkans as a consultant to the Center for Preventive Action's South Balkan working group, of the Council on Foreign Relations. This mission also visited Belgrade, Serbia, Pristina, Kosovo, Skopje, and other cities in Macedonia, and Tirana, Albania, meeting with the presidents and other government officials, as well as opposition leaders of these countries. They also had extensive discussions with academics, journalists, US diplomats, local human rights activists, NGOs, and representatives from the international community.

This research project with CRS has also benefitted, at the encouragement of the United States Institute of Peace (USIP), from collaboration with the World Peace Foundation in Cambridge, Massachusetts, which also received a grant from the USIP to examine the role of various indigenous and international NGOs in early warning and conflict prevention, representing different regions of the globe. The conference, "Non-Governmental Organizations (NGOs), Early Warning, and Preventive Action," which was held in Cambridge in April 1995, thus presented a useful opportunity for the Kroc Institute researchers to test a preliminary draft of the conceptual framework of this study before a wider NGO audience, and also to deliver preliminary reports on the case studies in development.

The research team expresses its appreciation in particular to Dr. Nick Mills and Dr. Joe Bock, whose vision spurred this project forward at its inception, and to Dr. Geraldine Sicola, former Director, Emergency Coordination, of Catholic Relief Services, and her assistant, Andrea Scharf, for their guidance, assistance, and feedback on drafts of the book manuscript throughout its development. Special thanks are due to Dr. Sicola for facilitating logistical arrangements and documentation which proved of special value in the preparation of the field research and development of the case studies.

This publication was prepared with financial support from the United States Institute of Peace through a grant to Catholic Relief Services–United States Catholic Conference Incorporated. The opinions, findings, and conclusions or recommendations expressed in this publication are those of the authors and do not necessarily reflect the views of the United States Institute of Peace or official statements, positions, or views of Catholic Relief Services-United States Catholic Conference Incorporated.

Professors Gaffney and Leatherman express their appreciation to the many individuals who so generously shared their insights, as well as time, and thereby greatly expedited their work in the field, and benefitted them significantly in the preparation of the case studies. Professors Väyrynen and Leatherman offer special thanks to Dr. Juha Auvinen, University of Helsinki, for his suggestions on an early paper outlining the study's conceptual framework. Professor Leatherman also expresses her gratitude to Professors Victor Friedman, University of Chicago, and Patricia Davis, University of Notre Dame, for their helpful comments on an earlier draft of her Macedonian case study, and also to graduate students of the Kroc Institute's International Peace Studies program, for their careful reading of early drafts of the manuscript.

The research team extends its deep appreciation to the United States Institute of Peace for generous support of the project. They also extend a special thanks to Sandy Krizmanich, for her competent management of the project's budget, and to Patricia Lynne, Marguerite Holleman, and Elizabeth Grandin, whose technical assistance has proved invaluable in transforming the team's joint efforts into a book manuscript. The team is particularly grateful to Hal Culbertson for his significant editorial help in different phases of the project. The individual members of the research team are, however, solely responsible for any of its shortcomings.

July 1998

1

CONCEPTUAL FRAMEWORK

1

THE PRIORITY OF ACTING PREVENTIVELY

The Discontinuities of the New World (Dis)Order

INTRASTATE CONFLICTS HAVE BECOME A PRINCIPLE THREAT TO PEACE AND SECURITY in the late twentieth century (Wallensteen and Sollenberg 1995). They have led to widespread destruction, collapsing states, environmental devastation, regional instabilities, growing numbers of refugees and internally displaced, and a high loss of civilian lives. But the international community is ill-equipped to overcome, much less avert, these disasters. The objective of this study is to focus decision makers' attention on how to prioritize and target local and international resources on societies' "breaking points" to keep closed the gates of war. The study addresses questions about where, when, and how the international community working together with local communities can proceed. Which conflicts merit attention? Which are likely to escalate and in what ways? How soon? Do the same criteria hold from one case to the next, from one continent or culture to the next? How can we increase the resilience of societies to violence? How can problems with building a consensus on the assessment, and then organizing and coordinating collective action, be overcome?

To be sure, there are substantial barriers to collective action. For the most part, the international community has been reactive rather than proactive on the matter of internal conflicts. Unilateral state actions and responses to them have been the primary pattern of international relations, while collective actions to enforce peace and security have been undertaken only in the case of gross violations of sovereignty and other pivotal international norms. In general, the pragmatic politics of traditional statecraft served to discourage early actions to identify intrastate problems and prevent their escalation into risky national and international behavior. Traditionally, collective international efforts have, at best, tried to manage the consequences rather than causes of violence and repression.

A main problem is that intrastate conflicts seem to require very different methods of early warning and prevention than traditional interstate confrontations. In interstate conflicts, preventive actions are targeted at the opposing state to deter or persuade it from behaving in an unacceptable manner, although these actions may also be intended to drive a wedge into the ranks of the adversary thus weakening its capabilities and determination. In intrastate conflicts the sanctioning actor has to choose sides and decide whether it prefers to punish the government and support the opposition or the other way around. The legal and political conditions for intervention also greatly differ in inter- and intrastate conflicts. Due to the norm of sovereignty and the greater complexity, and thus unpredictability of civil strife, the hurdles to external intervention into intrastate crises are higher. Moreover, the international community has lacked effective institutional machinery to enforce internal peace, making multilateral actions for early warning and prevention less likely than in interstate conflicts threatening international peace and security.

Nevertheless, the multilateralization of early warning and prevention of internal conflicts is now in its early stages. Conflict early warning and prevention are being introduced in the United Nations globally and the Organization for Security and Cooperation in Europe (OSCE) and the Organization of African Unity (OAU) in Africa regionally. These developments are an indication of the new importance attached to avoiding violence and ensuring compliance with international treaty obligations and norms. The weakening of traditional assumptions about the absolute nature of state sovereignty coupled by the strengthening of international norms and standards which protect individual and group rights and promote democracy have reduced impediments both to the development of collective preventive action and intervention in the internal affairs of nation states. Frequent failures of states and entrenched domestic violence have prompted the international community to develop responses, however inadequate, to restore order and stability. Thus, a new challenge is to develop a preventive international order which can augur the outbreak of violent conflicts and deal with their intrastate nature (see especially Evans 1993).

Although the number and complexity of UN peacekeeping operations expanded considerably immediately after the end of the Cold War, the international community's capacity for early warning and preventive measures in intrastate crises is still very limited. The limitations stem from the structural legacies of the Cold War restricting multilateral actions, while the growing number of interventions is a reflection of the proliferation of deadly internal conflicts. The structural view suggests that the lack of early attention and efforts to extinguish conflicts before violence erupts is due to structural defects in international cooperation. The alternative perspective is more optimistic. It implies that national governments and international organizations are, in principle, able to extinguish conflicts before they escalate, but have failed recently because action needed to limit and manage the overload of violent cases has taken precedence over prevention elsewhere. Or the situation may be as George Soros (1996, 77–78) bluntly points out: there is no general desire to prevent conflict.

Both of these accounts are inadequate in that they can justify inaction and fail to provide any sound policy advice. Instead, one should stress the imperative to develop new and more effective means of inventive diplomacy to identify and prevent the use of military force. Novel trends in international relations, such as the movement towards multi-polarity as well as the emergence of new actors and issues, provide an expanding political space for the resort to early actions to forestall mass killings. Despite claims to the contrary, the international community is learning from such cases as Bosnia, Cambodia, El Salvador, and Rwanda, inclining toward comprehensive, long-term, peace building solutions. We are, however, still far from having the capacity to keep all conflicts latent. In fact, conflicts regularly become violent and even intractable, and can be settled only with exhausting political efforts. Successful preventive action to defuse, manage, limit, and terminate violence is therefore a high priority; it helps to keep international relations peaceful and avoid considerable human, political, and economic costs.

Despite the weight of these moral imperatives and pragmatic considerations, early warning and conflict prevention face several major challenges, including problems of factual and political validity, consensus building, and the organization of collective action. First of all, there is the question of the analytical validity of different methodological approaches, and relatedly, the abilities of various actors (the academy, think tanks, intelligence agencies, the military, and the business community) to perform effectively in forecasting crises. There need to be tools for identifying the background causes of conflict, and understanding the ways they fuel escalation. Computerized approaches based on a myriad of indicators have the advantage of providing comprehensive information on deteriorating conditions. However, in the absence of context specific information, policymakers may have little indication of what actions are most needed to contain the (impending) violence, and how they should be deployed to have the maximum peace building effect.

Second, there are various hurdles to overcome in developing consensus for prevention, whether action is uni- or multilateral. Unilateral measures may be easier to launch, since they only require consensus within the government of one country. But the call for ameliorative actions requires consensus among policymakers on dangers which have not yet become acute. These appeals compete, often unsuccessfully, with other more pressing government business and concerns for attention. The difficulty of gaining even mid-level policymakers' attention is confounded by the fact that public pressures to act do not accumulate in the pre-escalation stage to the same extent as in later phases when violence has become manifest.

The barriers to multilateral action are similar, if not also more complex. Building an international consensus requires policy coordination on at least two levels: internationally among political leaders as well as within each of their governments and bureaucracies (cf. Putnam 1993). To the extent national assessments of the seriousness of a given conflict situation and the appropriate political strategies vary widely, they will yield only a limited political basis for collective action.

Remedies to collective action have traditionally depended on the effective coordination of preventive national responses, the rise of a leading power, or the establishment of a group of countries ("a concert") to mobilize and coordinate international actions. However, in the post-Cold War context, non-governmental organizations (who are often organized and operate transnationally) have increasingly assumed a more active role in the early identification of conflicts, establishing links with national governments and international organizations to alert them of the need for action (in which NGOs themselves often participate). Among these state and non-state actors involved in early warning, there already exists a dynamic, yet regulated competition both for organizational status and recognition. If channeled constructively, this can help overcome barriers to effective early action. However, in most fields, the relations of NGOs both with governments and local civil societies are still tenuous and their mutual cooperation limited (Bennett et al. 1995). Thus, the contributions and tremendous progress of the NGO community in recent years notwithstanding, in acute crises, the onus still remains ultimately on governments to organize effective national actions and coordinate them internationally to hinder the outbreak and escalation of violent conflicts and to provide resources for humanitarian relief.

In addition to problems of political validity and collective action, efforts at the early warning and prevention of deadly conflicts face another challenge: the exercise itself is politically sensitive, in part because the actors usually have quite different views on the conflict. Since they stand to gain or lose depending on how the issues are framed, the various actors will often try to manipulate early warning and prevention to serve their own interests. This "contaminates" early warning information by obscuring the real roots of the conflict, undermining its prevention, or redistributing the political blame and praise. For example, Ezell (1992, 93–94) shows that early news reports of the 1988 massacres in Burundi often were shaded by the government's line that exiled Hutu had returned and incited their kinship to massacre Tutsi. Such news served as a conduit for the Burundi government claims that its army showed remarkable restraint. Allowing reporters access to affected areas, and admitting such "bad news" as 5,000 dead, allowed the government to gain some credibility, and also minimized the atrocity when other sources, such as medical and church workers and diplomats estimated much higher numbers of casualties.

In reality, politics cannot be avoided in the warning and prevention of violent conflicts. One detects, nevertheless, an assumption of political neutrality underlying statistical and other "remote" methods of early warning. Although the analyst apparently avoids any practical involvement in the dispute by such methods, the parties involved are not likely to perceive the effort to provide generalized advice to relevant actors on the possibility of violence as politically neutral. Of course, in *conflict prevention* such a detached approach by the policymaker is impossible as it requires practical action to deter, dissuade, or persuade the parties to a conflict from using force or escalating it. Politics is not, however, only a negative factor; on the contrary, the international community can use it positively to prevent and extinguish violence.

Scholars, the media, intelligence agencies, as well as governments, international organizations and local community members can all make contributions to the early warning and prevention of conflicts. However, their capacity to do so varies, as does their access to information. Local actors can empower their own communities for positive change in ways that may prove more culturally appropriate, and hence also sustainable (Lederach 1995). However, they may face considerable personal risks as the conflict escalates or government repression intensifies. In addition to problems with the validity and reliability of information and the degree of openness in its use, there are also questions about how these actors' monitoring and reporting capabilities can be integrated with each other. While a universal or global system of early warning is unlikely to emerge, there is nonetheless a need to cast as wide a net as possible in the initial information gathering phase. Early warning and conflict prevention are not "objective actions," as much as informed and valid judgments of the situation.

As we shall see further in Chapter 2, early warning and prevention are also closely linked activities, because of the interdependence of the actions. Making sure the two activities work well together is an important prerequisite for at least two reasons: (1) targeting preventive action effectively depends on the quality and timeliness of the early warning information; and (2) in some instances, early warning serves preventive functions itself. To be effective, early warning and conflict prevention initiatives must also meet short-term and longer-term objectives. Over the short term the task is to contain and reverse escalation. The local parties have the primary responsibility for stopping the conflict and its escalation. The United Nations and other international organizations should help them in this task.

At the same time other initiatives must also target background causes. Development and humanitarian aid can ameliorate structural injustices and stabilize the society, but they can also exacerbate the existing differences and thus become a source of conflict. Because they are asymmetrical, foreign aid and intervention of third parties can add new political dimensions to power disparities, which the antagonists are likely to exploit. To avoid this risk, the donors should carefully assess the impact of economic aid on the regional, ethnic, and other conflicts in the recipient country. They should even carry out ethno-political assessments on the impact of external flows into the country (Reinicke 1996; Esman 1997).

The conflict management literature has traditionally focused on transforming conflict escalation by influencing the means the parties use. However, preventive action can target the other dimensions of internal conflicts, including social and material disparities, cultural tensions, and institutional failures of government. Which dimension merits attention first is a matter of political judgment, and also a question of time. Obviously, the imminent threat of the spillover of conflict, or the escalation of violence requires quick responses to contain them, and cannot wait for the longer-term transformation of the underlying causes of conflict.

This study takes a broad approach to early warning and preventive action. We assume they have a role to play not only in the pre-conflict phase of intrastate crises, but also in the intra-conflict and post-conflict phases as well. Although a phase theory helps to simplify conflict, categorizing prevention as an activity for the early stage of incipient conflict and conflict resolution for the final stage leading to reconciliation does not reflect reality. Emerging practice treats early warning and prevention more broadly. Interventions to address conflict necessarily have a *rehabilitative* dimension oriented to the past, a *resolutive* dimension oriented to the present, and a *preventive* dimension oriented to both the present and future.

In all phases of intervention, special attention must be given to managing the critical *side-effects* of third party intervention. For example, international assistance given indiscriminately to the victims of internal conflict, can, in fact, help the perpetrators reorganize, as happened in the case of the Hutu refugees fleeing Rwanda. In Bosnia, carving out "safe havens" which the international community failed to adequately protect, made the war's victims more vulnerable, as seen by the mass executions in Srebrenica. Peripheral vision is imperative to ensure the international community's efforts to expand the conditions of peace do not inadvertently fuel conflict, prolong the suffering of its victims, or make them more vulnerable. Peace actors, therefore, must not only monitor and promote intended consequences, but also manage the unintended effects of their policies.

There are no shortcuts, standard formulas for success, or universal principles for preventing conflict in all situations. Instead, the background conditions and escalation dynamics of each conflict have to be carefully differentiated throughout the conflict's life cycle. Although a set of indicators helps simplify the tasks of evaluating internal conflict, qualitative interpretation is essential to understand each society's "fault lines" and "breaking points." The first part of this volume groups these indicators in terms of *background factors*, including the material and structural, cultural, and institutional (especially political) sources of conflict. A second set of indicators is used to assess the *processes of conflict escalation* over the dimensions of space and time, including its spread horizontally and intensification vertically. Concepts such as "conflict accelerators," "signal flares," and "triggers" are used to evaluate the increasing seriousness of conflict. Chapter 5 on preventive diplomacy explains how military, economic and political instruments can target the escalatory dynamics, and background conditions of internal conflicts, noting both the strengths and weaknesses of these actions.

In the second part of this book, case studies on Burundi and Macedonia substantiate the arguments underpinning the analytical framework. By way of conclusions, we offer counsels of excellence evaluating these two case studies and findings on other intrastate conflicts to guide conflict prevention and peace building initiatives in this decade and beyond. By moving from a conceptual framework and case studies to policy recommendations, the guidelines have a relevance to policy making not always obtained by more traditional methods. Methodologically speaking, this approach allows us to retain an element of comparability, and draw some recommendations, while also enabling us to explore the particularities of each conflict setting, including case specific strategies and their cumulative effects on peace.

Policy Challenges

The book subsumes the characteristics of internal conflicts and the challenges of managing them under four main categories:

1. the multi-dimensional and multilevel character of internal conflicts

2. the problems of monitoring such conflicts for early warning and conflict prevention

3. the challenges of creating peace synergies to counter the negative, escalatory dynamics of intrastate crises

4. the limited resources in the international community to deal with a growing number of destabilized societies

A "toolbox" approach is used to help the reader explore the main facets of intrastate conflicts and conceive preventive actions. The final chapter summarizes the approach, deriving from each of the four observations a hypothesis for discovering the causal processes by which conflict either escalates or is prevented, and a criterion for designing and implementing early warning and conflict prevention. The main policy challenges can be summarized as follows:

First, the multidimensional and multilevel character of internal conflicts pose a series of challenges for the international community to ensure its response to internal conflicts is comprehensive. There is no hegemonic power or universal institution with the autonomy, resources and motivation adequate to meet all the demands internal conflicts place on the management of international peace and security. There must be a division of labor among governments, IOs, and NGOs, as well as local leaders and organizations so that all dimensions and levels of society are targeted to avert the outbreak and spread of violence. However, as we see shortly below, state and non-state actors have different interests and motivations, as well as resources at their disposal. This results in problems of collective action, including for the organization and coordination of early warning and conflict prevention.

Second, monitoring for early warning and conflict prevention depends on political access. While remote monitoring may be attractive especially because of the capacity of computerized methods to manage large amounts of data, the information generated often leaves a large gap between scientific findings and policy action. The need for culturally sensitive, politically astute and practical information, calls for *engaged monitoring*. For this to be possible, international actors have to gain access to the conflict by means of negotiated engagement with the conflict parties. The relationship the outside parties have with the disputants becomes a critical consideration.

A third policy challenge concerns peace synergies. In the same way that conflict creates its own negative synergies as it escalates, conflict prevention needs to launch simultaneous peace processes at multiple levels and along multiple dimensions (material, structural, cultural, institutional) of society. To support peace entrepreneurs and imbue peace with its own life, however, requires *cultivating networks* among the community of actors involved in early warning and preventive action as a source of power. However, such organizing may be highly problematic in civil conflict and collapsing states. The conflict dynamics pull individuals toward polarized positions, not toward moderate, compromising or middle of the road solutions. Although policy networks respond to the criterion of decentralized coordination to engage significant actors in the peace process and to counter negative conflict synergies, as well as to maximize the effectiveness of limited resources, the obstacles to their formation may be formidable.

Non-governmental organizations are key actors in building policy networks. Their prominence draws attention to the diffusion of power in an increasingly "multi-centric world" (cf. Rosenau 1990), where complex emergencies typically bring governments, international organizations and NGOs into contact with each other to exchange information, and ensure a division of labor in the delivery of goods and services. Many NGOs operate transnationally, and in partnerships with local organizations. For all of these actors, networks serve as a means to pass information and to exchange ideas electronically, and organize meetings, as with the Burundi Policy Forum in Washington, D.C. International issue networks are distinguished by the "centrality of principled ideas or values" that motivate their formation. As Keck and Sikkink note (1995, 1), "what is novel in these networks is the ability of non-traditional international actors to mobilize information strategically so as to gain leverage over much more powerful organizations and governments." Though they do not always succeed, this is what makes networks increasingly relevant in policy debates.

Of course, NGOs are no panacea. The response of the international community to internal conflicts will vary, in large measure, according to the interests of the major powers—and their willingness to commit resources. While networks are activated in response to a particular crisis, *coalitions* supply the political capital and often times financial backing to support and legitimize the operations in the field. Like networks, coalitions are also loosely formed groups, although as the coalition against Saddam Hussein in the Gulf War illustrates, they can also mobilize around specific policy objectives, and collaborate for their achievement. While there is somewhat of an overlap between the two terms, we use coalitions to refer to political activity centered around traditional intergovernmental politics, and networks to speak of the dense exchange of information and services among non-state actors and government bureaucracies and international organizations in response to specific crises that encompass a common issue of concern.

Mobilizing Pragmatists for Principled Action

As we noted at the outset, early warning has traditionally referred to the management of crises in interstate relations. There it has relied mostly on the unilateral monitoring of a state's behavior by the adversary, although some multilateral mechanisms and tacit cooperation between the parties have been used. If the monitoring process turned out alarming information, the subject government had to decide whether it should stay inactive or resort to positive or negative sanctions to prevent the attack by the other side. For its part, the Cold War encompassed norms and mechanisms to avert or control internal conflicts, as another means of superpower confrontation and competition. However, the end of the superpower era has resulted in significant changes in international responses to internal conflicts, especially in terms of the major powers' contribution, reaction time, methods for controlling conflict, and the role of governmental and non-governmental organizations.

As Väyrynen notes (1995, 364), "the Cold War was a bipolar rivalry for the primacy in relative strategic power and the legitimacy of competing ideological principles. It was also a managed conflict, in which the avoidance of open military confrontation was the first ground rule." Conflict between East and West was contained in part through a spheres of influence arrangement, arms control agreements and other security measures, as well as through managed bipolar economic and ideological/cultural competition. The alliance systems also served numerous purposes in addition to balancing power between the Western democratic and Eastern communist systems. Internally, they socialized member states into the dominant powers' political and economic system, though little coercion was needed to do so in the West, unlike the East.

The superpowers contribution to the management of conflict throughout the international system was primary, to the extent that the role of intergovernmental organizations was limited. The superpower rivalry greatly constrained the United Nations in peacemaking, though regional organizations to a lesser extent. Nevertheless, before regional organizations could become involved as mediators, they, too, needed the acceptance of the parties directly involved. Lacking the resources of a universal organization, or of the great powers, they played a less active role in peacemaking than might otherwise have been the case (Zartman and Touval 1992, 246–47).

During the Cold War, non-governmental organizations also had less autonomy to operate, as humanitarian assistance, and foreign aid in general, were additional instruments for the great powers to engage in the bipolar political struggle. However, maintaining strict neutrality among the contending parties in regional conflict was essential if NGOs were to deliver assistance. There was considerably less diversification of NGO roles during the Cold War period than since. In fact, NGOs had little role to play in conflict management. Human rights NGOs may be one exception, although their role was limited essentially to advocacy. The reaction time of both intergovernmental and non-governmental organizations to internal conflicts was relatively late: they were more likely to deal with its consequences than early warning and prevention, that is, mediating a peace settlement, or cataloging human rights violations after the fact, respectively.

For the superpowers, early warning mechanisms had their most obvious usefulness as trip-wires which came into play whenever a dispute threatened to undermine international stability. In the context of nuclear weapons, early warning referred to the technologies capable of detecting or even anticipating the launch of an enemy's ballistic missiles in a sudden surprise attack. Here early warning loses its deliberative functions. In the European context, the main objective of early warning during the Cold War was to control the dynamics of superpower conflict between NATO and the Warsaw Pact, especially to prevent a surprise attack that could lead to a nuclear showdown. The system relied on bilateral and multilateral mechanisms (crisis management centers, hot lines, confidence and security building measures, etc.) to inhibit the outbreak of inter-state conflict. The division of Europe into spheres of influence where the superpowers essentially determined the rules of the game provided its own mechanisms of control. The bipolar arrangement ensured that states' internal conflicts would be suppressed in the interest of bloc unity. Bloc-based mechanisms and policies, such as the Brezhnev doctrine, were also in place to contain by external actions intrastate conflict, if it did erupt.

Elsewhere early warning and strategies of conflict prevention were viewed through a geopolitical lens that colored actual or potential conflict in the shades of the bipolar rivalry. The recasting of liberation struggles, for instance, between the *apartheid* government of South Africa and the African National Conference, as a duel of capitalists against communists, illustrates such distortions. The Third World's overall acceptance of a balance of power under the Soviet and American spheres of influence arrangement was complemented by superpower overtures that sought to improve social conditions, to promote economic growth, and to enhance certain cultural affinities, related, for instance, to language, religion, and transnational ideological movements, like Arabism or Pan-Africanism. The superpowers were mostly concerned with how this influenced their orientation toward Eastern, Western, or non-aligned partnerships; they paid less attention to the complexities of many of these states' internal political alignments or struggles. Rather, the country's relative size, the extent of its resources, and the strength of its military, and its geographic location as a function of regional or global strategic configurations usually determined how much familiarity with its inner workings was needed. However, the abstract principles and formulas of foreign policy under the superpower detente were unreliable as a means of containing conflict, as the results of aggressive Soviet conduct in Indochina, the Middle East, the Horn of Africa, and

Afghanistan in the 1970s in particular, illustrate (Crocker 1992, 203). Similarly, the United States used military force in Central America and the Caribbean.

Conflict management was, above all, an exercise in pragmatic political judgments closely tied to the superpowers' strategic interests and global confrontation and competition. While this made it difficult to *resolve* intrastate conflicts, the limits to competition and the tacit cooperation also helped control and terminate them (Miller 1995, 53). The pattern shifted in the late 1980s, as the Cold War began to wind down and the superpowers cooperated to solve regional conflicts. Gorbachev's "new thinking," including the recognition of the influence of local factors, rather than US "imperialist machinations," made such cooperation possible, which the US was ready to reciprocate. The result was a superpower concert during the 1980s that succeeded in finding solutions to various regional conflicts, including in the Middle East, Afghanistan, and the Horn of Africa, as well as in Angola and Southern Africa (Miller 1995, 77; Hermann 1992). The efforts were more successful in part, because the conflicts were dealt with on a case-by-case approach, rather than as a function of global superpower confrontation, so that the regional context and local roots of conflict received attention the Cold War politics had neglected, and often, exacerbated (Crocker 1992). However, the collapse of the Soviet Union itself in late 1991 marked the end of this phase of the joint management of conflicts. As the remaining superpower, the US has vacillated between exercising a Pax Americana, organizing multilateral action for conflict resolution (as with its leadership role in the Gulf War coalition), and withdrawal and isolationism.

The variety of responses by the US and other great powers in the post-Cold War reflects the extent to which, under multipolar arrangements, policymakers calibrate national strategic interests on a case by case basis. Whereas the Cold War formula was based on maintaining a global balance of power, the initial (and persistent) lack of a concerted international approach to the conflict in the Former Yugoslavia (until the November 1995 Dayton Peace Accords succeeded in bringing an end to the violence in Bosnia, at least temporarily), reveals the difficulties of overcoming inaction and competition among great powers in a multipolar international system. The absence of a clarity of collective interests and divergent great power commitments pose significant obstacles to collective action. The delayed reaction time also imposes greater costs on the eventual containment and resolution of conflicts, while the scale of human atrocities and deprivation climbs.

The structural conditions of multi-polarity also give rise to a different set of assumptions about what constitutes pragmatic political action to deal with conflict in the peripheries. In fact, the starkest discontinuities may arise from the disengagement of great powers. The change is especially dramatic in Africa, where superpower involvement not only intensified the violence of intrastate wars, but had also artificially fortified the coherence and "stateness" of the adversaries, both governments and rebels. Now the international community can no longer assume the great powers will manipulate regional actors and commit resources as a means of conflict management. Instead, as Miller explains (1995, 63), disengagement means the great powers will reduce their political-security commitments outside their immediate areas of interest.

The spheres of influence arrangement translates into some division between major powers. But a division of labor not only provides justification for the other major powers to remain disengaged; it also remove checks on the abuse of power. One consequence is the great powers are unwilling to enforce systematically international standards and principles. This reluctance extends not only to conflicts in the peripheries, but also to conflicts that erupt within the territory of one of the great powers. For the US, the main justification is that any decision to uphold international norms must be backed up by a willingness to use military might to enforce them, should diplomacy fail. The underlying assumption is either that: (a) the US has no strategic interests at stake which would justify the use of force, which case may apply to conflicts in the peripheries; or (b) as the Chechnya case suggests, the US has too great strategic interests at stake to risk disrupting bilateral relations. Then principles of sovereignty and non-intervention in the internal affairs of other states can be invoked as a cover for inaction.

Inaction in the peripheries may also be justified on the grounds that the lack of national interests at stake makes it difficult to commit new resources, whether for security, economic, political, or humanitarian causes. Pragmatic "state centric" arguments for disengagement and isolationism also assume there is very little the international community can do between talk and military enforcement. The tendency to treat conflicts as unidimensional limits options for strategizing preventive action, and puts the burden on more costly measures down the road when the crisis escalates.

All this points to the fact that in theory, at least, peripheral countries are a serious limiting case where the employment of early warning and conflict prevention by major powers is concerned. The other kind of limiting case concerns those states with whom the North does have significant ties. Western reluctance to criticize Russian President Boris Yeltsin's handling of the Chechen crisis, or the Chinese for their human rights abuses, or conflict with Tibet, reveals that maintaining order, and ensuring the protection of the great powers' strategic and economic interests are the priorities.

Consequently, it seems there is only a narrow set of circumstances under which the great powers are predisposed to devote attention and resources to early warning and preventive action: cases where core national interests are directly threatened by an internal conflict, and yet involve relatively weak (typically peripheral) states where the intervention can be achieved without too great a cost. Macedonia and Haiti are such cases. Macedonia surfaces because of the threat of a wider regional destabilization pitting NATO members Greece and Turkey on opposite sides of the conflict; and Haiti because of the waves of refugees headed to US shores. The prolonged fighting in Bosnia, under close media coverage, finally proved too costly politically for the great powers not to get more involved to contain and resolve it. But in all these cases, the United States committed military resources, and finally ground troops only with great reluctance, and in the latter two interventions, only belatedly. Then there are the collapsed states which are mostly forgotten by the international community, such as Afghanistan and Sudan. While civilians are caught in the fray, rival factions are left to fight over the spoils of the state.

The Human Needs Perspective

The involvement of international NGOs helps to minimize the marginalization and even abandonment of strife torn and collapsing states by the international community. Their new roles in the front lines of conflict are partly a function of the superpowers' disengagement. At the same time, the policies of structural adjustment promoted since the 1980s, and more recently democratization, have both reduced the size of many states' civil services, while also placing greater burdens and responsibilities on civil society. The NGO community has stepped in to help states meet these new needs and overcome the limited capacities of their societies, in order to extend an international safety net. Their interest in preventive action has been increasingly compelled by the fact that they *have* to deal with conflict—if they are to have any role in development and humanitarian assistance. However, this has prompted a policy debate within the NGO community on whether, and if so, what kind of role they can play in conflict resolution, aside from their efforts to ensure the safe passage of food and provision of medical assistance, for example.

Their main concern is that an enlarged role could compromise their essential mission and neutrality. Maintaining neutrality in conflict situations is difficult, especially when the NGOs international presence is unwanted by some of the warring factions. For example, in Burundi, NGOs often have had to work "in the cross hairs." They are caught between speaking out to draw local public (and international) attention to the threats made against their personnel and programs (thus risking greater exposure and perhaps further undermining their perceived neutrality), and maintaining a wary, if also precarious silence, and carrying about their jobs (Buckley 1996a). Such dilemmas cause NGOs to question whether they should continue working in the host country at all. Their departure, however, is often a strategic gain for the warring factions, who can then act without fear of international scrutiny or reprisals. Then the suffering of the victims of the conflict—typically women, children, and the elderly, as well as the infirm—is multiplied as the temporary sources of personal security, food, water, shelter, and other basic assistance, possibly including provisional medical attention, evaporate.

NGOs are also concerned that humanitarian assistance may do more to prolong than to alleviate the suffering of innocent civilians, for example, when aid is diverted to support the warring parties (Prendergast 1996). The Rwandan case raises another question: Should NGOs always provide humanitarian assistance indiscriminately? By providing humanitarian assistance to Hutu refugees and the perpetrators of genocide alike, the international community's response helped the Hutu military regroup, and risked laying the groundwork for a new cycle of violence to begin. For such reasons, many NGOs acknowledge it is no longer sufficient to enter crisis situations wearing political blinders on the assumption that the moral purposes of their actions suffice to guide and justify their involvement. Consequently, there are calls for establishing common international standards, or mandates to protect their work especially among the victims of civil strife. More attention is also focused on improving coordination among NGOs so warring factions stand less to gain by playing one NGO off another.

A third area of concern centers on the coordination of humanitarian assistance among NGOs and the rest of the international community. Since the middle of the 1980s the United Nations has taken steps to create a preventive system to avert the flow of refugees and displaced people and to establish early warning systems in the areas of environment and food crises. Also outside the UN there is ample material available on economic, environmental, and food trends, which is sometimes specially fashioned to serve early warning functions (see, for example, Brown, Lenssen and Kane 1995). Nevertheless, the UN has mostly overlooked the development of early warning on violent conflicts. This neglect can be, in part, explained by their political sensitivity.

Traditionally, the international community has not intervened until conflicts have degenerated into violence, and pose a threat to the national sovereignty of its members, and the system of nation states itself. But today, Article 2(7) of the UN Charter, banning interference in the internal affairs of states, must be weighed against the principle of human solidarity with people and their rights, and the consequent need to provide assistance to those in need. Article 2(7) also observes that the principle of non-intervention into the internal affairs of states, however important, shall not prejudice the application of enforcement measures under Chapter VII. Even in this new situation, humanitarian intervention remains problematic; many legal experts still consider it inadmissible and, furthermore, non-enforcement measures of Chapter VII are not necessarily an exception to Article 2(7) (Gordon 1994; Arend and Beck 1993).

In his *Agenda for Peace* (Boutros-Ghali 1992, 15–16), the Secretary-General sees, however, early warning as a precursor to the identification of threats to international peace and security calling for a synthesis between broad-based risk information and political indicators to assess the seriousness of these threats. He also recommends that the Security Council invite, on the basis of Article 65 of the UN Charter, information on "those economic and social developments that may, unless mitigated, threaten international peace and security."

Early warning and conflict prevention were also specifically addressed in General Assembly Resolution 47/120 (1992) which "invites the competent organs of the United Nations . . . to consider implementing preventive deployment and/or establishment of a demilitarized zone" as a part of the efforts to prevent conflicts and achieve a peace settlement. Resolution 47/120 gives the Secretary-General a broad mandate to develop an early warning and conflict-prevention regime under UN auspices and more particularly under the Department of Humanitarian Affairs. The Secretary-General has also called upon the member states and regional organizations to provide information on confidence-building and other measures that may help forestall conflicts. The Secretary-General himself estimates he spends 20 percent of his time for early warning and preventive diplomacy (Boutros-Ghali 1993, 324–25).

One of the reasons for the Secretary-General's active involvement in conflict early warning and prevention is obviously that it backs up his mandate, under Article 99, to bring to the attention of the Security Council any matter threatening the maintenance of international peace and security. In fact, the Secretary-General cannot effectively utilize this right without an effective system of information gathering and analysis. In addition, the UN fact-finding activities can serve the purposes of conflict resolution by catalyzing the parties to imagine and identify peaceful solutions (Eliassen 1995, 407). In addition to the powers of the Secretary-General to bring matters to the attention of the Security Council, he can set up, on the basis of Article 34, investigative commissions to prevent the escalation of disputes and pave the way to their peaceful settlement (White 1993, 74–77).

Among regional organizations, the Organization for Security and Cooperation in Europe (OSCE) has developed a number of early warning and conflict prevention mechanisms. At the Helsinki summit of July 1992, OSCE states decided to activate political consultations and improve their work, associated with the establishment of the Crisis Prevention Center (CPC), in early warning and dispute settlement. Before that the Berlin Ministerial Council had, in June 1991, set up an emergency mechanism which was activated several times in the Yugoslavian crisis, although with scant results. The Rome Council, in October 1993, subordinated the CPC to the Vienna Secretariat thus streamlining the OSCE organization, but also limiting the CPC autonomy. So far the success of the CPC has been modest at best. On the other hand, the nine long-term missions of the OSCE, established since September 1992, have succeeded somewhat better in preventing the escalation of conflicts (Estonia, Latvia, and Macedonia) or managing the post-conflict situations (Moldova and Ukraine), while they have been less successful in preventing or even ending violence in Bosnia, Chechnya, Georgia, and Tajikistan.

Case studies on the peace efforts in Tajikistan, Nagorno-Karabakh, and the Georgian territories show how dependent both the UN and the OSCE are on the cooperation of the local parties and the policies of the regional power, in this case Russia. The local and regional constraints have been so strong that, in the absence of vital interests by the major powers, the UN and the OSCE have repeatedly failed to institutionalize the peace process, not to speak of the early warning and prevention of violence (see Roy 1995; Paye and Remacle 1994). Within the OSCE, the most successful actor has been the High Commissioner on National Minorities (HCNM), established in Helsinki in 1992 to provide "early warning" and "early prevention" in national minority conflicts (Greco 1995, 10–11; Rosas 1995). "Early warning" is exercised by the HCNM visits to member states to contain and de-escalate tensions, while "early prevention" relies on alerting the OSCE to cases which are so serious that the High Commissioner cannot solve them on its own (van der Stoel 1994a; The Role of the High Commissioner 1997).

Whether, and how intergovernmental organizations respond depends, however, on building a consensus among its member states on the assessment of the situation, and organizing for collective action. Those organizations with limited resources, as is the case of the OAU which has also started to develop some early warning and prevention mechanisms, will also require logistical and financial support of the great powers, as efforts to organize an African intervention to forestall the escalating domestic crisis in the aftermath of Burundi's July 1996 coup, show (for background, see Evans 1997b).

Reconciling Different Imperatives

The key question is not whether pragmatic state centered thinking or the human needs perspective prevail in any given situation, or in general, but rather how the interaction of governments, NGOs, international organizations with each other and with local actors, shapes responses and influences the outcomes to intrastate conflicts. Their interaction has not yet been systematically studied, though pioneering work points to the importance of a synergistic relationship. NGOs, states and international institutions often need each other to have an impact in a given issue-area. This is evident, for example, in the case of NGOs working on environmental issues (Princen 1994). They helped shape the "epistemic communities" that "led to an increase in state capacities to manage the market, both domestically and through the creation of international regimes" (Risse-Kappen 1995, 293–96).

NGOs can enhance the impact of governments and international organizations on the early warning and prevention of internal conflict by: (1) increasing access to parties in conflict, and flow of information about them; (2) improving the comprehensiveness of response; (3) amplifying the impact of peace strategies through their own networking; and (4) creating conditions for great power engagement in larger scale preventive and rescue operations. To these ends, NGOs often work in a partnership role with governments and international organizations, though they can also contribute by remaining on the sidelines to critique failures in government responses. Obviously, to some extent a partnership role precludes the latter, so NGOs must weigh the advantages and drawback of their involvement, particularly as it effects their perceived impartiality by the parties, and hence, capacity to deliver primary services.

NGOs have a leading role to play in getting the state centered world to take action because they are typically already on the ground where crises are emerging, and thus close to important, if sectoral and partial, information. Nonetheless, NGOs' partnerships and close contact with local chapters, national organizations, and/or other NGOs, as well as the delivery of their services in the local community puts them in touch with the problems at hand, often more so than embassy staff or officials in the international diplomatic community. This means NGOs may have important early warning information and monitoring capabilities.

NGO information and lobbying help to prioritize state interests, and encourage the channeling of resources to deal with humanitarian crises and conflicts. Their role in mobilizing media attention is important: it helps get the attention of governments focused on issues which might not find their way onto a crowded agenda; and it leverages action through public awareness and support. NGO relationships with international organizations help them gather crucial information, strategize and coordinate interventions, and implement policies. NGOs strengthen the capacity of governments and international organizations to respond, since in so doing they can channel resources through, and draw on the networks and partnerships that NGOs have already established on the ground or can quickly set up.

Nevertheless, NGOs' relationship to both the local and international contexts of crisis situations is often quite complex. They interact not only with other actors at the international level, but also in the host countries. The complexity of NGOs' relationship to the parties to the conflict in the host country may constrain their flexibility as far as early warning and conflict prevention is concerned. For example, the losers of domestic power struggles typically appeal to international NGOs to act as their international allies, while the winners use the ploys of sovereignty and the discourse of non-intervention to protect their privileged position, as the Burundi case illustrates. The competing interests and often illicit goals of warring factions can put NGOs into a perilous position.

Indeed, NGOs must often navigate a complex web of local and transnational ties, which the various warring factions forge with the underworld of transnational arms dealers, rogue intelligence services, and mercenaries, as well as their ethnic kin living in outlying regions or abroad. The latter often have their own organizations (including military formations and other resources) that the local leadership draw on in an attempt to achieve their objectives. Judgments have also to be made about which other NGOs are legitimate and can be trusted as local partners in the assistance operations. The South African based organization "Executive Outcomes," describes itself in NGO-like terms as committed to assisting countries with water purification, construction and medical services. In fact, it provides military training and work for South African commandos in Angola and Sierra Leone. Its activities have tended to protect the production and trading of diamonds and other valuable resources by which the governments of these countries have been funding their war. In return, Executive Outcomes have received their own hefty compensation, including access to these valuables (Reno 1998, 61–63, 129–39).

The core missions of NGOs vary greatly, from the delivery of humanitarian and development assistance, to conflict resolution, civil society, and the protection of human rights. This division of labor helps the international community target the various dimensions and levels of conflict, including structural cleavages, cultural tensions, as well as problems with institutional legitimacy and democratization. Though not without flaws, such coordination has been a central feature of the international community's efforts to contain the Bosnian conflict, and to rebuild the country and its political and civil institutions in the post-conflict phase.

Of course, as the Bosnian conflict also shows, the same transnational linkages which strengthen the international community's capacity to intervene and influence local developments in crisis ridden countries, may also weaken the latters' capacity to manage the situation on their own terms. This is often the case when the regime is identified as the perpetrator of violence in the internal conflict, and hence targeted by the international community for punishment and/or reform, as with international sanctions on Serbia, or Iraq, or the establishment of the war crimes tribunal in the case of the Former Yugoslavia (which has delegitimized the Bosnian Serb wartime leadership). Conversely, for opposition forces, the international-ization of the conflict through the establishment of transnational ties with NGOs and international organizations, as well as third party governments is one important means of strengthening their position vis-a-vis the ruling elite. Here the establishment of the international war crimes tribunal for Rwanda could be said to serve the interests of the ruling Tutsi.

The role of international incentives in such cases must also be carefully evaluated. In newly democratizing and weak states, there are generally weak domestic incentives for political leaders to behave properly. In fact, there may be more incentives to behave poorly and to play up the ethnic factors, both for personal and political gain. Then international incentives can be fragile. Even in Europe, which is richly endowed with international insti-tutions, and comparatively speaking, resources, incentives can turn out to be a currency of limited fungibility. For example, membership in such Eu-ropean institutions as the Council of Europe, NATO and the OSCE, has been used as positive inducements to encourage the democratic process in transitional states, and avert ethnic conflicts. However, the incentive effect can wear off as soon as states join. From then on, efforts to mold new behaviors entail real costs for the institutions (that is, funding to support structural reform).

Strengthening civil society through the coordinated efforts of NGOs and their networks may emerge as one significant area where the interna-tional community can make an impact on conflict prevention and peace-building. Short term emergency responses are important, but the fo-cus ultimately needs to be on a long-term strategy to help societies in distress become more resilient to the structural, cultural and political tensions that threaten violence. As the case of South Africa illustrates, a strong society (held together more by class structures, perhaps than civil), supported also by highly committed, transnational movements and networks, can help keep a country together that is undergoing tremendous social transformation, even when the political institutions themselves are perceived as illegitimate by the majority population. But states with strong civil societies have greater capacity to rebound from disaster and widespread social strife. It can make all the difference between recovery and collapse, as a recent study on collapsed states in Africa shows (Zartman 1995).

Whether there is any international response to a country threatened with the specter of civil war and possibly collapse, depends often on the role various types of NGOs play in awareness raising, including, for example, garnering international media attention. These efforts in themselves do not constitute any remedies to the situation at hand, though they may be a necessary first step for mobilizing political will and bringing together the coalition of actors needed to carry out any preventive actions. The important point is that no fixed "global system" of early warning is likely to emerge. Unlike the system of sovereign states organized in part through various alliance systems, in the multi-centric world, actors retain a high degree of autonomy. This makes the patterns of their interaction, even with states and international organizations, quite fluid. It is apparent that different coalitions will form in response to specific contingencies regarding emerging crises.

Thus, the effectiveness of early warning and conflict prevention is more likely to depend on the coordination of appropriate actors and their networks. Drawing collectively on the information and expertise of actors working on the ground, both NGOs and international organizations, like the OSCE, which deploys missions of long duration to countries with potentially destabilizing problems, is important. In Burundi, substantial international engagement in preventive actions in the mid-1990s may inhibit the outbreak of genocide, whereas in the past the decision by the international community to ignore such gross violence, or only belatedly condemn it, was probably a crucial permissive factor in the escalation process.

In the event government leaders determine they, too, must act, NGOs can test the waters, and create the coalitions that help make such action politically viable. For their part, governments may seek out the involvement of NGOs to raise media attention, public awareness of and education on the issues, and to garner support. In such cases NGOs work in partnership with government policymakers. Their services are critical to political leaders in democratic societies, who must justify the commitment of national resources, especially for military and peacekeeping operations, to the electorate.

The Benefits of Foresight

As our case studies on Burundi and Macedonia show, the central actors in conflict early warning and prevention are national elites (including those of the opposition), third party governments and international governmental, and non-governmental organizations. They have at their disposal different methods of gaining information and acting on it for the purposes of early warning and conflict prevention. However, preventive diplomacy is inherently contingent, and resistant to systematizing. This means that systematic, universal and mechanistic approaches to early warning (that is, macro data sets, refugee flow models), are bound to fail. There is little to be gained by treating political issues as essentially technical matters.

Recent innovations, such as the establishment of networks of early warning actors, like the Burundi Policy Forum, have their risks, as well as promises. As we emphasize throughout the study, there is always the question of neutrality not only for governments and international organizations, for whom it has traditionally been a crucial factor in the execution of any third party roles, but increasingly for NGOs. The neutrality/impartiality of the latter can be compromised by too close association with government officials and policies: among other things, it can undermine their acceptance by the parties. Their active collaboration also diminishes the supply of independent actors in civil society, who play an important role in making normative critiques of government policies, and also in the positive case, legitimizing and supporting them.

In both the conceptual and empirical work in this study, we employ a broad definition of preventive diplomacy to encompass both pre-, intra- and post-conflict prevention. This also means that the purposes of intervention vary. We see clearly there are limits to the costs major powers will incur to promote these objectives, all the more so in peripheral areas of the world where they have practically no strategic interests at stake. Burundi's small size, its remote, landlocked location, and its relative paucity of exportable material resources have contributed to its overall neglect by the international community, at least until the mid-1990s. Little external pressure countered the rise of the minority ethnic oligarchy whose hold on power has been punctuated by a succession of ethnic bloodlettings under the leadership of authoritarian military regimes. In contrast, the primary motivation of the international community (the US, and its Western allies) to take preventive action in Macedonia stems from their appreciation of its sensitive geo-strategic location, in addition to the inter-connectivity of its internal conflict dynamics with regional tensions. Internal conflict alone probably would not have justified international action. For, not unlike Burundi, Macedonia is also a state on the periphery—in fact, a periphery within the Balkans, which is itself on the southern periphery of Europe. Moreover, Macedonia has little in the way of material resources which imperilment would have drawn international concern.

Although the media plays a key role in elevating certain crises to the attention of the international community and forcing them onto the international agenda, generally speaking, humanitarian concerns alone mobilize minimal international efforts of a rescue nature, much less those of a preventive character. In fact, with the international agenda already crowded by crises, there are serious obstacles to convincing policymakers they should divert attention and resources to problems not nearly as commensurate as those facing them at any given moment, or which are in the media eye and also clamoring for attention.

There is good cause, therefore, to seek to instill in the major powers the priority of acting preventively. Institutionalizing such a norm will admittedly make the international agenda even more crowded at the outset. However, the long-term benefits of foresight should outweigh the temporary stresses on the system, as can be surmised from the application of such principles in other social spheres, such as medicine, or more to the point, epidemiology, where preventive action must operate in the global context to be effective.

2

ORGANIZING FOR PROACTIVE INTERVENTION

The Search for an Early Warning Model

EARLY WARNING AND CONFLICT PREVENTION ARE BASED ON PROACTIVE RESPONSES to potential threats to national and/or human security. Preventive diplomacy has a long history both in bilateral and multilateral international relations. Traditionally, it has relied, among other things, on measures to maintain the balance of power, deter the potential aggressor, and organize various types of diplomatic and military interventions to hinder the outbreak of violent conflicts between states. To underpin preventive actions, policymakers have tried to detect signs of whether a war with another state is imminent.

A substantial body of literature exists that tries to understand the causes of war, or its likelihood. For instance, empirical studies on interstate wars have been utilized to find out systemic properties, national attributes, and patterns of national behavior which correlate with the risks of war and help to identify them at an early stage (Singer and Wallace 1979). Correlational models try to establish inductively relations between violent outcomes and their structural causes, such as alliances, nuclear proliferation, or economic conditions. Deductive, structural models define the causes (that is, scarcity, identity, and relative deprivation) of global and local environmental conflicts, mediated by various social effects (Homer-Dixon 1991 and 1994).

While inductive correlational models help to establish invariances and specify international and national factors associated with inter-state war, they have serious limitations for understanding how to develop models of early warning for intrastate conflicts. First, correlations and causal relations in international wars may change over time, requiring periodic updating of models (Gurr and Harff 1994, 4). Second, the structural conditions that correlational models specify tend to be remote or underlying, not proximate causes of violence. Third, correlational models do not help us understand the dynamics of conflict escalation or how different management approaches introduced at different points of time may alter the conflict development. Thus, these models are unable to provide early warning analysts with a framework which would help them devise carefully targeted policy responses (Singer and Wallace 1979; Homer-Dixon 1991 and 1994; Gurr and Harff 1994, 4).

The effort to develop early warning indicators of *intrastate* conflicts is not entirely new, however. Scholars have utilized, for example, such variables as internal cleavages of society, organizational strength of actors, existence of democratic institutions and external intervention to predict the extent and intensity of protests and rebellions (Gurr and Lichbach 1979). Yet, the need remains to develop a more effective early warning system which is empirically valid, simple enough to use in practice, and politically feasible. Some new steps have recently been taken in this direction both in terms of theory development and policy applications; one can even speak of the emergence of a new cottage industry in the field (see, for example, Rupesinghe and Kuroda 1992; Gurr and Harff 1994).

The early warning of intrastate conflicts has been permeated by the search for the most effective indicators, methods, and information systems by which material, social, and cultural conditions and processes of conflicts conducive to aggressive actions can be identified at an early phase. However, there is a mechanical bias in much of the early warning literature. It presumes that given appropriate methods and a reliable data base violent conflicts can be detected and their escalation prevented. A correlate of this tendency is to suggest that in spite of all obstacles and constraints decision makers are able to make correct policy choices if only they use high-quality procedures in problem solving. It is the task of experts to develop such procedures and "sell" them to decision makers. Such a view is advocated, for example, by Janis (1990).

One of the problems with such mechanical approaches, however, is the vast quantity of inconsequential information they produce, such that, as Boutros-Ghali has noted, it becomes difficult to locate vital indicators (Boutros-Ghali 1993, 325). These approaches also generally overlook the fact that early warning is essentially a political activity; on the one hand it is a form of practical reasoning, which can be used to promote specific ends, while on the other hand it relies on political norms that reflect community preferences. For instance, early warning is based on the norm that the avoidance of violence is desirable in all circumstances. The comparison of social reality with such normative standards leads necessarily to subjective conclusions. One cannot say, however, that early warning is entirely arbitrary as it tries to emulate objective decision making, assessing probabilities and risks of violence (cf. Holdsworth 1989). Early warning combines an effort at the objective analysis of conflict risks with their normative assessment and the advocacy of specific political ends.

In the early warning and prevention of conflicts, normative queries seek answers to questions such as: How much and what kind of violence is acceptable? Should the parties be treated equally in conflict prevention? What types of preventive measures are justifiable to contain the danger of escalation? These and other normative issues may be perceived differently, and hence risks assessed differently, by those actors who are in charge of monitoring and those who are supposed to take preventive measures.

To answer these questions, we need to move away from the mere observation of regularities to a generative causal analysis of conflict. An analysis of the generative connection between the background structures and observed consequences produces a dynamic, causal explanation (Dessler 1991). Early warning and prevention of conflicts can be effective only when based on a dynamic view of the causes and development of conflicts as manifested in a selected number of representative, or perhaps most serious, cases.

Some progress is being made in these areas. Sequential, response, and conjunctural models are better suited than correlational models to tracking the development of conflict over time and for identifying appropriate points in conflict cycles where intervention may make a positive difference on the outcomes. Sequential models outline the likely course of developments that lead to conflict escalation. Some models give particular attention to background and intervening conditions and accelerators (which are "special events outside the systems parameter that includes international, internal and intervening conditions"), and others to conflict cycles. Response models identify "the points in conflict processes in which strategic interventions or 'responses' are likely to make a difference in outcomes" (Gurr and Harff 1994, 4–5; Gurr and Harff 1996). As for intervention models, one should make a distinction between structural interventions focusing on material environmental and economic conditions fostering violence, and policy interventions intended to change the course of conflict dynamics. Their relevance is recognized by those who say that the quality of early warning is secondary and the nature and timing of warning, that is, intervention, as well as its reception is primary (Gordenker 1992, 3).

Conjunctural models have been of special interest. They may help the analyst interpret how different combinations of conditions ("conjunctures") lead to widespread protracted conflicts, massacres or, alternatively, accommodation and various types of constructive outcomes (Gurr and Harff 1994). An example of the potential of these models is Vasquez's theory of war which stresses the conflict dynamics preceding the outbreak of a war and the multiplicity of its causes and contexts, including domestic prerequisites and territorial relationships, and routes to it (Vasquez 1993).

Ultimately, the early warning process cannot be described by any single and supposedly objective model; on the contrary, various cognitive and organizational models of politics have to be considered in the development of early warning mechanisms. Recognizing this, our efforts to develop theoretical and conceptual aspects of conflict early warning have been inspired by three additional sources of ideas on early warning: human rights, famines and internal displacement, and information processing and policy making.

Human Rights

Increasing attention is being given today to preventing human rights violations, underscoring that the real purpose of reporting human rights offenses "must be deeper than ex post facto determination of compliance with human rights treaty" (Dimitrijevich 1993, 20). The efforts to prevent human rights violations by NGOs amounts, from the governmental perspective, to early warning. The failure of these efforts increases pressures to resort to stronger preventive actions by governments. However, a basic problem with the current intergovernmental methods of early warning and prevention of human rights violations is that they are not based on any systematic review of the situation prevailing in various countries (Beyer 1992). In addition to the lack of systematic information on human rights situations in individual countries as a basis of action, current international strategies to protect human rights are essentially reactive. The United Nations must first receive information on violations before it can act to avert them (Ramcharan 1992, 272–73). According to critics, even if the United Nations responds, its reactions have often been, at least in the past, based on agency-specific decisions and their limited implementation (Beyer 1992, 21).

In Europe, the OSCE has been the linchpin in the monitoring of human rights. The Final Document of its Vienna follow-up conference of 1989 established a Human Dimension Mechanism at the governmental level, which was subsequently elaborated in OSCE meetings in Copenhagen in 1989, and Moscow in 1991. It created a political obligation to exchange information and respond to inquiries made by other OSCE states on the compliance with human rights agreements. However, the use of this mechanism is predicated on the willingness of governments to activate it. Unfortunately this willingness has been recently fading and there has been special reluctance to apply the mechanism in the relations between states in Western Europe and North America. Selectivity diminishes the general applicability of monitoring instruments, of international standards, and of the legitimacy of international institutions. It also creates an impression of two classes of governments: those civilized and not needing the CSCE political procedures and new democracies whose behavior must be supervised Bloed (1993, 73–74, 87–88).

Governmental influence is more limited in the case of the OSCE High Commissioner on National Minorities. While politically accountable to the governmental bodies of the OSCE, the High Commissioner has an independent and flexible mandate to reduce tensions associated with the position and rights of national minorities (for an analysis of the HCNM's role, see Zaagman 1994; The Role of the High Commissioner 1997).

Fact-finding, monitoring, and early warning of human rights violations offer some obvious lessons for the early warning of violent conflicts. In both cases there is a need to develop standards and criteria to monitor tensions and abuses. There is also a need to avoid compartmentalized approaches in which narrow bureaucratic or ideological interests steer the process of monitoring. Both in monitoring conflicts and human rights there is also a common need to develop a "generative explanation" between the background conditions and political outcomes which they foster. According to Jongman (1994, 68) such outcomes, which he calls "signals," can be observed in past behavior and possibly predicted by experts for the future.

Nevertheless, lessons on the early warning and prevention of human rights violations have limited value in the development of conflict early warning indicators. There are well defined standards against which human rights violations can be judged, but these do not exist for judging the worsening of conflicts. Moreover, there was at least in Europe of the early 1990s a greater consensus among governments to accept the introduction of the principle of enforcement in humanitarian issues that let it prevail in inter- and intrastate conflicts. And the dynamics of escalation in the violation of human rights and violent conflicts are different. In tense situations, the likelihood and severity of the escalation of violence is greater than in the human rights abuses, although they often go hand in hand. This also means that monitoring for conflict prevention requires not just short-term rapporteur missions or fact finding inquiries, but rather missions of longer duration (such as those deployed by the OSCE) with a broader political mandate that links monitoring and fact-finding with confidence-building, and the search for political solutions. The multilateral efforts also need to be systematic, impartial and, non-selective—which is seldom the case in the national monitoring and may be also wanting in actions initiated by international organizations.

Famines and Internal Displacement

The forecasting of famines involves elaborate mathematical models to predict the size of food stocks, the consumption needs of the population, and other variables. Early warning has, however, been a secondary concern in famine prevention: the early warning of a famine is often issued only when mass starvation has become a stark reality. Instead, early warning should have been "geared to warning about the erosion of the subsistence basis of the victim's society" (Walker 1992). Rather than information on the parameters of famines, the key issue should concern the ability to detect the crisis early on and the preparedness of governments to respond to such threats by effective and concerted action.

The wide dissemination of information on socio-economic erosion is one way of eliciting a reaction from governments and relief agencies. In fact, one of the main lessons to be drawn from the efforts to forecast famines is that publicity may matter more than the specific actions taken. A range of administrative, journalistic and political communications can thus serve the early warning role and have a preventive function as they prompt governmental and non-governmental actors to engage in earlier actions to ameliorate the situation (Drèze 1990, 159–60 and Ravallion 1990, 263–66). This means the function of early warning is not only to provide decision makers with forecasts on the likelihood of famines, violence and other social ills, but also to force them to act. By making the risks public, it increases the transparency of the crisis and creates public expectations and pressures that governments should act to prevent the disaster.

Contingency planning is an important lesson from the early warning of famines. With contingency planning, policymakers can prepare in advance for necessary actions and envisage their timing (Drèze and Sen 1989, 264). Once conflicts begin to escalate, integration becomes more difficult and compartmentalization of activities often becomes the norm.

The findings of a study on internally displaced people basically arrives at the same conclusion as the evaluations of famine forecasting. With some gaps, the prevailing standards to protect displaced people are quite adequate. The pervasive problem is their inadequate implementation. To remedy the situation Deng (1993, 137–40) issues a call to action and recommends a three-tier system: (a) monitoring, reporting and early warning; (b) intercession, dialogue and mediation; and (c) eventual humanitarian collective action.

The establishment of the Office of Research and the Collection of Information (ORCI) in 1987 was among the first attempts to develop an early warning system for the United Nations and to provide the Secretary-General with advice for action in these areas (Ramcharan 1991). The ORCI mandate included specific provisions for early warning regarding refugees and displaced persons, but little was accomplished through 1992 before the office was dissolved. Following its demise, the newly created Department of Humanitarian Affairs (DHA) was designated the focal point for consultations on early warning of the new flows of refugees and displaced persons. Several UN agencies participated and by 1994 they had held seven inter-agency consultations, gradually reaching a consensus that factors conducive to refugee flows include oppressive rulers, human rights violations, inter- and intra-state wars, epidemics, famine, terrorism, economic plight, and degradation of the environment (Dedring 1994, 98–100). The UN could follow up on this with an early warning system based on common reporting formats and, especially, the capacity to make mature, analytical political judgments on the basis of the information gathered. But such an effort will have to overcome both suspicions of governments and inter-departmental differences within the UN. So far, UNDP has been among the most active agencies in planning a global early warning system (Dedring 1994, 101–103; Dedring 1995, 20–23; Peck 1998, 71–75).

Political Risk Analysis

The third source of ideas for early conflict warning and prevention is the sovereign risk analysis. It focuses primarily on the probability and intensity of political events that can jeopardize the stability of a country. Demonstrations, strikes, and armed civil conflicts are examples of such events. Political risk analysis is interested, in the first place, in the impact of political instability and turmoil on the working conditions of transnational business within a particular country and especially in financial losses that may follow.

There is little consensus among the experts on how the concept of a political risk, and its scope and intensity should be defined. However, a reasonably valid and concise definition of sees political risk as an event that "threatens a firm with financial, strategic or personnel loss due to the non-market forces" (Kennedy 1987, 5). Often a political risk analyst starts with the prospects for the stability of the executive leadership, but may also consider the efficiency and impartiality of governmental institutions (that is, extent of corruption, bureaucratic red tape, and incompetence in public institutions, or independence of the judiciary). Other political forces have to be scrutinized too, especially those opposing the government (for surveys of the political risk analysis and its methods, see Overholt 1982; Raddock et al. 1986; Stapenhurst 1992).

Political risk analysis has relevance, albeit limited, for the development of early warning indicators. Some factors are relevant, however, for developing early warning indicators to identify the potential for violent internal conflict at an early stage. These include the social and political analysis of domestic conditions that have a bearing on a nation's proneness to conflict. Both the social and economic inequalities and challenges that can exceed the carrying capacity of the government, as well as the latter's legitimacy need to be considered (Raddock et al. 1986, 7–37; Kennedy 1987, 40–45). The lessons to be gained from risk analysis differ, however, from those derived from human rights monitoring and famine forecasting. In the case of famines, the public pressure for governmental action plays a major role, while the results of risk analysis are intended for company executives rather than governments or public opinion. On the other hand, corporate decisions to withdraw investments from a country or the imposition of sanctions are clear signals to the government that they should mend their ways and/ or restore stability. Political risk analysis has, by definition, a manipulative task to safeguard and advance the interests of corporations.

Models developed for military and intelligence purposes have a similar function; they are supposed to provide a detailed picture of political power structures which helps to identify internal cracks in the target country. They can in turn be manipulated either to maintain stability or induce a change in the preferred direction. For instance, before invasion, the US Department of Defense commissioned computer models on both the Iraqi and Haitian society to predict the "effects of social, political and economic actions on various sectors of society" (Nairn 1994, 347–48).

In general, the analysis of political risks offers too narrow a perspective to understand threats to peace and security in their entirety. It is primarily interested in the potential governmental instability and its impact on business operations. The business perspective obviously downplays other relevant concerns such as human costs and cultural implications of violence as well as the alternative ways of resolving the conflict. In addition, the integration of the results of risk analysis into corporate decision making differs from the utilization of early warning information in governmental bureaucracies or non-governmental organizations. Finally, the opportunities for and constraints on preventive action are not comparable in the corporate and in public and private political worlds.

Information and Policymaking

Lessons from such models as the cataloging of human rights abuses, forecasting of famines and internally displaced, as well as political risk analysis all point to the importance of information and its utilization. The sources of information may vary from mass media through intelligence agencies and non-governmental organizations to high-level policymakers. The processing of information from mass media can be automated because of its large volume, while more singular information has to be assessed personally. However, the collection of information for early warning is seldom unrestrained. In addition to the perennial problem of access, there are always queries concerning the reliability and validity of data. A real but seldom recognized problem concerns the norms that govern the collection of information. In particular intergovernmental organizations have to operate within the limits of norms imposed on them by governments and intra-organizational routines. This may mean, among other things, that only public sources of information can be utilized, while other sources are off limits.

Another area of information problems concerns the summarization of information by appropriate criteria or categories. Information in general, and political information in particular, makes sense only after it has been interpreted. Therefore, an "early, early warning system" needs at least implicit criteria to arrange data to underpin policymaking. These criteria should tap the breaking points of societies fueling violence as well as the escalatory and constraining dynamics in conflicts. Model-building is useful, but it should not unlink real-life information and policymaking.

In early warning the continuous and comprehensive monitoring of the situation is a precondition for effective political advice and preventive action. Monitoring is a process in which socioeconomic and political conditions of target countries are analyzed in terms of their conflict propensity. While actions violating the norms of peace, democracy, and human rights can be defined and detected with relative ease, another problem remains: Where is the threshold of violation which justifies the use of preventive and punitive actions by the international community? A related problem concerns the assessment of the escalation risk inherent in different types of internal instabilities. Understandably, research interested in collective violence and human insecurity focuses primarily on major misdeeds, that is, genocides and mass murders (Rummel 1994). But should early warning try, in the first instance, to detect signs of genocides and thus help in their prevention? Or should early warning monitor a larger array of potential conflicts (Alker 1994, 119–21)? The latter would help to warn about lesser violence, which still may result in the loss of thousands and thousands of lives, and also detect crises which later on can escalate into mass murders.

There are both empirical and ethical grounds to justify a broader approach. Empirically, it is impossible to know in advance whether in a vulnerable and failing society one political group will try to strengthen its position by mass murders or whether its goals are more limited. Moreover, large-scale violence has its own dynamics which cannot be predicted solely from structural background conditions. Ethically, one can make an absolutist argument that every human life deserves to be saved by preventive measures if at all possible. But even if more relativistic thinking is followed, one can say that while the decimation of a small community of people may not quantitatively figure among the worst genocides of the century, it means a loss of a unique element of humankind.

Finally, one has to ask about the purpose of early warning and how information should be collected, processed, and used to serve the relevant goals. Early warning information can be used to issue a technical warning of a likely crisis to "whom it may concern" or, alternatively, the message can be directed to a particular target group. Such a warning can be either private or public, quiet or loud. Communications of business risks are usually quiet and private, while the monitoring of human rights and famines yields louder public information. If it is loud enough, an early warning is converted into pressure politics prompting governments or other actors to initiate specific policies to rectify the situation. Ultimately, early warning has the function to enhance three instruments: prevention, mitigation, and preparedness (Thoolen 1992, 173). Technically, preparedness can exist even without any early warning capacity, but it helps to target the available resources to prevent disasters or mitigate their consequences. In the case of violent conflicts, prevention is the main objective, while mitigation has the task of alleviating the consequences of violence.

Prerequisites of Early Warning

For early warning systems to be effective, the initial information gathering phase of early warning should cast a fairly wide net to gain as complete a picture as possible, and keep it up-to-date. It has to gauge social reality in a valid manner that is *also* usable in everyday political practice. This means that: (1) the instruments of early warning systems have to be streamlined and contextualized according to relevant criteria; (2) the information produced by them must be user-friendly and tailored to specific decision needs; and (3) the main early warning messages must be continuous and consistent (Spencer 1994). We also argue for replacing the mechanical view of early warning with a more realistic understanding of the multiple and complex political consequences of such action. This presupposes the consequences are well understood and their adverse effects are minimized.

Departing from a structurationist perspective, we also call for "engaged sensing." This point of departure is informed by the methodological assumptions we see underpinning early warning and conflict prevention. Whereas the objectivist perspective assumes that structures largely constrain actors, the structurationist approach contends agents and structures interact and effect each other as 'codetermined' or 'mutually constituted entities' (Wendt 1987, 339). Early warning and conflict prevention are dynamic processes. The interaction of early warning systems and parties to a conflict influences the way the conflict develops, including changes in the latters' goals, demands and behaviors, and perception of the issues at stake. Policymakers need to be aware of these developments, and understand their implications for the effectiveness of early warning and conflict prevention.

For these reasons, early warning systems have to be capable of producing nuanced interpretations of the behavior and stakes of the parties to conflict. This generally requires personnel involved in early warning on the ground (which also means that the engaged actor has negotiated either explicitly or implicitly its access to the conflict zone) or contact with local actors in the conflict area. It also means that local monitors need to be culturally sensitive—though not culturally indoctrinated. The question is not only of *cultural*, but also of *political* sensitivity: policymakers and practitioners have to know how to navigate between different expectations and requirements. Hence, cultural awareness and a capacity for making context specific evaluations of the conflict and its political components are essential. There is also a need to put the deeper understanding of local and national developments into a broader perspective, including how they relate to the regional setting. In any event, early warning and prevention can never be "objective" actions in which the accuracy of information and the effectiveness of actions alone are decisive. They form a morass in which the understanding of, for example, socioeconomic structures and cultural values by a scholar or decision maker is important, but not sufficient. He/she must also be aware of the objectives and operations of the parties to the conflict to be able to provide a valid judgment of the situation.

Another prerequisite for preventive action is an early warning system which gathers information in an anticipatory fashion and carries out analyses of the potential for conflicts to develop. In contrast to traditional approaches by which NGOs and the news media typically monitor and report on human rights violations and atrocities ex post facto, preventive action is, by definition, a pre-emptive enterprise. This imposes special requirements for the gathering and use of information for early warning.

When scholars are involved in the process, in contrast to the related activities of intelligence agencies and business enterprises, it also should be an open and accountable endeavor. However, this can lead to other problems. First, the actors collecting "time-urgent" early warning information must recognize that, through their network of contacts, they become involved in quite a variety of political developments in which they cannot always stay neutral. As a result, their preventive activities may be perceived as serving the cause of one party over the other. Any incidents or problematic developments mentioned in reports can be magnified in importance through the manipulation of media, or public pronouncements by one party as a propaganda tool against the other. Such problems are not insignificant, since they undermine governments' support for preventive diplomacy. As Boutros-Ghali reports in the 1995 Supplement to the *Agenda for Peace*, states collectively support preventive diplomacy, but are often reluctant to contribute to it, especially if they are one of the antagonists.

Another important consideration is whether early warning notification should be conveyed through public or private diplomacy. This concerns both the "who" and "how" of early warning. "Going public" with an early warning can itself exacerbate the conflict; this may be the case whether governments, intergovernmental bodies, or NGOs issue an early warning. Some disputants may be encouraged to exploit a conflict situation for enhanced status and attention to their cause, or other gains, which they expect from the added media exposure. Early warning then leads to the outcomes it aims to avert. Early warnings of ethnic cleansing, for example, may well lead the targeted communities to decide to leave. At the very least, this will result in the massive displacement of peoples, and possibly create refugee flows. Worse yet, instead of forestalling adverse developments, such warnings can fulfill the very aims of the perpetrators of such policies. Issuing a public early warning could also disrupt other efforts of quiet diplomacy carried out within international organizations, or by other third parties.

As observed earlier, monitoring and reporting on conflicts can have unintended consequences, affecting how the parties perceive their stake in the conflict, and its resolution. Consequently, early warning requires considerable diplomatic finesse, and sensitivity to the implications of such action given the political context. Because of the politicized nature of such activity, NGOs whose primary activity is service related will probably be constrained from issuing early warning statements, whether publicly or privately. Confidentiality must be weighed, however, against the necessity of mobilizing the political will of other governments or non-governmental actors to take action and commit the necessary resources to avert violence. Thus, early warning faces some of the same requirements as impartial mediation in conflicts in which violence has already broken out—unless the purpose of early warning is to help one party win the conflict.

We draw on a structurationist perspective to inform not only the methods of early warning, but also the approach we bring to the analysis of early warning information. In our opinion, a successful early warning system should combine the use of generalizable models and in-depth case studies involving local engagement. Early warning requires models specifying the key criteria by which the present and future degree of stability in a society and its breaking points, can be assessed. Case studies help to approximate the timing, mode and consequences of social and political explosion. In this study, we are interested in the particularities of conflict, but the testing of similar parameters relating to the background factors and escalatory processes of conflicts across different cases allows us to retain an element of comparability. Indeed, we need comparisons to show how the background conditions, conflict processes, and outcomes differ from one case to another and how these differences shape the success or failure of early warning and preventive action.

Gathering and Assessing Early Warning Information

For both analytical and practical reasons, the early warning of conflict needs a wide network of on-going information gathering. It should cover both the historical evolution and present circumstances of the targeted societies. The collection and selection of necessary information requires core analytical and institutional competencies by which the incoming information can be assessed and utilized. Early warning is necessarily a decentralized form of transnational action because of the multitude of actors, issues, methods, and targets involved. To be effective, an early warning network requires nodes which crystallize the information and convert it into warning signals, or "red flags." Early warning is ultimately an evaluative process that leads to a political judgement about whether or not to take action. The main *actors* involved are academic scholars and policy analysts, non-governmental organizations, news media, intelligence agencies, and governmental policymakers. They all have their strengths and weaknesses in gathering and assessing information for early warning.

Roughly it may be said that there are three critical issues in the collection of early warning information; access to information, its validity and reliability, and the degree of openness in the utilization of information. The role of different actors in the collection of early warning information can be summarized by Table 2.1 below.

This summary is naturally open for criticism. For instance, the assessment concerning the degree of access by different actors to information depends on what sources we are thinking of. NGOs tend to have extensive access to the local society and less so to the higher echelons of policy making, but with governmental experts it is the reverse. Scholars are usually handicapped in both respects, while the media and intelligence agencies can reach out to both levels of society. One may also query whether the reliability of information is as high as suggested by the summary; for example, the bureaucratic nature of intelligence agencies may badly distort

TABLE 2.1   **Actors in the Collection of Early Warning Information**

	Access	*Reliability*	*Openness*
Scholars	Low	High	High
NGOs	Medium	Medium	Medium
Media	High	Medium	High
Intelligence	High	Medium	Low
Governments	Medium	Medium	Low

information and the casual organization and sectoral focus of some NGOs may leave important gaps in it.

Usually, scholars, NGOs, and the media only produce information and occasionally issue early warning, while the preventive action tends to be the prerogative of various governmental agencies (foreign ministries, the military, and intelligence agencies) which are, at the same time, also involved in the collection and assessment of early warning information. This leads to at least three critical questions: (a) the nature and quality of early warning activities within governmental agencies and their relationship with preventive diplomacy; (b) the relationship between open or semi-open organizations (academy, media, and NGOs) and the executive actors involved in preventive operations; and (c) the potential role of NGOs in preventive actions, especially in their "bottom up" variant.

NGOs can make important contributions, since they are often closest to the action, and can provide information on the stakes different parties may have in a developing dispute. Thus, both indigenous and international humanitarian NGOs are often uniquely positioned to identify early warning signs as their sources of information include parties to which governments and media may not have an access in the early phases of conflict. However, there are also some important limitations to the role of NGOs in early warning. In cases of humanitarian intervention, the information produced by a NGO reflects the interests and views of the population it serves and the arrangements it has made to gain local access. In addition, NGO information is filtered through the organization and its partners—in some cases governments with their own stakes in conflict. Still more problematic, at the earliest stages of a crisis, information disseminated by NGOs and news reporters can be quite superficial and partial (Ezell 1992; DeMars 1994).

There is also the risk that early warning activity could undermine the parties' perception of the NGO impartiality. This is more likely to be problematic for NGOs which are not specialized in monitoring, reporting on or resolving conflicts, but for which the delivery of vital services is the primary goal. The personal safety of NGO workers is also an important consideration. For instance, there is a need to have stronger safeguards to protect individuals and NGOs which avail themselves of international human rights complaints procedures, and their legal representatives, against adverse action or penalties (International Helsinki Federation 1994; Friends World Committee for Consultation 1994). If the military requires a casualty-free operational environment, peace brokers, human rights activists, and relief workers are certainly entitled to similar safety. The murder of Fredrick Cuny provides an example of risks faced by a visible aid worker, especially if the expert becomes tangled in political webs (Shawcross 1995;

Anderson 1996). In sum, there can be little doubt that greater involvement of NGOs in early warning activities—in what, in reality, amounts to intelligence gathering and intervention in domestic affairs—will also be treated as highly political, and all the more so where early warning is most critical.

News reporters may also have certain advantages in early warning, and can themselves be trained for rapid deployment as fact finders—an idea Ezell (1992, 90) considers an essential element of early warning to prevent genocide. He emphasizes the importance of careful investigation rather than reporting speculative information, and preparing reporters in interview techniques and survey methods to make good use of refugee testimony as a source of eyewitness accounts, rather than anecdotes (Ezell 1992, 110–11). At the same time, genocide can be a brief and spasmodic series of events in which there is little time to send in reporters, or if they are already on the spot, their access to information is limited, as was the case in Rwanda (Hilsum 1995). If the atrocities have already broken out, early warning information by journalists, if it is timely enough, can only be of use in limiting violence by helping governments to prevent its further escalation. Especially in high-profile conflicts, such as the Gulf War, the opportunities of journalists to collect reliable information can be severely restricted by "press pools" and other arrangements (Fialka 1991). In such situations journalists can only witness the escalation and do very little to prevent it.

There also is the challenge of integrating systematically the monitoring and reporting capabilities of NGOs and media with other (inter)national means of intelligence gathering, reporting, and analysis. Recent proposals call for linking NGO monitoring and reporting with formal international and regional systems for early warning. The Commission on Global Governance recommends specifically the establishment of a new global machinery through which early warnings could be articulated (Commission on Global Governance 1995, 92). There also have been proposals made by NGOs within the context of the Organization on Security and Cooperation in Europe (OSCE) to enhance their role in early warning and the prevention of conflicts, including by extending to them the right to activate OSCE human rights mechanisms (Netherlands Helsinki Committee 1994, 18). The OSCE has begun to move in this direction.

The Interface Between Early Warning and Conflict Prevention

Early warning and preventive action are closely intertwined forms of action due both to the relations between actors involved and the interdependence of the actions undertaken. Hence, the notion that early warning is supposed to pave the way to prevention may be too simple. The way early warning and conflict prevention work together is critical. Some forms of early warning have preventive functions themselves. Early warning is an evaluative process that leads to a political judgment about whether or not to take action. Thus, a decision to issue an early warning "notification" is, in fact, one type of action: it conveys the message of the risk of imminent escalation of conflict to violent means. It alerts the conflicting parties that their actions are closely followed by outsiders. An early warning notification also sends a signal to third parties that it is time to start preparing for preventive moves. Issuing such notification may, however, be destabilizing because it adds pressure on the antagonists to reach their goals before measures preventing it are started. Therefore, international policymakers often emphasize less visible "early, early warning" (Evans 1994; van der Stoel 1994). The objective is to gain time, and enhance the possibilities to employ a low-profile, "early" preventive diplomacy, and other non-coercive and non-military preventive measures. The resort to more visible and coercive forms of "late" preventive action means the "early" prevention has failed. Thus, prioritizing and targeting preventive action also depends on the quality and timeliness of early warning information.

These different forms of preventive action have their parallels in mediation strategies (cf. Princen 1992). Early action is, in effect, "impartial prevention." Like the neutral form of mediation, the success of early prevention depends in part on the antagonists' perception of the third party's credibility and acceptability to act in a non-partisan fashion. As Max van der Stoel has argued, early preventive action is aimed at "encouraging and supporting efforts by contenders to seek accommodation." In contrast, late preventive action is like power mediation. "Muscular prevention" influences the course of events by tempering the interests of the parties by rewards and punishments. Its objective is to "persuade parties to abstain from violence when eruptions seem imminent" (van der Stoel 1994, 9–12). Late prevention thus aims at finding ways of averting the escalation of conflict, or thwarting inadvertent conflict. Its success depends in part on power projection, which must be credible to the protagonists. The functions of muscular prevention include containing and de-escalating tensions, and other negative developments. This may be accompanied by efforts to promote dialogue, confidence, and cooperation among the parties, and to persuade them to forgo the pursuit of gains through unilateral means.

Monitoring and reporting also create an interface between early warning and conflict prevention. First, more contextualized and nuanced monitoring and reporting on the sources and dynamics of conflict escalation help policymakers to interpret information, and is vital for the development of effective conflict prevention strategies. Second, early action carried out by local diplomatic missions and non-governmental actors can help dissuade or inhibit perpetrators from carrying through with violent action. An international presence can be established at a relatively low cost and low level of political risk, but can make an important contribution.

There are, however, always obstacles to surmount for launching preventive action. Many urgent crises crowd policymakers' agenda, making it difficult for less serious situations to gain their attention. Similarly, justification must also be made for the expenditures of preventive action, when other crises already place heavy demands on governmental budgets, and those of international organizations. Nevertheless, monitoring and reporting can put pressure on decision makers and thus commit them to sustain action either unilaterally or collectively. While often an attractive option, media coverage to leverage such action by the international community may not always be advisable. One or more of the antagonists may see the coverage as hurting their cause, or alternatively as enhancing it. Either way, they could be encouraged to further escalate the conflict. These are among the unintended consequences which third parties must seek to avoid or at least minimize.

Third, when early prevention does fail, the failure itself can help policymakers judge whether a certain "threshold" has been reached that justifies or necessitates an early warning notification, and the recourse to more coercive measures. In this sense, early warning and conflict prevention function on two different, though inter-related levels. Prevention of conflict at one level serves early warning purposes on another level (and vice versa). In the protection of human rights, the failure of monitoring and early preventive efforts by international officials gives a signal to the governments that the situation is deteriorating and requires preventive action with muscle. On the other hand, the usefulness of early warning continues even if violence has broken out as there is a need to prevent the deterioration of the crisis into even more large-scale hostilities.

Conflicts: Cyclical, Multidimensional, and Multilevel

To develop effective strategies for early warning and preventive action, analysts and practitioners need a nuanced understanding of conflicts, including their background causes and escalatory dynamics. The literature has typically treated these factors in relation to a multi-phase conflict cycle. The cyclical models depart, as a rule, from the distinction between latent and manifest, or violent and non-violent phases of conflicts, but they may contain as many as seventeen phases ranging from durable peace to open conflict (Reychler 1997, 57–61). Here violence can be defined as the use of coercive power to alter the behavior of other actors to comply with the user's preferences. In latent conflicts there are certainly differing interests and attitudes, but only violent action makes them manifest. The process of manifestation is usually associated with social change altering the position and preferences of actors, giving rise to new actors and issues, and thus changing the political agenda of the community. The phase model assumes that if efforts to solve the differences early in the conflict through such methods as persuasion, negotiation, and arbitration are not tried or they fail, the relations between parties may deteriorate. They are likely to turn to threats and coercive means to resolve the dispute, provoking a crisis which can potentially escalate into a large-scale use of force. Sooner or later, one side wins the conflict or it enters a stalemate when violence can be terminated by an agreed settlement.

Cyclical models are, as a rule, uni-dimensional and organized along a temporal axis. They lead us to think of conflicts in terms of their successive stages in which various corrective actions can be undertaken to avert the further deterioration of a dispute. Miall (1992, 40–43), for example, makes a distinction between prevention, regulation, and ending as phases of the conflict cycle (see also Nikolaïdis 1996, 31–36). In the first phase, conflict prevention aims to maintain stability by the good management of social relations, sensitivity, and social justice. In the second phase, threats to stability become visible and the mechanisms for early warning and conflict containment should be activated. If early warning indicates a sufficiently high likelihood of violence, various measures should be applied to prevent the outbreak of violence. If they fail, the parties should make their best effort to limit, resolve and ultimately terminate the violence. The resolution of conflict then requires initial understandings, de-escalation initiatives, and negotiated agreements (Kriesberg 1992, 4–5). Finally, social and material damage produced by violence should be repaired by reconstruction and reintegration to create a new basis for continued reconciliation (Berdal 1994).

The phase model of conflicts is useful in that it specifies targets for external involvement; first in early warning and prevention, then in conflict resolution, and finally in post-conflict peace-building. However, the model provides rather simple, and perhaps too obvious precepts for action. Therefore, several caveats are needed. First, instead of being uni-dimensional, conflict processes are usually *multidimensional* and unfold in a disjunctive manner. There are internal tensions within a conflict process, hinting both to threats of escalation and opportunities of resolution. Second, the phase models tend to focus primarily on the *means* to manipulate the conflict process, but neglect other relevant dimensions such as goals, interests, and internal conditions of the actors involved. Following Zartman (1991, 513–16), we see these dimensions of conflict as unfolding along their own trajectories, although there may be synergistic effects among background factors, and between the different elements in the escalation process.

Third, the cycle models fail also to take into account the *multiple levels* to every conflict and the continuing shifts between them. In reality, the individual, group, nation, state, and the international level are intertwined in a complex and dynamic manner with each other. Whether, and how actors are drawn into a conflict depends both on the structure of the system, the nature of the situation, and the broader historical and cultural context in which the conflict evolves. Fourth, there are usually multiple *issues*, across which the nature and salience of conflict varies (Northrup 1989, 58–60; Diehl 1992).

Issues refer to the objectives, values, and interests motivating parties to use violence, while stakes identify more concrete positions which they have developed in specific issues (Holsti 1991; Diehl 1992; Esman 1994). While the parties may agree on the issue in conflict (that is, education for the ethnic minority in its own language), they may well have different stakes in the way the matter is settled. What is at stake also depends on the position of actors in the larger social and political structure, their interests, goals, and the means used. For example, political leaders may, as the instrumentalist perspective suggests, play up inter-ethnic tensions within and between countries for their own political purposes, even though at the base of society relationships between members of different ethnic communities are not especially acute. Such differences must be evaluated carefully, if early warning and conflict prevention are to be effective. Thus, the emphasis we put on issues and stakes is directly associated with our conception of the political and strategic nature of the early warning and prevention of conflicts. Stakes in conflict motivate actors to hide and manipulate information and elicit such actions by governments and international bodies that favor them over the other parties to a conflict.

Fifth, the phase models allude to conflict processes and dynamics, without specifying how they lead to different outcomes. Which types of behaviors drive and accelerate the greater destructiveness of conflict and which, on the other hand, decelerate such a trend? How do specific types of behavior affect the outcome of conflict on its different levels and dimensions and what kinds of interactive effects exist between them? Is it possible to identify a set of conditions and processes which tend to trigger the outbreak of widespread violence in intra-national conflicts and assess how it could best be forestalled?

The predominant managerial literature on crisis response fails to give us many guidelines for action. Rather than depicting conflict as the key problem standing in the way of effective crisis management (with the main focus on effective crisis response), we need to put our attention first on the dimensions and dynamics of conflict processes that lead to political crises, and on this basis look for effective responses ('t Hart 1992). Our approach

is to develop a set of conceptual tools to answer questions about how conflicts start and develop, and to assess what kinds of interventions can help
prevent, ameliorate, and terminate them. Following Buzan's (1995) theoretical distinction between structure and process, we devise a box of tools
that helps us differentiate between the *social and material background* and
the *escalatory dynamics* of conflict. As a rule, one can say that background
factors are a necessary but not a sufficient condition for the outbreak of
violence; conflict can hardly erupt without the existence of socio-economic
and political grievances. They are not, however, sufficient to prompt escalation of the conflict process. On the other hand, conflict processes can be
sufficient, but not usually necessary conditions for escalation.

Both background conditions and dynamics of violence differ between
structural, material, institutional, and identity conflicts. In *structural conflicts* tensions stem from such conditions as social hierarchies and cleavages,
or territorial divisions. Structural conflicts result in the marginalization of
some groups and the privileging of others, along class, ethnic or gender
lines, for example. In *material conflicts*, the scarcity and allocation of resources and demographic and environmental pressures lead to adverse social
effects that shape politics and potentially lead to violence (see, for example,
Homer-Dixon 1994). In *institutional conflicts*, the political struggle mobilizes the ideological values and material interests of the people to fight for
the control of the state, the resources it commands and, in that way, hegemony and autonomy within society (see, for example, Esman 1994). In
cultural or *identity conflicts*, violence is embedded in the socio-economic
and cultural cleavages of society, but reproduced in the perception of threats
to the individual and group core values and belief system (that is, myths
and memories) leading to the resort to force to defend or augment them.
By examining the dynamics of identity conflicts, we also see how the different *levels of conflict* (from the individual to group, national and
international levels) are activated, and various actors are mobilized.

The distinction between background factors and escalation dynamics
also has a practical side: it is associated with the difference between long-term
and short-term conflict management strategies. The amelioration of background causes of violence requires *long-term strategies* focusing on equitable
and sustainable economic development, the establishment of strong and
legitimate political institutions, the relaxation of cultural tensions, and the
strengthening of social practices to resolve peacefully deadly disagreements.
Engaged monitors, particularly individuals who are culturally sensitive,
politically aware, and know well the needs of the society, can provide valuable early warning information that prioritizes and targets resources where
they are most needed and have the greatest chance of amplifying peace. For
example, given the role that the media played in exacerbating inter-ethnic

fears and tensions in the Former Yugoslavia, the training of journalists in cultural sensitivity and multi-culturalism were wisely given a high priority in the preventive measures introduced in Macedonia.

Short-term strategies are needed when the outbreak of violence is imminent and there is not enough time to wait for the long-term strategies to have an impact. Here, engaged monitors need to be able to judge how conflict is intensifying, that is, whether it is spreading horizontally to mobilize more actors, or to achieve more extreme goals, or whether it will intensify vertically, as the parties become more polarized and they turn to increasingly violent means. Whether early warning notifications should be issued publicly at such junctures is a critical question. Again, it is important to ensure that such action does not inadvertently precipitate what the perpetrators themselves seek. Short-term solutions almost always are political by their nature and require that the leaders of the opposed groups cooperate to thwart off violence, for example, by sharing power, accepting an external mediator, or peacekeeping troops. Thus, short-term strategies usually favor a "top down" approach, or preventive action with muscle. Meanwhile, long-term strategies can also operate "from below," strengthening social, economic, and political structures of peace through impartial preventive action. "Bottom up" solutions tend to be more effective and durable as they change the society and do not just temporarily paper over the differences between the leaders of contending communities. However, both bottom up and top down approaches can have a socializing effect, for example, by reinforcing democracy and civil rather than ethnic conceptions of citizenship.

In short, the multidimensionality and multiple levels of conflict make for phases and escalatory dynamics that are seldom neatly ordered; rather they overlap and are contingent on each other. The matters are further complicated by the fact that types of conflict issues can vary with actors' interests and ideologies and their disagreements on how to accomplish even a shared goal (Druckman 1993, 26–29). Therefore, in designing conflict early warning indicators and preventive measures, there must be attention to the constant interaction across levels, issues, and dimensions. To simplify the analytical tasks, the *phases* of conflict can be divided between pre-conflict, intra-conflict, and post-conflict stages in which the first and third phase are predominantly non-violent. Each of these three phases can be explored in terms of the distinction between *background factors* versus *process*. While in the pre-conflict phase background factors tend to shape processes, the outbreak of violence is such a fundamental trigger that it also transforms the social context of the conflict.

Preventive action has to be tailored to different phases, with their characteristic structures and processes, types and levels of violent conflicts. In terms of phases, preventive action has three basic objectives: (1) to prevent latent disputes from developing into hostilities, and to find means to resolve them non-violently when they do; (2) to hinder the further escalation of violence; and (3) to avert a breakdown and relapse into violence during the post-conflict peace building phase. Different preventive policies and tools apply to each of these objectives. The task of early warning is to detect the development of potentially violent conflicts and provide adequate time to find out preferably non-coercive means by which the acute escalation of a crisis can be avoided and the conflict channeled constructively.

Preventive strategies can be divided into *external* versus *internal* ones, depending on who has the main responsibility for action, and *muscular* versus *impartial* ones, depending especially on the means used in preventive action. Internal prevention happens among the parties to a given conflict, while in external prevention third parties become involved. In the pre-conflict phase preventive strategies are primarily internal and non-coercive, relying on bargaining between the main parties to the dispute. Ideally, this means that the parties institutionalize a process or create mechanisms that permit a mutual dialogue to address their long-term relationship and transform the root causes of the conflict. In the intra-conflict phase, the opportunities for an internal settlement diminish and the need of external involvement increases. External involvement in most cases has been non-coercive, comprising efforts at mediation and reconciliation between the parties with the objective to prevent escalation and, ultimately, to stop war. Here early warning should pinpoint the likelihood that its perpetrators aim to escalate the war by crossing salient qualitative or quantitative limits. Such notification should give time for the international community to try to prevent the escalation. In the post-conflict phase, the reconstruction and reintegration of a war-torn society cannot succeed without the internal commitment of the main parties to accomplish these goals. At the same time external, non-coercive economic and political assistance is vital for success. The post-conflict early warning should alert policymakers to any breakdown in the peace building process that could relapse into violent confrontation. The objective is to create stable conditions for the long-term peaceful management of society (cf. Conflict Management Group 1994, 6).

The bottom line of the above argument is that early warning and prevention are both strategic actions. Therefore, in addition to means, which the traditional cyclical models of conflict stress, we have to pay attention also to causes and goals of action. The reliance on means in model building can lead to circular reasoning. It can be avoided if the strategies of early warning and prevention are designed to reflect the underlying structural, material, identity and institutional sources of conflict (that is, socio-economic, territorial and cultural conditions) on the one hand, and the dynamics of the conflict processes, on the other. In looking at conflict dynamics, both the issues over which the conflict is waged and the stakes that actors hold in them are particularly important as they provide a measure of the seriousness of the conflict and the lengths to which the parties are ready to go to reach their goals.

Both the early warning and prevention of conflicts may be short-term activities, while conflict resolution and peace-building usually demand more time. Thus, the time span and urgency of these two phases of conflict are different. This also means that the nature of politics—that is, issues and stakes—are different in these phases. In early warning and prevention the stakes are associated primarily with tactical advantages and public images, while in conflict resolution and peace-building they concern more the long-term allocation of political power and material values. This conclusion is not surprising as it simply states that with the exacerbation of conflict, it casts a longer shadow and its impact on the parties becomes more pervasive and long-lasting.

Alert messages and preventive measures must be both materially capable, politically feasible, and focus on malleable factors ("independent variables") whose transformation can prevent the escalation of conflict. As a rule, socio-economic, territorial, and cultural background conditions of conflicts may merit attention in early warning, but their transformation requires too much time and effort to provide a feasible approach in the political environment in which risks are high and expectations of action are immediate. Therefore, preventive strategies must primarily focus on the dynamics of conflicts, while early warning should probably utilize both sets of factors.

Conclusion

There are many obstacles to making early warning and conflict prevention a regular practice in the management of international peace and security. States have to make a commitment to manage the causes, not just consequences of violence and repression. Identifying and acting early on them to prevent conflicts needs to become a priority. Nevertheless, emerging conflicts are overshadowed by the great number of full-blown intrastate crises crowding the international agenda during the 1990s.

With the shift toward multi-polarity, there is an expanding political space for preventive action. A more diverse group of actors is also becoming involved in the collection of early warning information, but there are still problems with access to information, its validity and reliability, and the degree of openness in its utilization. There will also always be trade-offs between the need for timely evaluations and systematic analyses drawing from a deep knowledge of local conditions. The latter will translate more readily into concrete policy initiatives, but are of little use for preventive action if they are not forthcoming in a timely fashion. The international community also has to overcome the challenge of integrating systematically the monitoring and reporting capabilities of NGOs and the media with other international and national means of intelligence gathering, reporting, and analysis.

The interface between early warning, including its monitoring and reporting functions, and preventive action is especially critical. However, numerous obstacles stand in the way of translating information about potential crises into collective action, including the problems of factual and political validity of the assessment, building a consensus on it, and then organizing an appropriate response. While the barriers to NGO—governmental cooperation have been lowered in recent years, in acute crises governments still have the main responsibility for organizing preventive action.

Early warning and conflict prevention have a role to play in the pre-, as well as intra- and post-conflict phases. In the intra-conflict phase, the first priority is to contain the proximate causes of violence, and to deal with its immediate consequences including preventing its spill over into neighboring regions and providing humanitarian assistance to victims. There are, however, many impediments for mobilizing preventive action with muscle. More readily available are the kinds of actors and resources which can be deployed to target background or antecedent causes of conflict. Such efforts should be introduced not only in the pre- and post-conflict phases, but also, to the extent possible, in the intra-conflict phase in order to lay the groundwork for a durable peace. Conflict transformation depends on containing escalatory processes over the short term, while altering the underlying structural conditions over the long term, including the material, cultural, and institutional dimensions of conflict. Of course, short term strategies are needed when the outbreak of violence or its spread is imminent and time is too short to wait for the long term strategies targeted on background conditions to take effect.

Ultimately, there needs to be more of a preventive developmental approach taken to targeting international resources on vulnerable and poor societies. In practice, vast resources are spent instead on rescue missions which do little to bring durable social and economic justice and political stability. Those conflicts on which the international community targets preventive action with muscle are more often the exception than the rule.

3

THE EARLY WARNING TOOLBOX:
CUES FROM BACKGROUND CONDITIONS

Introduction

IN THE PREDICTION, PREVENTION, AND RESOLUTION OF INTRASTATE CONFLICTS, the successful identification of the potential sources of violence requires a viable theory of conflict. Such a theory must contain at least structural, institutional, and cultural elements relating to the domestic context, and also provide a means for evaluating potential destabilizing factors emanating from the international environment. Marc Howard Ross (1993) has, in particular, developed, compared, and empirically tested structural and psycho-cultural explanations of conflicts, while Jeffrey Ian Ross (1993) has made a distinction between structural, psychological, and rational accounts of terrorism. Göran Therborn (1991) argues, in turn, that human action can be explained either by the attributes of the actor, its structural location, or cultural belonging.

Thus, there seems to a fair amount of agreement that structural and cultural approaches are most relevant in exploring the roots of violent conflicts. Actor attributes obviously matter only in a relational, and thus in a structural context, and may not need independent treatment. Rational accounts rightly notice the instrumental aspects of violence and have to be utilized, therefore, in the analysis of the escalation of violent conflicts and efforts at their prevention. Rationalist explanations are less helpful in considering the background conditions of violence. However, structural and cultural conditions have to be linked with the institutional dimensions of conflict, especially those concerning the legitimacy and effectiveness of political institutions.

Structural Perspectives

Structural explanations suggest that the conflict proneness of society depends on its organization, that is, how various social groups, their interests, and resources are related to each other. The changing distribution of economic and political resources, and access to them, among the social groups are of special relevance as they define the social infrastructure in which ethnic and other forms of social mobilization take place. Resources provide means to compete both in the public and private spheres for social and economic privileges available in the society. The competition and its outcomes are shaped by the political opportunity structure, that is, incentives and restraints, of the society.

The structure of society as such is, however, too broad a notion to provide a basis for a selective and clear system of early warning indicators. Therefore, some of its central characteristics must be singled out for special attention. In addition, a distinction should be made between deeper systemic conditions (that is, geographic location, level of development, and the type of political system) and factors precipitating violence (that is, cultural and historical facilitation, the distribution of grievances, and the lack of institutional legitimacy) (cf. Ian Jeffrey Ross 1993). Because of the effort to develop strategies for the early warning and prevention of conflicts, this analysis focuses on precipitating, or facilitating causes of violence rather than its deeper structural roots.

Entitlements and Their Failures

The structural aspects of society in our early warning model are conceptualized primarily in terms of entitlements, territory, and cleavages. All human beings face what Amartya Sen has called the "acquirement problem," that is, the dilemma of how to establish and maintain command over various economic and social resources. In every society individuals and groups have a certain endowment of commodities to which they are legally entitled, and the society usually offers an opportunity to exchange them. By their endowment people have the right to acquire a "bundle" of available commodities. If people cannot meet their legitimate basic needs, an entitlement failure occurs either as a consequence of the unavailability of necessary commodities, inadequacy of the individual endowment, or the breakdown of exchange relations (Drèze and Sen 1989, 22–25; Sen 1990, 34–52).

The *entitlement system* is linked with the property rights of the society. In terms of these rights, the failure of entitlements means that they are not honored and adequate access to food, shelter, education, and other necessities is denied. Such discrimination may be due to the violation of law when an extra-entitlement transfer of property rights takes place (Sen 1981, 45–51). In fact, some authors have criticized Sen for neglecting the abuse of power as a main reason for entitlement failures. For instance, food and other necessities are often used as instruments of war. The critics argue that power and politics must have a more central place in accounting for human misery and entitlement failures (Rangasami 1985; de Waal 1990).

In the present analysis the key question is whether the entitlement structure can provide early warning on simmering and potentially escalatory conflicts in society. The entitlement approach has been used to account for the background causes of violence, but its explanatory power remains still uncertain and is no doubt difficult to test (de Gaay Fortman and Kortekaas 1994; Väyrynen 1994, 14–19). Empirical research has suggested that material inequality alone is not a sufficient reason for the outbreak and escalation of ethnonational conflicts, although it may play a greater role in other types of conflicts and in situations in which the discrimination of indigenous minorities is compounded by environmental stress (Gurr 1993, 34–60; Gurr 1994b, 358–59). However, factors pertaining to economic development and political system are better predictors of violence than environmental degradation which have a stronger impact on small wars (Hauge and Ellingsen 1998).

The distribution of and access to material entitlements provides a measure of inequality and opportunity in society. If the access to basic entitlements is very skewed and rights to satisfy basic needs are not honored, the society is obviously prone to conflicts. These conflicts are due either to the inability of the society to deliver necessary commodities to satisfy entitlements ("scarcity conflicts"), or to the fact that some groups have privileged access to them while other groups are deliberately denied them ("discriminatory conflicts"). The latter approach brings in the analysis of the use of power in society.

In *scarcity conflicts* individuals and groups are competing for absolute amounts of insufficient resources, while in *discriminatory conflicts* the rivalries concern the relative shares of resources. In scarcity conflicts the amount of resources, either in absolute or per capita terms, is either fixed or declining, while in discriminatory conflicts resources are growing, but they are distributed in a highly skewed manner.[1] Then the abundance rather than scarcity of resources is the cause of the conflict. The ultimate question in scarcity conflicts concerns the power to decide who will survive, while in discriminatory conflicts the question is more of who prospers in the process of accumulation. One can submit that both of these conflicts can be approached in the framework of rational, instrumental action in which material goals loom large. It is also fair to assume that intermediary social factors, such as agricultural production and the disruption of social institutions, further facilitate the spread of violence (Homer-Dixon 1991, 90–98).

In disintegrating communities social control can be maintained by repression or challenged by rebellion against the oppressive government. Probably conflicts of scarcity are more intense than those of discrimination.

Therefore, it is important to check whether the nation's economy is growing or declining and whether the ecological and demographic stresses have crossed the limits of tolerance. While justice is a pertinent issue in both types of conflicts, its implications are starker for scarcity conflicts in which the stake is about survival. In fact, the access to entitlements provides an indicator for social justice: the more blocked the access the more unjust the society. The notion of justice is relevant for early warning because it indicates the degree of responsiveness, compassion and, thus, legitimacy in society.

In traditional agricultural societies a critical entitlement, and thus an indicator of conflict potential, is the distribution of and access to *land* as a basic source of living. Conflicts over land often concern absolute gains and ultimately the survival of the parties to it. Competition for land may take place within the dominant type of economic activity or between different types of activities. In the former case small peasants and big landowners have competing claims over the ownership of agricultural land and access to it (the conflict in Chiapas, Mexico, clearly belongs to this category). In the latter case the land conflict occurs either between the nomadic herdsmen and farmers or between agricultural and industrial uses. The loss of cropland, due to industrial expansion and soil erosion, together with the stagnating land productivity leads to declining grain production and may lead in heavily populated countries into a serious food crisis. In that regard an early warning on the coming food crisis in China, with all of its adverse political consequences, has been already issued (L. Brown 1995).

Rapid population growth and the scarcity of land increase social pressures and fuel violence also in many African countries. Rwanda is a prototypical example of how land scarcity fostered confrontation between the cattle-herding Tutsi and land-tilling Hutu. Sons of landless Hutu peasants were easily recruited in death squads, *interahamwe*, in charge of atrocities against the opposing Tutsi community of cattle herders (Ruanda 1994). In Kenya violent struggles between Masai, Kalenjin, and other nomadic tribes of the Rift Valley whose lands have been invaded by Kikuyu, Luo, and Luhjya farmers, and the other way around, have demanded altogether 1,500 lives since 1991, and 300,000 people have been displaced. Over time, the rivalry for land has been intensified by hostile ethnic rhetoric by the Moi government and claimed hundreds of lives since early 1995. Historically, the colonialists favored the cultivators at the expense of the pastoralists whose interests were, however, defended by Kenya's first president, Jomo Kenyatta. This created a sense among the Kikuyus of grievance and resentment which had been exploited by Moi (Press 1995; Berkeley 1996).

Land scarcity does not, of course, necessarily lead to violence. As long as the entitlement to land is reasonably well honored in the rural areas and it is not directly associated with ethnic divisions, inequality in land ownership can remain a secondary factor in precipitating opposition and unrest. This argument is consistent with the finding by Midlarsky (1988) that patterned rather than generalized inequality is a better predictor of violence, at least in Latin America and the Middle East. Patterned inequality exists when land holdings in the upper portion retain their size, but are subdivided into mini-lots in the lower portion. Such a process leads to a discriminatory conflict between the social top and bottom, and intensifies the scarcity conflict at the bottom.

In urban areas, an important indicator of social inequality and thus conflict proneness is the access to gainful *employment*. It generates a permanent stream of income and provides, together with education, which is the single best predictor of individual salaries, a springboard for upward social mobility. The skewed distribution or lack of permanent employment opportunities is a sign of fragmenting social structure. People earn their living, if at all, from short-term and part-time jobs which do not provide an economic basis for coherent social organization and children's education. In terms of employment opportunities and salary levels there are, especially in countries like Brazil, strong differences between the urban and rural people and between the dominant and minority ethnic groups (World Development Report 1995, 41–46).

Obviously, a rapid rate of urbanization and the ensuing rise in the number of urban poor increase demographic pressures in cities and thus contribute to social explosiveness, especially if the country simultaneously experiences an economic crisis and external economic intervention (Auvinen 1993, 34–46, 143, 150–53). As mentioned, a deep *urban-rural gap* in living conditions is an important signal of a society's fragmentation. In fact, three different conflict dimensions—intra-urban, intra-rural, and urban-rural—emerge in this context and cannot be separated from each other. The impoverishment of the countryside encourages people to move to cities where they join the burgeoning underclass of shanty towns. This exacerbates tensions, especially criminality, between the urban proletariat and wealthy elites. Large-scale movements of people may also bring ethnically distinct new and old immigrant groups into contact and lead to fears and hostility.

It has to be stressed that the social marginalization and geographical mobility of people as such do not usually lead to large-scale, instrumental violence. Its outbreak requires either "political gasoline," such as economic crises and competing political or ethnic identities, or social tensions, such as those manifested in the spread of drugs, prostitution and other forms of social disorganization as well as in the privatization of violence by organized crime and armed gangs. Such violence is no less real in its consequences than political or ethnic violence; yet, its early warning and prevention requires quite different approaches. The insecurity of Karachi, Moscow, Los Angeles, or Sao Paulo speak volumes about the potential of privatized, disorganizing violence—molecular civil wars," to use Enzensberger's (1994, 42) expression—in urban centers.

In usually tranquil rural areas, the conflict potential can be increased not only by steep inequalities in land ownership, but also by the existence of foreign-controlled mining or oil producing enclaves. Valuable natural resources provide assets by which the parties to a crisis can amass power and fund their military activities and repression (of which Angola, Burma, Liberia, and Zaire provide examples).

Ambitious economic programs, rapid population growth, and the ensuing need to mobilize resources and increase agricultural production displace people, destroy the environment, disrupt social institutions, and increase, though only over the long term, the potential for civil strife (Winnefeld and Morris 1994). If the direction of mobility is from the over-populated agricultural regions to more easily degraded coastal and other areas, one can speak of ecological marginalization as a cause of conflict (Homer-Dixon 1994, 15–16).

As mentioned earlier, structural conditions or the extent of "collective disadvantage" (Gurr 1993, 126) as such seldom foment violence. Inequalities can be activated by negative triggers such as the collective feeling of *grievances* which are due either to a sudden drop in economic conditions or the denial of entitlements to a particular group or both. The pre-existing structural, cultural, or institutional divisions deserve attention, especially if the society is in the throes of a major economic crisis, thus pushing socially and/or ecologically marginalized people over the edge. A high degree of internal coherence, firm self-identity, and easily mobilized resources can trigger a disadvantaged group to act, even by violent means (Gurr 1993, 126–28; Gurr 1994a). The Yugoslavian case provides supporting material; favorable responses to ethnic propaganda were strongest in the regions most suffering from the economic recession and failures of restructuring in the 1980s (Woodward 1995, 202–203).

Territory

The territorial structure of society provides another set of structural factors which help to identify conflicts at an early phase. *Territory* refers here to the spatial arrangement of power and resources. In a social sense, territory is differentiated; that is, it is divided both in terms of property rights, functional uses, and structural features (such as center and periphery). Territories can be classified according to their users and uses, and these classifications are communicated as markers to other actors. In terms of classifications and signals, territories are either closed (territorial states) or open ("commons"). Territorial conflicts concern both the control of and the access to spatially defined pieces of land. Such conflicts are not only about territory in the material sense, but also about the norms and rules of access and utilization (Väyrynen 1993; Ruggie 1993).

In terms of ideology, territory is not only national or otherwise propri-etary, but embodies a broader sense of belonging. Territory provides the spatial marker for including and excluding people. Territoriality as a strat-egy of political control is a means of regulating access to different kinds of resources, entitlements, rights, and obligations. Groups tend to perceive incompatibilities stemming from territorial conflict in zero-sum terms. This is, however, too restrictive a view, not because territory cannot be divided, but because identity, ideology, and rights are equated and always connected with a broader social-political system and vision. Therefore, while sover-eign territory is usually indivisible the ideological dimension fosters overlapping spatial demands.

Woodward points out how in ex-Yugoslavia the nationalist argument led to territorial aggrandizement which provided, in turn, the basis for claims to political authority, economic resources, and citizenship. The ter-ritorialization of conflict started from the patriarchal rural culture, but spread also to cities. This development ultimately linked the present tensions with historical struggles for land. The historical-territorial confrontation, rather than ethnic or religious hatred as such, reinforced the quest for national homogeneity and sovereignty over political power and material assets (Woodward 1995, 205–208; Woodward 1995a, 236–46).

In general, most social forms have a particular spatial fixity. Agnew notes that "the proximity or distance, the uniqueness or the plurality which characterize the relations of social groups to the territory are therefore of-ten the root and symbol of their structure" (Agnew 1989, 46). For example, the political anchoring of the Serbian identity in the Kosovo region has exacerbated the inter-ethnic conflict there between the Albanians and the Serbs (the former outnumbering the later 9:1). In the West Bank and Gaza the struggle for land between Israeli settlers and Palestinians, who claim to have ancestral rights to it, provides another example of how the problem of territory not only causes conflicts, but is a symbol of them.

Each territorial unit has its social structure and special identity, such as group loyalty and national sentiment, attached to it. Territoriality is a background element that interacts with both structural conditions (that is, access to entitlements) and cultural dispositions (that is, attachment to land as a part of national identity) to increase or to reduce the proneness of society to violent conflicts. Territoriality is most inflammable when it has an intimate association with structural and cultural conflict elements. If a nation is relatively homogenous such an association is not internally divisive, but it may result in external expansiveness to project the national values to other nations.

Problems arise in such cases when societies are constituted by a rich mix of ethnic groups, each claiming overlapping and contested pieces of territory. Historically, in the Balkans several nations have claimed greatness and the public memories of these claims live on. The problem is that "there is simply not enough real estate for all these claims of greatness, their territorial ambitions are mutually incompatible" (Mojzes 1994, 42–43). Against this backdrop, it can be hypothesized that especially in traditional societies conflict proneness is higher if the parties to a conflict share or compete for the same territory. This spatial intertwining increases points of friction which can accumulate over time into a pervasive and enduring confrontation. Efforts to divide the territory in sovereign parcels may deteriorate rather than solve the conflict. On the basis of similar reasoning Mazrui (1995) concludes that the most volatile combination of ethnic geography is one in which ethnic diversity flourishes without corresponding territorial differentiation.

The vulnerability of society to violence increases further if the groups are economically and politically in unequal positions. In such cases the conflict is not only derived from incompatible national or ethnic identities, but also from the differential access to degrees of control over a given territory. Thus, in Bosnia the Serbs felt that the Owen-Stoltenberg plan gave too much of its industrial potential to the Croatian-Muslim coalition, while in Krajina they were unwilling to give back to the Croats those pieces of territory, especially Eastern Slavonia, which have natural resources and industrial capacity.

Tensions are further compounded if different groups share claims to the same territory which has significant but different historical meanings for them. The tendency of such a conflict to become intractable results from the way nationalist agendas construct and interpret space. They tend to transform territory into a political space to which people feel loyalty, and which serves to define and communicate to others their identity (Väyrynen 1993, 166). In internal conflicts there is a tendency to separate various groups from each other and thus sharpen territorial boundaries. Such a separation is often accompanied by the stereotyping, scapegoating, and even dehumanization of the enemy which give rise to the dialectics of demonization of the other and the sanctification of the self (Ryan 1996, 148–53). If the parties cannot distance themselves by secession or irredentism, the risk of "cleansing" to preserve ethnic purity increases.

As hinted above, Rwanda is a pertinent example; rather than distinct ethnic groups, the Hutu and Tutsi, often sharing the same territory, had different socio-economic endowments. The majority Hutu have been cultivators, suppressed in the colonial system, while the minority Tutsi have been privileged cattle-keepers and the colonial *comprador* group (Shoumahoff 1994; Hilsum 1995). Rwanda and Burundi both provide evidence of how the competition for limited resources in a given territory is a major source of conflict in a land-dependent economy. Another territorial reason for resorting to (pre-emptive) military force is the fear of secession by an entire region, such as Southern Sudan, Eritrea, Shaba, or Biafra in Africa.

In industrialized societies the sharing of territory does not usually increase the conflict proneness. On the contrary, territorial intermingling tends to increase interdependence and communication, lessen tensions, and create a mutually advantageous division of labor. Thus, the deterritorialization of society is a sign of its decreasing proneness to conflicts. For example, the recent search for a peaceful solution to the Basque conflict has emphasized non-territorial solutions such as new political ties, transfrontier arrangements, and representation at the European level (in the "Europe of regions").

Social Cleavages

The third dimension in the background conditions for the outbreak and escalation of violence is the cleavage structure of the society. The probability of violent conflicts is supposed to increase if social, economic and political *cleavages overlap* and thus reinforce each other. In such a situation there are few social, cultural, and economic bridges between the groups that would reinforce mutual concerns, shared identity, experiences, or goals. The control of territory is an exception as its sharing may increase contacts and exacerbate mutual tensions. On the other hand, *cross-cutting cleavages* prevent conflicts as they create multiple loyalties, mutual dependencies, and common interests (Coser 1956). Then the sharing of territory can reduce rather than increase conflicts. Cyprus, Northern Ireland, and South Africa have been often regarded as societies in which overlapping cleavages increase their propensity to inter-communal conflict.

In mapping the cleavage structure of society the basic categories are divisions based on ethnic, national, religious, and other cultural identities on the one hand and on economic and socio-economic and territorial divisions on the other. It appears that conflicts over identities are more intense, while the impact of material inequalities is, at least over a short term, more limited in molding conflict dynamics. However, struggles for political power remain the most central element in intra-state conflicts (Gurr 1994b, 354–59). Therefore one possible strategy to warn early on violence would be to identify first the main parties to the conflict, analyze their mutual relations in the field of identities, and finally check whether the structural background conditions reinforce or mitigate the contention for political power.

An underlying assumption of structural theories is that groups or individuals in the same social and structural positions have common interests regarding such concerns as security, power, and wealth. These concerns, though not unitary, are intrinsic to the structural position of the group and its ability to serve the members. The fortunes and misfortunes of an individual are, as a rule, tied to the group. Thus benefits or threats to the group's position affect the individual and integrate him/her more closely to the collectivity (Marc Howard Ross 1993, 37).

Ultimately, the conflict proneness of society depends on the intensity and nature of *grievances* felt by individuals and groups. The unequal distribution of entitlements, tension-ridden social cleavages, perceived social injustices as well as political and cultural discrimination provide indicators by which the society's breaking points, and thus the sources of violent conflicts, can be identified. As these examples show, grievances tend to have multiple sources, and also multiple targets, and change over time. Grievances usually have an impact only after they are mobilized by a political organization into collective interests and actions (Jeffrey Ian Ross 1993, 325–26; Gurr 1993, 68–70). As to structural theories, they identify the loci and direction of violent conflicts, while cultural theories may address better the problem of their intensity and proneness to escalation.

Cultural Approaches

Culture and Identity

The cultural perspective suggests that conflicts are shaped by shared and opposed fears about human existence and identity, and their projections to the future. Cultural theories, which have both a collective and individual psychological dimension, focus on such dispositional factors as cultural inheritance, mode of socialization and social learning, religious values as well as ethnic and other social identities. Ethnic and religious tensions are especially relevant in the cultural context as groups involved in them draw on identity markers or use certain cultural traits to designate self-identity and sustain community boundaries (for an overview of these theories, see Marc Howard Ross 1993, 51–69).

Contrary to a common perception, religious, linguistic and other cultural boundaries are not always rigid; groups may use different markers over time, as new needs arise for expanding or restricting group membership or restructuring of inter-group relations. Thus, ethnic "endowment" has both expressive and instrumental components. Psycho-cultural dispositions are intermingled both with the social structure and its cleavages as well as territorial control. For example, territories and social positions, and entitlements associated with them, can be "ethnicized"; that is, they can be captured for a given ethnic group by discriminating against another group (Väyrynen 1994, 15–17).

As Marc Howard Ross (1983, 10) argues, "psycho-cultural dispositions shape how groups and individuals process events and the emotions, perceptions and cognition that the events evoke. Dispositions link particular events to culturally shared threats to self-esteem and identity." The presence of threat and discrimination heightens the importance of maintaining and protecting the social identity of a person or of a community. The experience of *threat to social identity*—whether ethnicity, nationalism, race, gender, or religion—that is a part of a person's own core construct of self, can result in a protective response encouraging group mobilization. When social identity is defined among groups in mutually exclusive terms, each side may perceive the fulfillment of the other's identity and needs as the equivalent of its own destruction (Northrup 1989, 66–67). This leads, as Michael Ignatieff points out in the Yugoslavian case, to the conclusion that "if you can't trust your neighbor, drive them out. If you can't live among them, live only among your own." (Ignatieff 1994, 36–37). This maxim succinctly spells out the basic logic of ethnic discrimination and cleansing; throughout the entire Yugoslavian tragedy, safety was considered to be attainable only in homogenous political entities.

Myths and Memories

Psychological and cultural tensions are difficult to measure in cross-cultural investigations. However, their escalatory potential can be gauged by asking whether there are historical memories which capture the essence of the conflict and in that way keep the fear and animosity alive. Memories shape learning and responses to stimuli, but also create *myths* whose selective presentation remind people of the past struggles and grievances even if they do not have any direct effect on the present generations at all. Myths, folk histories, and group grievances, passed from one generation to another, serve as ideologies or cultural models through which threat perceptions are filtered and interpreted (Agnew 1989, 47).

As an example one can mention the massacre of Armenians by the Turks in 1915–17 when some 1.5 million Armenians were executed and died on death marches across Turkey. Dudwick (1993, 264–65) argues that "it is impossible to exaggerate the significance of this event for contemporary Armenian thinking . . . the memory of the genocide served as a virtual 'charter of identity' even among the families who had not experienced it directly." Generally, it has been suggested that genocides are works of powerful historical memories of suffering and wrongdoing, transferred by socialization from one generation to another, which are reactivated in a particular set of circumstances (Hirsch 1995).

In the Balkan context, Stokes (1993, 231–32) argues that "the importance of the Kosovo myth to Serbian politics is not to be found in its actual historical qualities, but in its selection by the nationalists as the appropriate symbolic universe of Serbianness." It refers to the mythically heroic battle of Kosovo Polje fought by the Serbian warriors against the Turks on June 28, 1389, and its historic outcome: domination of the Serbs by the Ottoman empire.

The battle was not an isolated historical incident, but a part of the larger pattern; the Serbs face suffering and treachery and die as victims in war, but they are not ultimately defeated. As Prince Lazar in Kosovo Polje, they choose through death the empire of heaven to be able to resurrect Greater Serbia in the future. The historical persistence of this myth in Serbia is remarkable and can be understood only through the central role of the Orthodox church to keep the idea of Serbia alive (Judah 1997, 30–47). The Serbs have been repeatedly denied the fruits of their sacrifices. This perception of historical injustices has reinforced myths that alter defeats into mental victory. Mojzes (1994, 39–40) calls this "the crucifixion and resurrection syndrome; because of steadfastness despite suffering we rise as victors."

On the sixth hundredth anniversary of the battle in 1989, the myth of Kosovo Polje was as much alive as ever and shaped the Serbian attitude towards the Muslims of Bosnia and the ethnic Albanians of Kosovo (Kaplan 1994, 35–39). The Kosovo myth serves as a selective frame which is not time bound in its interpretation of the Serbian experience. This property of the myth reflects a more general tendency to "destroy the sense of real time. Concepts of the past and the present are so intermixed that a grievance of long ago is perceived as a present affliction" (Mojzes 1994, 40). The past is strongly present in today's Bosnia where Serbs and Croats refuse to live together with the Muslims as experiences in Sarajevo and Mostar so clearly show. Myths tend to overcommit and entrap people to a particular destructive course of action. A "sacrifice trap" is especially risky, because it easily leads to hero-worshiping in which violence is justified not by its original reasons, but by the loss of life itself (Ryan 1996, 154–55).

As a consequence of the selective framing, the style of nationalist discourse which emerged among the Serbs "isolated only one strand of Serbian experience, the religio-romantic strand, and shut out others, such as the liberal strand" (Stokes 1993, 231). This may help explain Serbian intransigence in the Bosnian war to yield to international pressures to cede territorial gain in a peace settlement, especially the Vance-Owen Plan. (The Bosnian

Serbs had finally to agree in late 1995, because of the military advances of the Croatian-Muslim federation and NATO bombings). The strength of the Kosovo myth reveals also a psycho-historical trigger of violent conflict when other circumstances permit its unleashing. In this context it is relevant to remember that to strengthen his own political position, Slobodan Milosevic skillfully mobilized, starting from the more nationalistic countryside, the primordial feelings of Serbs in Kosovo by appealing to cherished nationalist symbols.

The selective interpretation of history is reinforced by the feeling of being victimized. This tendency can be also called the "Kozara Mountain syndrome." In these mountains, in the region of Banja Luka, Nazi German and Croatian Ustashe forces killed thousands of Serbs in the summer of 1942, while the rest were taken to concentration camps. According to Robert Block (1994, 51) the "Kozara massacre still burns in the memory of the local people. As a result, Serbs from this region are some of the most insecure, and hence militant, of all."

The feelings of insecurity and injustices can lead to the *totalization of ideology* as happened in Rwanda where Hutu ideology insisted that Tutsi should have no place in the country and be returned to their original home which supposedly was in Ethiopia. The ideology and the imperative to disseminate it was crystallized in the "Hutu Ten Commandments" published in *Kangura* magazine. The tenth commandment says that "the Hutu ideology must be taught to every Hutu at every level. Every Hutu must spread this ideology widely. Any Hutu who persecutes his brother Hutu for having read, spread and taught this ideology is a traitor" (Hilsum 1995, 164–66, 170).

In Yugoslavia, the Jasenovac concentration camp where the Ustashe mass murdered some 250,000 Serbs is a constant reminder of the cruelty of Croats during World War II. In the 1960s a memorial was established by Tito, a Croat himself, to tell about these atrocities. Croats felt victimized, however, because in their view their suffering in the Serbian hands were not similarly emphasized. In the early 1990s the Croatian leadership failed to publicly condemn the brutalities of the Ustashe state, which had far-reaching and negative political consequences for peace in the region. In fact, a major reason for the escalation of hostilities in Yugoslavia has been that different parties have not come to terms with their historical relations; "the past remained unmastered and unforgiven . . . [and] aggression begins in denial" (Ignatieff 1994, 31–35; see also Boban 1992).

Psycho-political grievances may also spring from the popular feeling that a nation has been betrayed historically. Such a betrayal should be compensated by returning a nation or a territory to its original condition or status. This feeling is widespread among the Russians in Crimea which was ceded by Moscow to Ukraine in 1954. Now a popular movement is demanding the return of the Crimea to its rightful Russian context. Another example of the impact of the feeling of betrayal is the independence struggle of Eritrea. It was motivated by the fact that Western powers gave it to Ethiopia in 1960 even though Eritrea had never before been a part of it.

Institutional Legitimacy and Mobilization

Legitimacy

The unequal access to entitlements, overlapping social cleavages, and historical memories do not necessarily lead to violence. They can be tolerated as long as there is a perception that the institutions of state and society function in a relatively evenhanded way. In other words, violence can be contained if the social and political institutions are considered *legitimate* and just in their treatment of all major social groups.

The Yugoslavian example again provides relevant evidence. Ethnic hatred intensified in its multiethnic communities in the early 1990s only after it became clear that the federal structure, its effectiveness and legitimacy were collapsing. Ethnic communities started feeling themselves vulnerable to the alleged aggressive intentions of opposing groups. The sense of vulnerability and fear have been most pronounced among the national groups which became minorities in a foreign country, such as Serbs in Croatia. The situation turned from bad to worse when former Communist elites started manipulating nationalist emotions to strengthen their grip on political power. In a word, "ethnic hatred is the result of the terror that arises when legitimate authority disintegrates" (Ignatieff 1994, 23–28).

The breakdown of political and institutional legitimacy is not only a necessary but also a sufficient condition for the slide of a society into turmoil. The relationship between socio-economic inequities and collective violence is mediated by the degree of strength and legitimacy of the societal institutions. Obviously, legitimacy is also connected with the degree of democracy in society's governance, although it has also been argued that a rapid transition from authoritarianism can increase hatred and prejudices.[2] The erosion of legitimacy is not an abstract political process but is usually connected with the fragmentation and weakening of state structures. If the society is relatively stable and it is not ridden by any major overlapping cleavages, the weakening of state power does not need to have any immediate consequences. In fact, it may be a natural course of developments in a mature democracy. If, however, deep divisions between differing identities and interests exist, the central state may not be able to keep centrifugal forces in check, and thus the escalation of conflicts into violence begins.

The developments in Russia bear witness to this tendency; the decentralization of political control has permitted the rise of an informal economy, dominated by crime syndicates, and led to the increasing volatility in the peripheries, whether within (Chechnya) or without (Georgia and Tajikistan) Russian borders. In general, the weakening of central structures activates historical memories of political self-determination and mobilizes movements demanding the restoration of autonomy (Gurr 1993, 76–82).

In political risk analysis the declining legitimacy of the regime, due for instance to the disaffection of the "anxious" middle class, is seen to open the door to struggles in the leadership succession, and thus to instability (Raddock 1986, 6–14; Overholt 1982, 51–60). From a different vantage point de Gaay Fortman and Kortekaas (1994, 23–31) point out that, in addition to "direct resource-connected entitlements," also "institutional entitlements" should be considered. Institutions create rules and procedures in society and thus shape the distribution of resources and entitlements. Hence their partial and unjust management fosters opposition and conflict. Thus, the legitimacy of social and political institutions seems to be a backdrop against which people fathom the inequities and injustices of society. As declining legitimacy also hints to cracks in the state monolith, it provides opportunities for groups to increase their own political power and collect more material wealth (Holsti 1996).

The Role of the State

The role and nature of the state in the escalation and management of conflicts are central factors for understanding the degree and nature of political legitimacy. In the international periphery, states tend to be weak; they are "quasi-states." Relatively speaking, such states may be strong in the local context, yet unable to perform many of the standard state functions (Jackson 1991; Jackman 1993). Peripheral states may have strong repressive capabilities, but little ability to deliver and protect entitlements, except through clientelism and corruption. Zaire was a prototypical case of a country where the corrupted state ruled over a fragmenting society and economy until Mobutu's rule finally collapsed in late 1996.

This duality of the peripheral state machinery may exacerbate conflicts. The assets of the state encourage parties to rival for the control of its economic perks and repressive capacity, while on the other hand the rulers do not have enough positive power or commitment to curb violence and destitution. Demographic and environmental pressures undermine further the coherence of peripheral states and their ability to deliver political and material goods (Homer-Dixon 1994, 25–26). The end result can be the emergence of a warlord polity in which the state loses its established function and disintegrates into predatory fiefdoms (Reno 1998).

Authoritarian state structures are more often a sign of political weakness than of strength. Over the short term, authoritarian states can, however, be more stable because of repressive measures, while less institutionalized and established democracies face both political protests and outright rebellion (Auvinen 1993, 46–55, 168–69). In the global context, the difference is not necessarily only between authoritarian and democratic states, but the real zone of turmoil may be located in the zone of transition. In transitions old and new power structures clash with each other and lead to a battle between authoritarian and democratic institutions. Therefore, their war proneness can be higher than in other cases (Mansfield and Snyder 1995).

In general, the strengthening of the democratic state is an important precondition for the management of domestic conflicts and external threats to sovereignty. Such a policy would be manifested, for instance, in the reinforcement of the nation's economic infrastructure, its civic institutions, and ties between them. Popular control does not necessarily prevent conflicts, even in mature democratic states, but it affects the intensity of conflicts by limiting them to protests and demonstrations. In authoritarian political systems conflicts escalate more easily and thus become more destructive (on the importance of democracy for social stability and conflict resolution, see Singer and Wildawsky 1993; Welsh 1993, 55–58).

Opposition and Mobilization

The state's weakness due to its lack of legitimacy gives licence for the *opposition* to act. The strength of opposition depends on its ability to mobilize social and organizational capacity. The escalation of latent disagreements into manifest conflicts involves the *mobilization* of pre-existing groups into political action. Mobilization can be both inner- and outer-directed and either expressive or instrumental in terms of its ideology. It usually has several goals; for example, to increase the group's autonomy within the current political unit, weaken its political elite, or secession. Often the mobilization of one group results in the counter mobilization by its adversary, thus accelerating the escalation process. Such processes can provoke a crisis, and challenge the regime legitimacy (Esman 1994, 28–40).

In fact, crises typically contain elements of de-legitimation, involving the breakdown not only of institutional arrangements, but also of familiar symbolic frameworks underpinning the pre-existing political order. Crises can thus be conceptualized as a perceptual category: a crisis comes into being when a sufficient number of influential individuals or groups perceive significant changes in their environment prompting cognitive dissonance. In other words, as 't Hart argues (1992, 4–5), at the individual level the affected person holds onto "familiar beliefs sustaining the existing order and personal stakes in it, and, on the other hand, significant, repeated and undeniable disconfirming information that some things are seriously wrong."

These contradictions are played out also at the societal level, as individuals and groups articulate their definitions of the situation, and make different claims about the causes and consequences, while advocating alternative and often conflicting strategies for dealing with it. In reality, this tension between the established past and the uncertain future boils down to the argument that there are, in the end only two parties in a political system; the "party of change" and the "party of status quo" and the distinction between them cuts across the traditional left-right classifications.

Inevitably, crises have also an affective dimension, in that they challenge previously held world views, and generate anxiety, and personal and collective insecurity, often compounded by experiences of material damage, human suffering, or gross injustice. The challenge to the state arises when the perceived changes call into question the past, present, and future functioning of particular aspects of the government, and often the knowledge, status, and authority claims of those officials seen to be responsible. Such challenges to the legitimacy of social and political institutions also fuel mass mobilization. Crises are thus junctures when the institutional legitimacy and governing capacity of society is at stake.

To understand the direction that a crisis of regime legitimacy is likely to take, it is also important to explore the institutional capacities of major social groups and the degree of their unity in various phases of the conflict. Unity is a pertinent issue both among the elites and the grassroots organizations. If the elite is united, it tends to resort to repression to eradicate protest, while cooperation in the grassroots undermines the success of repression and in that way exacerbates the conflict. The openness of society and access to its decision-making bodies is an indicator of its ability to address grievances in a cooperative manner. Openness has the desired positive impact only if the state has a minimum of institutional capabilities to cope in a reasonably equitable manner with the pressures emanating from the civil society.

The more scarce the legitimate institutional means to redress grievances, the more likely it is that conflict management will become destructive. In fact, the destruction of public institutions is a sure sign of troubles to come as it makes possible the further polarization of society, along with the use of ties, propaganda, and hate-inciting media (on the Yugoslavian case, see Mojzes 1994, 53–59). Indeed, such strategies aim at the manipulation of perceptions and emotional distress. By then, the parties to a conflict have probably acquired weapons, and the more lethal they are the greater the destruction. The establishment of rival military units is an indicator that the society is already in the state of latent or manifest civil war. Such a development is a sign of the collapse of public security which in the Yugoslavian interregnum was "the first casualty" (Woodward 1995, 207).

Summary of Early Warning Indicators

The foregoing analysis reveals the demanding nature of any effort to develop a system of early warning indicators. On the one hand, these indicators must be derived from a viable social theory and have general validity across a spectrum of cases. On the other hand, the applicability of early warning indicators is necessarily dependent on temporal, historical, and cultural contexts. Therefore, it is impossible to use the same set of indicators to tap the explosiveness of each and every conflict. Moreover, all indicators carry political implications which can be overlooked only with impunity.

It should also be recognized that indicators tap different levels of society. While we think that the emphasis of early warning should be on national societies, international factors cannot be neglected either. Therefore, Table 3.1 suggests the following topology of early warning indicators. Our hope is that the indicators can be used so consistently that a basis for comparative inquiry and assessment on the proneness of conflicts to escalate can be laid.

Against this backdrop it seems that the development of an early warning system for the effective identification of emerging conflicts calls attention to at least the following background factors:

1. The degree of *structural tension* in society: the deeper the social tensions, the higher the probability for the outbreak of violent conflicts. Structural tensions can be gauged by such indicators as the distribution of income and land ownership, inequities in social development, especially access to gainful employment, and economic gaps between different social groups and regions, especially between the urban centers and the rural peripheries.

2. Shared or divided *territory:* conflict is more likely if different communities share the same territory, especially if structural and cultural tensions are already fueling their confrontation. Segregation can help to maintain peace, but when disputes along ethnic or national lines arise, it may also provide conditions which facilitate ethnic mobilization, polarization of disputants, and accelerated conflict processes. Thus, territorial *identity* can function as an aspect of social identity and ensuing in-group bias and hostility towards out-groups (Northrup 1989, 66). Threats to any part of the core construct are sometimes classified as "intangibles." They

TABLE 3.1 **Dimensions, Levels, and Issues of Conflict**

	Dimensions			
	Material	*Structural*	*Institutional*	*Cultural*
Intranational Level	Control of resources; demographic pressures; environment	Social hierarchies and cleavages; territorial divisions	Legitimacy and control of political and military institutions	Dominant and oppositional value systems; historical myths and memories
International Level	Technological position; external economic integration; military capabilities	Position in the center-periphery structure; territorial centrality	Recognition by other actors; organizational memberships; networking capacity	Appeal of values and culture; normative influence; historical reputation

are about the actors' perceptions of needs or concerns with image
or status, legitimacy, and presentation (Bercovich and Langley 1993;
Druckman 1994, 48–50), and as such do not lend themselves to
compromises, without the parties in some way sacrificing the essence of the matter at hand.

3. The nature of *social cleavages:* a main issue is whether the divisions
    in society create a crisscrossing pattern based on a complex divi-
    sion of labor and multiple loyalties or whether they divide social
    groups in mutually exclusive collectivities. From the standpoint of
    conflict prevention it is particularly important that material, insti-
    tutional, and identity cleavages do not overlap, but provide a basis
    for the emergence of a viable civil society.

4. The *legitimacy of political governance:* democratic and equitable
    national political institutions are important protective shields of
    group rights. The effectiveness and acceptance, or at least the tol-
    erance of these institutions by the majority help to maintain stability
    and an atmosphere free of unnecessary fear. The decline and
    delegitimization of political institutions jeopardizes public order
    and opens the floodgates to violence. If this leads to the establish-
    ment of private armed gangs and the rise of a warlord system, the
    probability of violence increases considerably as the situation in
    Afghanistan, Liberia, Somalia, and Yugoslavia illustrates.

5. The degree of *cultural tension,* the feeling of historical grievances,
    and, in general, the history of conflict in society reflect the extent
    of value incompatibilities within societies. Such conflict factors
    can be revealed by exploring tensions between different ethnic,
    religious and political values, interpretative frameworks, myths and
    ideologies, and the history of confrontations generated by them.
    Often the amount of past conflict is the best predictor of new
    conflicts to break out.[3] Instead of learning how to avoid conflicts,
    people and states tend to repeat the past errors.

6. In a conflict-prone society there is often a high degree of *militari-
    zation and governmental repression* to which the aggrieved
    population tends to respond, sometimes actively, sometimes apa-
    thetically. The response depends on the degree of mobilization and
    the organizational capacity and other resources of the population,
    including the degree of unity among it. A low degree of organiza-
    tion and mobilization helps repressive governments keep their
    power and subjugate the people. As the Haitian example shows
    the protection of people may require external intervention and
    enforcement of basic human standards.

Notes

1. Homer-Dixon (1994, 8–10) uses the concept of "environmental scarcity" which has three separate components: scarcity of renewable resources, their unequal distribution, and population growth. While his approach permits a dynamic and interactive analysis of environmental conflicts, he does not make a necessary distinction between conflicts over absolute and relative gains.

2. Similarly, Esman (1994, 30) argues that "periods of political transition such as the dissolution of multinational states or rapid decolonization accelerate ethnic mobilization, because resultant uncertainties about security or the distribution of power often generate perceptions both of threats and of fresh opportunities." The demise of the state's institutional legitimacy is nonetheless a precipitating factor.

3. This is the premise of PANDA (The Protocol for the Assessment of Nonviolent Direct Action) which uses event data on nonviolent political actions to forecast the possibility of their escalation into violent confrontations. PANDA has been developed by Dr. Doug Bond at Harvard University; see Doug Bond and William Vogele 1995. Profiles of International "Hotspots". Program on Nonviolent Sanctions and Cultural Survival, Harvard University (mimeo).

4

CROSSING THRESHOLDS: MECHANISMS OF CONFLICT ESCALATION

The Complexities and Dynamics of Escalation

THE CONFLICT RESOLUTION FIELD HAS TENDED TO TREAT THE ESCALATION OF conflict as a question of means. Simple phase models of conflict highlight changes in adversaries' tactics and resources. The models track how disputes evolve into crises and violence and war erupt. Diplomatic efforts have traditionally operated from this model, deploying short term efforts to contain violence and settle issues. Less attention has been given to understanding how root causes fuel the escalation, or developing a more complete picture of how conflict escalates across dimensions other than the parties' means.

The limitations of diplomacy to achieve durable peaceful outcomes to contemporary conflicts and to prevent others from turning violent, means there needs to be innovation in traditional ideas and practices. We need to go beyond the containment of violence and negotiation, to transform social injustices, perceptions, cultural tensions, deep rooted hatred, and issues of institutional legitimacy (Lederach 1997). A more discriminating approach has several practical advantages. It can help policymakers target resources in context specific ways. Limited resources can be used more efficiently, and the key breaking points in society can be targeted for specific preventive measures. At the same time, thinking about the long term transformation of society and the underlying causes of conflict become part of the initial operation, rather than remaining delinked from attempts to avert, control or de-escalate the violence.

How conflict escalates depends partly on the kind of structural, cultural and institutional factors fueling it. For example, structural conflicts with principles of social justice at stake tend to encourage rigidity in the aggrieved parties' positions. Cultural conflicts involving a community's sense of endangerment can lead to zero-sum thinking ("if the other group survives, we perish"). Televised coverage revisiting former atrocities can be used to exploit these fears, and create more psychological barriers to communication between adversarial communities. The lack of legitimate political or legal channels for redress can lead aggrieved parties to use violent tactics.

These are essentially static descriptions of the influence of background conditions on escalation. But conflict is dynamic, so we must also have a sense of its development over time. Escalation tends to collapse the time horizon, accelerating the pace of events. The events themselves exceed thresholds. Whereas the background conditions provide indications of the potential for extreme violence, accelerators (propaganda, violent rituals, or symbolic acts) warn of its impending and quickening development. The logic is that accelerating events worsen the conflict in the presence of background factors, but have less serious implications when these are absent. Other indicators of a collapsing time horizon include signal flares (warning statements) and escalation triggers (events or actions that remove existing safeguards and spark the violence). Accelerators, signal flares, and triggers are conjunctural factors—they draw our attention to key turning points in the conflict. They mark events that surpass previously set limits. The more such sign posts, the more intense or widespread the deterioration.

The first part of this chapter operationalizes the concept of conflict escalation, developing a number of indicators that can be used in the field by practitioners to judge whether a conflict is worsening or is being managed constructively. The second section relates how our three categories of background conditions (structural, cultural, and institutional) fuel escalation processes. However, intrastate conflicts do not follow a single trajectory on the road toward conflict escalation. They typically unfold in a disjunctive manner. There can be different levels of intensity along different conflict dimensions. So we look for signs of conjunctural factors in the ways the parties express their needs, in the degree of unity of their movements, and the kinds of goals and means they use. The aim is threefold: (1) to help peacemakers judge where and how a society's tensions are accumulating; (2) to encourage thinking to maximize the peace effects of a given intervention; and (3) to anticipate negative side-effects and develop contingency plans.

Conceptualizing Conflict Escalation

Richard Smoke has defined escalation as "consisting in the crossing of saliencies, which are taken as defining the limits of conflict. As a war escalates, it moves upward and outward through a pattern of saliencies that are provided situationally" (Smoke 1977, 34). Sometimes escalation is seen as a "homogeneous process" in which the stakes and means used are gradually increased, while Smoke, following Thomas Schelling, suggests that steps,

TABLE 4.1   **Dimensions of Escalated Conflict**

Vertical Dimension (Intensity)		*Horizontal Dimension (Expansion)*			
Behaviors	Choice of Means	Issues	Goals	Actors	Geographical Scope

small or large, taken by the parties to cross salient limits are the defining characteristics of an escalation process (Smoke 1977, 30–32). These may include drawing new states into the disputes, or the resort to especially lethal weapons.

Escalation can be understood either as an automatic process embedded in the dynamics of conflict or as a series of strategic unilateral moves by the parties involved. In both cases there is an interactive or reciprocal element in the escalation of disputes into deadly violence and war (cf. Smoke 1977, 21–30). It is often assumed that reciprocity drives escalation in more relentless ways, while the lack of it assures stability. However, it makes sense to treat escalation and reciprocity as independent dimensions of conflict behavior.

Zartman argues that passage from one phase to another in conflict escalation is preceded by a stalemate. It forces the actors to rethink their goals and means, and if they prove unrealistic or inadequate, a redefinition of the situation is needed. "Stalemate is the key both to the escalation process and the shift of ends, means, tactics and leadership" (Zartman 1991, 516). Stalemates are pivots of conflict dynamics which can lead both to escalatory and de-escalatory processes. For conflict resolution to be successful, it is important either to maintain the current stalemate or support de-escalatory tendencies. The stabilization of the situation involves both making the status quo more attractive and raising the costs of escalation.

Conflict escalation can be conceptualized along two axes: vertical and horizontal (see Table 4.1). *Vertical escalation* refers to the increase in the intensity of the dispute in terms of the conflict behaviors, and means used. They may involve actions that range from "the imposition of economic, material, social, political or symbolic cost, with no physical injuries or deaths, to an action that explicitly includes threats, risks or actual human deaths." Such indicators provide measures of the intensity of antagonism (Bond and Vogele 1995, 4). The intensity of the conflict increases as more and more actions take place outside the framework of the country's political and legal system. The number of victims and damage caused provide graphic indications of the vertical escalation. Its control thus aims to limit the human and physical destruction caused especially by the use of military force.

Horizontal escalation expands the geographical scope of conflict and brings into the sphere of non-violent or violent action new groups, communities, or states. For example, demonstrations provide evidence of the mobilization of support for a cause through public participation. Such events are "precursors to, and sometimes accelerators of, the escalation of conflict to violence" (Bond and Vogele 1995, 4). The horizontal expansion of conflict may also involve the spill over of conflict in regional contexts. Historically, states have become regularly involved in intrastate conflicts in neighboring countries. This is reflected in the connections by factions of an internal war with external powers, for example (Heraclides 1990; Hammarström 1994). Under the rubric of horizontal escalation, we may also think of the expansion in the number of the issues at stake (issue proliferation), or in their size ("issue inflation"), and also in the parties' goals.

Generally, at the outset of a conflict, the issues at stake tend to be discrete and more narrowly defined. As the conflict persists, both the size and number of issues tend to grow, if for no other reason because the failure to achieve early solutions itself becomes a new source of grievance. The concept of a "metaconflict" has been used to describe the situation when the initial issues at stake have become greatly outweighed by new issues which the escalation of conflict produces (Rubin, Pruitt, and Kim 1994, 72, citing McEwen and Milburn).

In contrast to issue proliferation, "issue inflation" concerns the size of the issue. The size of the issue has a lot to do with its framing. A particular incident, such as an inter-ethnic skirmish or murder may be treated as an isolated event. However, as conflict escalates, it is more likely to be perceived by the parties as a manifestation of inter-ethnic tensions, an attempt to settle ethnic scores, etc. This is a transformation of the issue frame from the specific to the general (Rubin, Pruitt, and Kim 1994, 72). This often involves treating the issue at stake as a conflict between large rather than small units (that is, a conflict between ethnic groups, rather than individuals, a conflict involving inter-state security, rather than the welfare of groups within the state) (Deutsch 1991, 37). The parties may differ completely in their perception of the issues at stake, how the issues are framed, how large they are, as well as the referent principle that underpins them. The framing of an issue in big terms, rather than as a discrete incident, also implies that the solution to the conflict must be all the more encompassing (structural or social change), rather than more narrowly conceived (the arrest and conviction of the perpetrator).

In sum, both vertical and horizontal escalation embody salient limits whose crossing drives the escalation of conflict by inciting fears that lead to reciprocation. Hence, action-reaction sequences are at the core of the precipitating causes of escalation. These dynamics take various forms as suggested by the "aggressor-defender" and "conflict spiral models" (Rubin, Pruitt, and Kim 1994, 73–76). In crisis situations, the first task of preventive diplomacy is to contain and supplant the escalation dynamics with more positive forms of social interaction. This is the main objective over the short-term. However, sustaining peace depends on transforming the background conditions that fuel escalation, and this calls for a long-term commitment. Peacemakers should exercise care that short term interventions do not undermine prospects for working towards a lasting peace. This means the long-term objectives should be in view from the outset (Lederach 1997).

Impact of Background Tensions on Conflict Escalation

Structural Conflict

Entitlements, territory, and cleavages are key structural aspects of society. Entitlements reflect the distribution of and access to resources and opportunities in society. They are a measure of social justice and equality. Whether inequalities in entitlements become activated and fuel social unrest depends on such negative triggers as the feeling of grievances. The rise of collective violence generally depends on preexisting lines of opposition, which may be structural, cultural or political. The more these lines exist along multiple, and deep overlapping cleavages, the more mobilization leads to the total polarization of society. This intensifies conflict in a number of ways, including by increasing group cohesiveness (that is, actor expansion), limiting communication between the groups, and encouraging the development of "runaway norms."

Polarization of society is more likely when the conflict runs along preexisting cleavages (pitting urban dwellers against rural people), and is likely to be especially intense when it develops along multiple, overlapping cleavages (competing territorial and ethnic identifications, and statuses). A special case concerns groups competing over territory for access to entitlements, social welfare, and/or for reasons of individual and collective identity. Territorial disputes are generally perceived by the groups as zero-sum, raising barriers to the search for integrative solutions. Territory can also interact with cultural conflict to raise the parties' perception of the stakes. Cultural elements may include different historical memories and meanings attached to the territory, symbolized by cultural monuments, or historic battle fields, which are often ritualized through myths and their reenactment. These factors also make problem solving more difficult. For one thing, the presence of cultural elements tends to expand the number of issues at stake, and also to transform the specific issues at stake into larger issues, and into matters of principle. Furthermore, conflicts with cultural elements may also bring in ethnic kin, increasing the numbers of actors involved. This can lead to the conflict's geographical spread as well. Territorial elements of structural conflict intermingled with identity conflicts may also lead to goal expansion. If the group's initial demands are not met, they may then push for autonomy, self-determination, secession, or the overthrow of the state.

Identity Conflict

Conflicts involving cultural tensions tend to reduce to threats to identity and group survival. Thus, they have a strong psychological dimension, influencing both perceptions and affect. Culture provides the vehicles through which groups express themselves, and identify who they are as a people. Conflicts that threaten the group's right to use these vehicles, whether they be language, history, dress, schooling, rituals or territory, are perceived as threats to the group's members' core sense of self. Culture also frames how the group perceives its adversary and the issues at stake, linking individually perceived threats to self-esteem and identity to the collectivity. Adversaries may use historical memories, myths and rituals both to demonize and threaten the opposition, and increase its own group cohesiveness. Milosevic's full scale re-enactment of the Kosovo Polje battle in 1989 on its 600th anniversary had the effect of mobilizing the Serbs, while dehumanizing the majority ethnic Albanian (mostly Muslim) population of Kosovo. By televising of the event, Milosevic used the media to reinforce historical fears, anxieties and myths of endangeredness. Cohen (1995, 130) documents how this propaganda campaign encouraged minority Serbs in the Knin region to mobilize and form military subunits.

Cultural dispositions also influence the extent to which a group is likely to engage in contentious behavior. Perceptions of endangeredness or threat to survival induce high concern for a community's own outcome, and low concerns for its adversary. Serbian myths of crucifixion and resurrection not only communicate messages about the resilience of the Serbian people, but also about who is to blame for their suffering. The same can be said for the feeling of victimization experienced by the Serbs in the aftermath of the atrocities committed by Nazi German and Croatian Ustashe during World War II. Blaming indicates who is responsible and who must be punished. The feeling of provocation to punish arises from the anger blaming produces. As Rubin, Pruitt, and Kim (1994, 77–78) explain, such behavior encourages aggression, including the desire to retaliate in order to deter such behavior in the future. Conflict is especially likely to escalate when one group sees its enemy's contentious behavior as breaking accepted social norms, as illegitimate or atypical of how others behave, and not attributable to chance or extenuating circumstances.

Negative attitudes also reduce empathy and interfere with

communication—since people avoid contact with those towards whom they feel hostility (Rubin, Pruitt, and Kim 1994, 86). They also foment greater intra-group cohesion (Druckman 1994). Negative emotional responses also tend to fuel issue inflation—transforming issues from specific to more generalized concerns. The deindividuation and dehumanization of the enemy plays a central role in this: the group faces not just a specific threat from the opponent, rather a diabolical enemy (Rubin, Pruitt, and Kim 1994, 84; Northrup 1989). While anger and blame produce retaliatory spirals, fear produces essentially defensive spirals.

Nationalism and religious nationalism can be used to translate grievances and historical memories into political demands and goals. It is in the domain of political (or religious) leadership that blaming, anger, and fear are given a meaning, and the negative emotions turned into action in the service of a just cause. Nationalism and religious nationalism are functionally similar, "both serving the ethical function of providing an overarching framework of moral order, a framework that commands ultimate loyalty from those that subscribe to it." They both can give sanction to martyrdom and violence. Moreover, those who have not had power before may find the empowerment granted by religious violence especially appealing (Juergensmeyer 1993, 166).

The mobilization of individuals to collective action and violence involves changes in their psychological state. Northrup identifies four stages. First comes the perception of threat, then the distortion of incoming information, and third, rigid interpretations of the world. As people experience individual and collective threats to identity, they become vulnerable to propaganda and its dehumanizing effects. Dehumanization makes violence increasingly tolerable. As Northrup explains (1989, 74), "it is more difficult to harm something or someone who is like-self, and easier to harm something or someone construed as not human or inhuman ('not-self')." In addition, dehumanization by opposing groups is mutually reinforcing in a negative direction. In Bosnia, hostile acts undertaken by the Muslims or Croats against the Serbs made the Serbs' earlier dehumanizing propaganda about their enemies a "self-fulfilling prophesy." This fact, taken together with the politics of blaming and victimization, gave ethnic Serbs further "justification" for their violent actions, including "ethnic cleansing."

Cultural conflicts are characterized by the breakdown of norms that govern inter-group relations. While there are international humanitarian standards to which governments are held accountable for their behavior in wartime, it is less clear whether, and if so how, these can be applied to opposition movements which engage in domestic struggles. The normative ambiguity and uncertainty that has accompanied the passing of the Cold War international order makes the present juncture more problematic, as opposition groups break old limits, criteria, and principles, and try to establish new ones (Zartman 1997, 5–7). The lack of consensus means there will be fewer constraints both on the means used, and the kind of destruction and physical harm inflicted, as Bosnia or Rwanda illustrate. Because there are no widely accepted standards about appropriate solutions, third parties have more difficulties getting the parties to settle their conflict, as Richard Holbrooke, US emissary, experienced in early 1998 trying to find solutions to the conflict in Kosovo or Cyprus.

Identity conflicts tend to deal with such intangibles as identity, status, loyalty, integrity, authority and reputation. In addition, because cultural survival is often perceived as being at stake, identity conflicts, such as those played out in Kosovo, Macedonia, Chechnya, Rwanda, or Burundi, are likely to encompass questions of power, participation, and control over the group's own destiny. If the conflict persists, the issues at stake are likely to grow, since the group will demand more autonomy and control over its own affairs the less responsive the government is to its needs. This process is likely to transform the specific issues at stake into larger issues, and into matters of principle, which underlie the pursuit of autonomy, self-governance, secession or self-determination.

The experience of a collective threat to the group's identity generally encourages group mobilization. The particular form of mobilization depends on the group's cultural, political, or religious institutions. New rounds of conflict are often played out through preexisting groups, especially those formerly engaged in communal protest action (the Croatian Ustashe or Serbian Chetniks, or the neo-nazi movement). Conflicts with cultural elements are also more likely to expand both in terms of numbers of actors, as well as geographically, though this mainly depends on neighboring kin states prepared to support the cause.

In addition, because of their emotive impact, cultural conflicts have a rather different dynamic than inter-state wars fought between organized militaries controlled by the state. These armies usually depend on drafted personnel rather than volunteers. In the case of cultural conflicts, a fallen rebel soldier may be replaced by a brother or other kin—even by women and children (such as the war in Sudan and elsewhere in Africa). Government efforts to repress the opposition, especially through indiscriminate means that adversely effect civilian targets tend to breed more opposition, and hence new recruits for the rebel forces.

Institutional Conflict

The breakdown of political and institutional legitimacy is not only a necessary, but sufficient condition for the outbreak of social violence. Hence institutional sources of social conflict have a direct impact on escalation:

their collapse removes the remaining checks on centrifugal forces. Institutional conflicts are about political struggles mobilizing ideological values and material interests of the people to fight for control of their own destiny. Protracted social conflicts involve deprivation of basic human needs, while a dominant group monopolizes control of the state at the expense of other communal groups, often marginalized and oppressed (Azar 1990). While they can intermingle with structural causes (entitlements or territorial issues), institutional conflicts are fundamentally about status, legitimacy, and power. The main issues at stake are thus matters of principle and influence. This means institutional conflict involves "big issues" that tend to be intractable. The goals of the opposition can vary from the more limited aims of gaining more participation in the system and access to its rewards, to achieving cultural and/or political autonomy, control of the state itself, self-determination, or secession.

By limiting the access of the opposition to the state and its institutions and resources, the dominant group in control of the state deprives society of common social norms and constructive methods to find solutions to social problems, the South African apartheid system being an extreme case. At the same time, they force marginalized groups to mobilize and pursue extra-legal methods to attain their goals. Of course, groups are far more effective in escalating conflict than individuals. The group structure serves functions which individuals cannot alone do. The tasks can be delegated, ranging from the development of the group's ideology, its demands, goals, and strategy for attaining them, to the recruitment of new members and their socialization to the group ideology, and the development of special subunits, including armed forces (Esman 1994, 33–34).

The degree of unity among the opposition is important for understanding the volatility of background factors on conflict escalation. Group cohesiveness is important because it encourages adherence to group norms, discourages dissent, and multiplies the psychological effects of the conflict, particularly the negative attitudes and distrust towards the adversary. The adoption of contentious tactics enhances group cohesiveness and militancy. The change of group leadership from moderate to more militant individuals also marks a stage in the escalation (Druckman 1994, 54–58). But if the group itself is not sufficiently accepting of these changes, militant sub-groups and more radicalized factions may splinter off from the main movement to challenge its leadership. This pattern is evident in the emergence of the Kosovo Liberation Army which appeared on the scene in 1996 to challenge Ibrahim Rugova, the ethnic Albanian's "shadow president" elected in 1992, who has led a non-violent protest movement against the Serbs. Factionalization also encourages competitive nationalism, as each group is forced to take more radical positions to demonstrate greater loyalty and

commitment to the cause. Moderate voices are branded "traitors." Democratic elections can exacerbate these dynamics, by encouraging public
competition between the rival factions of a splintered opposition (Mansfield
and Snyder 1995).

Institutional conflicts have a particularly important impact on the expansion of actors, and the escalation of means. The mobilization of the
opposition and degree of cohesiveness and radicalization are key indicators
of strength. The society itself becomes more polarized as threats from the
state promote greater cohesiveness within the opposition group. Group
think dynamics reinforce cohesiveness and contribute to the movement's
radicalization. The overall result is a shift towards more extreme positions
and goals.

The most intense conflicts have a volatile mix of background causes
that overlap and reinforce negative conflict dynamics. Institutional conflicts, for example, often interact with structural and cultural sources of
conflict that generate structural changes in society. Once established, these
changes are exceedingly difficult to transform and resolve (Rubin, Pruitt,
and Kim 1994, 99). Among the most serious situations are societies with
deep overlapping cleavages caused by social injustice, and inequalities that
are territorially demarcated and reinforced along existing (or mobilized)
ethnic and/or religious lines. If these groups also hold on to deep seeded
grievances, then the potential for conflict escalation is higher. Polarization
of society is propelled by distrust and suspicions, and aggravated by the
lack of communication and transparency in the contending parties' relationship. Fear about the other's motivations and actions breeds conspiracy
theories, reinforcing negative emotions and instilling more fear. Isolated
from one another, the contending parties often perceive the situation as
completely different realities: as their paths cross less and less with the escalation of conflict, the groups may, in fact, live out different realities. The
polarization of community relations also places great strains on individuals
and families who do not share one or another of the contending ethnic or
nationalist identities—whether because they are of mixed ethnic or religious heritage, or for ideological reasons, or both. As the movie on social
tensions in the Republic of Macedonia, Before the Rain, depicts, the polarization of community relations forces non-participants to "choose sides."
This contracts the safe space in society. These tensions can lead to the break
up of marriages, and the ruin of extended family ties.

Collapsed states such as Somalia, Liberia, or Afghanistan are the
extreme instance of societies that have failed to deal with accumulating
tensions and escalating violence. Collapsed states are distinguished by the
absence of any effective civil society to rebound and assume the governance and other organizational and authority functions of the state in the

aftermath of its breakdown. As Zartman explains (1995, 8), "the whole cannot be reassembled and instead the components of society oppose the center and fend for themselves on the local level. Organization, participation, security, and allocation fall into the hands of those who will fight for it—warlords and gang leaders, often using the ethnic principle as a source of identity and control in the absence of anything else."

The breakdown of political processes and institutions produces structural changes in the conflict which prove difficult to reverse, and repair. Insecurity, polarization and confrontation between groups also breeds negative attitudes and perceptions which tend to persist. They are reinforced by self-fulfilling prophecy, the rationalization of contentious and violent behavior, and selective perceptions. War economies often result. The entrenched leadership have vested interests in violence, not peace. They become stakeholders in the perpetuation of chaos, not in the transformation of conflict. This means "they have incentives to resist conflict resolution and for starting new conflicts" (Rubin, Pruitt, and Kim 1994, 109). The resistance of the Bosnian Serb leadership to accept and adhere to the provisions of the 1995 Dayton Accords, and the tensions and violence in Mostar between Croats and Muslims illustrate this point (K. Brown 1995).

A dilemma peacemakers face is whether to include the radical leaders at the table and risk enhancing the legitimacy of their positions and goals, or exclude them and push them further to the margins and possibly toward more violent actions. But the factionalization of power in many contemporary conflicts means that even when the military leadership is included, they are not always able to exercise effective control over their community. The US emissary Richard Holbrooke learned as much in dealing with the divided ethnic Albanian leadership in Kosovo as the crisis there rapidly escalated in June 1998.

Collapsing Temporal Horizon

While the preceding discussion is essentially static, in reality background causes impact on conflict escalation in a dynamic process. The critical element is the collapse of the temporal horizon: the pace of conflict events accelerates out of control. Whereas background conditions provide indications of the potential for extreme violence, accelerators warn of its impending and quickening development. *Accelerators* are events that "rapidly increase the level of salience of the most volatile of the general conditions" (Tomlinson 1994, 4, citing Harff), including the parties' sense of insecurity, threat, injustice, or lack of confidence in existing institutions. The acceleration means thresholds are being exceeded faster than new constraints can be negotiated and put in place. This temporal aspect of escalation can be gauged in terms of three types of conjunctural factors: signal flares, conflict accelerators, and triggers.

Signal flares are statements and actions that warn of increasing confrontation and violence. They often involve the invocation of salient limits, or setting of (new) thresholds. Peacemakers may invoke them to warn about limits above which the conflict must not be escalated if violence is to be averted. Militants may invoke them to warn of preparations for violent responses. Political leaders may also use symbolic acts, such as resigning, as a means of dissociating themselves with the turn of events, and signaling their sense of imminent danger. Either way, adversaries use signal flares to draw the line, and stake out a position in relation to the threatened consequences.

The limits they set may concern the geographical scope of the conflict, the entry of new parties, or an escalation in the use of means. Cultural norms as much as historical experiences and meanings attached to them may underpin expectations about where thresholds lie. The example of the outbreak of inter-communal conflict in Bosnia and elsewhere in the Former Yugoslavia led the parties in Macedonia to set rather low thresholds: any clash between ethnic groups (even street brawls) were perceived as possible triggers for the outbreak of violent conflict.

The cultural and political context of conflict are key to understanding the potential dangers of conflict escalation and society's resilience. To understand thresholds in relation to the conflict, we should ask such questions as What political, strategic, symbolic or material elements shape the identification of a given threshold? What are the consequences if other parties do not accept and adhere to the same threshold? Can thresholds be set so they do not invite actors to attempt to push beyond them to gain attention or to test an early warning system? How can shared understandings of a given threshold be arrived at among a community's leaders, governments, and other stakeholders in a conflict, including external actors, and NGOs? Of what significance are low thresholds, versus higher ones? How does the potential for the spill over of conflict relate to stakeholders' designation of thresholds? Do leaders tend to signal lower thresholds?

Conflict triggers are, generally speaking, any decisions or actions that undermine the stability of the situation and the possibilities of the constructive management of conflict. Trigger events exceed salient limits, and in so doing, ultimately tear down the capacity of society and its institutions to cope with the social tensions. They are by definition acts that take place outside of the political system. Bond and Vogele (1995, 4) refer to this as "extra-institutional" political behavior. The parties' may resort to violence, and unilateral decrees, irrevocable commitments, and hostile and intransigent positions. These acts can involve the violation of the other group's entitlements, the destruction of its political institutions, the invigoration of historical grievances and the tearing down of the societies' cross-cutting ties.

Conflict triggers break down into two types, according to the time frame they imply with respect to the worsening of the conflict. The less immediate are the "trip wire" events. They may be necessary, though not sufficient conditions for the outbreak of violence. When trip wires are pulled, they remove existing safeguards that keep the conflict stalemated, contained, and the door open to a solution. Their loss undermines society's existing normative and institutional frameworks which could provide for continued dialogue between disputants, or supply referent principles for reaching compromises. Pulling trip wires makes conflicts "ripe" for violence.

The more immediate triggers are the "sparks" that actually set off the conflagration when they are thrown into this "ripe" situation. For example, in the Yugoslavian conflict, the breakup of the communist party and its political organization acted as a trip wire: it removed the last ties that were holding the country together (Stokes 1993). The slide towards intranational conflict had already been marked by the increasing disintegration of the country's political structures through successive stalemates and new conflict cycles. The collapse of the collective presidency ended the political stalemate, while disintegration of the Yugoslav Peoples Army, based on territorial defense, facilitated the establishment of national guards by the republics. The mobilization of the latter was the spark that triggered preemptive military action and led to war between the Serbs and Slovenia, and Croatia, and later between the Serbian, Croatian, and Muslim factions in Bosnia-Herzegovina (Cohen 1995).

Accelerators, such as propaganda, misinformation, rumors, or symbolic violence, often accompany trigger events and intensify their effect. As Stokes (1993, 249) notes, by late June 1991, when the political disintegration of Yugoslavia was imminent, "the public opinion in both Serbia and Croatia had been completely inflamed by vigorous campaigns of disinformation and propaganda. Each side ran hours of television stories showing mass graves from World War II being dug up and describing the bestial atrocities committed, always by the other side of course, in gruesome detail."

In the case of Bosnia, a Serbian demonstration of national symbols provoked fire from gunmen, and led rapidly to the erection of barricades throughout Sarajevo, and activation of paramilitary units. This spark set off the war; but any such event could have conceivably ignited the situation, as the safeguards had already broken down in Bosnia, while unilateral preparations by the various parties for the violent action proceeded (Cohen 1993). The Bosnian example recalls the fact that the breakdown of the government's monopoly of violence and the establishment of rivaling private armies or militias by the parties to a conflict is a sure sign of dangers ahead.

Escalation Across Different Conflict Dimensions

Preventive efforts are likely to be more effective if they are selectively targeted on those dimensions where tensions are accumulating most rapidly and dangerously. The parties' needs, unity, goals and means are the four dimensions along which we look for evidence of conflict accelerators, signal flares and triggers pointing to the rapid deterioration of the situation. Disputants frame conflicts in ways which allow them to communicate their grievances and articulate their *needs*. However, framing rarely consists of straightforward statements; moreover, parties are likely to change the way they frame their needs and grievances as the conflict escalates and as their goals change. The initial articulation of the group's position is likely to occur in response to a perceived threat, although in the absence of threats political entrepreneurs may seek to create them by manipulating information, or invoking historical grievances that allow them to mobilize the group and press for governmental attention to their demands (Esman 1991).

Protest movements often first search for an appropriate outcome by calling the attention of the government to their existence and insufficient share of society's benefits (Zartman 1991, 514–15). At this stage, the government's role and primacy are appealed to—not contested. However, the numerous asymmetries which characterize the relationship between governments and marginalized groups (asymmetries in the distribution of power, resources, legal standing, and structural position; asymmetries of access to institutional mechanisms; and asymmetries of goals and needs) means that at the outset the government is unlikely to entertain negotiations or bargaining as an avenue to seek solutions (Mitchell 1991).

Even though the early stage in the life cycle of conflict may be the most propitious moment to manage the conflict constructively, the goal orientations of the two parties are typically at odds, with the opposition seeking significant changes, and the government the maintenance of the status quo (Mitchell 1991). The result is often that governments "do too little, too late" (Zartman 1991, 515). In response to increasing pressure, governments often provide options which would have been more appropriate to the previous stage, but which may no longer satisfy the demands of the protest movement (Zartman 1991, 513–15). Thus, responses are often insufficient to decelerate the conflict processes, or contain them. As a result, groups tend to consolidate and present procedural and substantive demands. Their goal becomes one of being involved in the distribution of benefits. They want to control their own resources and destiny.

At this juncture, the government can work to suppress or eliminate the opposition; alternatively, the parties can work to set up processes which defuse the conflict, or they can choose courses of action which fuel the escalatory dynamics. Judicial inquiries, the formation of expert commissions, and other methods of official investigation are often designed to de-politicize the conflict or crisis situation in an effort to determine the cause of the problems, and possible solutions. These are among the methods governments have of counteracting the attending processes of de-legitimation of social institutions, political processes, and government leadership. Bargaining, negotiation, and other means of administrative or political accommodation (new elections, a new political pact, the appointment of opposition members to the cabinet, and more far-reaching institutional changes) are also alternatives for responding to the needs of the opposition, while relegitimizing state institutions. However, it should be noted that in a tense situation, elections may result in further destabilization, because of their tendency to act as a census, encourage radicalization and polarize the parties.

Failing sufficient response to its growing demands, in the next phase the opposition is likely to abandon collaborative efforts, and seek alternatives based on unilaterally imposed solutions (exit, secession, or self-determination, or the overthrow of the government). Abandonment of the collaborative endeavor is probably a signal the groups see no common ground among their positions, and no possibility of shaping a common future given their goals. They will either separately or both together determine that there are no legitimate or acceptable institutional frameworks, or political processes by which they can continue to interact and search for solutions. This moment is a critical challenge to the legitimacy of the state's political and social institutions, and the government's authority, power, and legitimacy. As these are undermined, additional trip wires are created that make the outbreak and rapid escalation of violence more likely.

Often governments' efforts to counter insurgent movements lead to an escalation of armed force. The Sri Lankan government's attempt to outmaneuver the Tamil insurgency through heavier weaponry spawned a domestic arms race. The scenario is repeated in other intrastate conflicts as rebel forces overtake the government troops and their supplies, or acquire them through bribery and government corruption. The development of transnational cultural movements, in support of domestic opposition causes (as in the case of the Tamils in Sri Lanka), and their involvement in illicit businesses (that is, drug smuggling) adds complexities to the conflict, for example, by providing insurgents with lucrative funding for their cause and outpacing governmental resources.

Conjunctural factors are also intensified by the degree of *unity* of an opposition movement. Mobilization depends on recruiting community members, and raising financial and other resources for political action. Mobilization of an ethnic, religious or other type of identity group, or a protest movement requires an awareness of what is at stake for the group. Generally it is the work of political entrepreneurs to shape awareness and recruit participants. Thus, mobilization is a process by which a community becomes politicized, and gains means to pursue it goals.

Surprisingly little has been studied about the mobilization of ethnic and other identity communities, despite the increasing salience of such actors in intranational conflict (Esman 1994, 29). However, Esman (1994, 30) hypothesizes that " 'defensive' mobilization in response to a clear and present threat to a group's established position will produce more rapid and aggressive collective action than 'offensive' mobilization to exploit opportunities for uncertain future benefits." For this reason, he argues that typically "ethnic entrepreneurs choose to highlight real or imagined threats to the community's status, security, and well-being." Nevertheless, mobilization is likely to be a result of a combination of mixed motives and incentives which are shaped by the political opportunity structure, ideology, organizational efficiency, and the resources and strategies of the community. The latter includes preexisting communication and organizational networks which bring their own set of resources.

The political opportunity structure provides the institutional context in which a movement shapes its strategies and tactics. The prevailing norms, incentives, and constraints of the political opportunity structure establish the legitimate boundaries or limits within which protest and accommodation can be worked out. They give the context in which the opponents mobilize, organize, participate, press their claims, and attempt to gain access to political authorities, redress for their grievances, and seek benefits (Esman 1994, 31–32). In terms of understanding conflict dynamics, a critical question is whether a movement works within these limits, or crosses them. Threats about crossing such thresholds are important "signal flares": actions that cross such thresholds significantly escalate the conflict and can trigger the outbreak of violence.

Ideology is important for the way it frames the parties' stake in the conflict, provides justification for their goals, and motivates the members to mobilize and push their claims. Although nationalism is often defined as the political ideology behind ethnic mobilization, some scholars differentiate nationalism from ethnic ideologies. Nationalism is typically defined as "an ideology that proclaims the distinctiveness of a particular people and their right to self-rule in their homeland," which, as an expression of ethnic solidarity, "tends to glorify a people's history, accomplishments, and aspirations; to preach the obligation of loyalty to the community, its institutions, and symbols, and to warn against external threats" (Esman 1994, 28).

As hinted above, the leadership of parties to intranational conflict is also a critical variable in the intensification of conflict. Political entrepreneurs play a key role in recruiting adherents to a movement, mobilizing resources, promoting the group ideology, and framing the issues. The leadership of political movements also tends to shift as the groups in the government or the opposition reconfigure and strategize new approaches. Over time, and in the absence of any constructive solutions, these changes are likely to result in more antagonistic, and less flexible individuals assuming leadership responsibilities (Zartman 1991). When even more nationalistic and radical political contenders are runners-up in an election, this leaves incumbents with little room to maneuver to reach any accommodation with their opponents.

Political entrepreneurs may contribute to the escalation of the conflict through a variety of strategies which center on the manipulation of information, and the struggle to impose on the adversary its own definition of what the conflict is about. In this struggle, information and communication are basic tools over which governments often attempt to exercise exclusive control, in an attempt to ensure their definition of the situation prevails, and to justify their objectives and course of action. The government leaders may also control information, media and channels of communication "to mask" a crisis situation. Their objective may be to buy time, or to keep the situation from further escalating. Such strategies can also backfire, by increasing the government's "credibility gap," especially if the situation worsens while no effective remedies are found in the meantime ('t Hart 1992). Serious crises can also be masked by displacing crisis perceptions onto other events, such as disasters, or international conflicts. Some experts suggest Saddam Hussein's redeployment of troops to the Kuwait border in October 1994 was intended to mask a growing crisis of his regime's legitimacy and control.

Opposition parties who seek to instigate change may find it to their advantage to aggravate a sense of social crisis in order to create a political and psychological climate more favorable to non-incremental changes. For both governmental actors and opposition movements, there is also a type of "self-binding" logic about framing issues as crises, and for dramatizing the seriousness of the situation. Extreme courses of action are more likely to be accepted when the threats are personified and the enemy is depicted in diabolical terms. To these ends, stakeholders can appeal to deep-rooted threat biases in the way people perceive their environment. The logic of such extreme measures is to externalize internal conflicts ('t Hart 1992, 8). The lack of objective and factual information about events contributes to the public's tendency to distort the situation, while disinformation can be used to promote stereotyping, and dehumanization of the adversary.

The intensification of the conflict can happen accumulatively, or with suddenness. The parties choice of *means* plays a central role in these escalatory dynamics. As a general rule, the escalation of means involves the turn from methods of dissent which are within the bounds of the society's political and legal system, to extra-institutional actions. The latter typically involve the crossing of salient thresholds, although other acts which are not necessarily illegal in some societies (the publication of hate propaganda), may nonetheless cross salient limits. The main assumption is that the accumulating actions weaken the political system, while the trigger type events (trip wire and sparks) create crises, break the system down, and open the way toward violent conflict.

The key consideration is whether or not the actions involve a "determinate" process, that is some procedure or method which is institutionalized in society, and to which the parties have, at least tacitly, given compliance. As Bond and Bennett (1994, 2) explain, "the outcomes of determinate behavior or routine political action (sometimes dubbed 'normal' politics) are always prescribed by some norm, procedure, practice or routine. Also, the outcome of a political action is bound by the system parameters for conflict resolution and is, therefore, a function of interaction and performance only within the constraints set by existing power relations." Societies which have adequate institutional mechanisms (legislative methods for finding solutions, including inter-ethnic councils, ombudsman, human rights commissions, or other routinized procedures for redress of grievances, such as a well functioning judicial system) have a greater capacity to manage conflict constructively, than those societies which lack these instruments.

The early warning of conflict is especially concerned with societies in which there are few or no functioning institutional mechanisms to manage its conflicts, and in which political action is therefore taking place largely outside the political process. Bond and Bennett (1994, 2) characterize this as "direct political action," which "is always unilaterally initiated; it never requires the cooperation or consent of another party; and it is always associated with some risk and/or sanction. Thus every direct political action yields outcomes that are not bound by existing practice or procedures. Such outcomes are a function of the actors' strategic interaction and performance independent of the system's directives, and thus less constrained by the existing power relations, if at all."

The extent to which opposition forces can engage in direct political action, such as protests, demonstrations, boycotts of elections and referendum, depends on the tolerance of the regime, and whether it resorts to repressive policies which make action costly for participants. For government authorities, economic instruments include blockades, embargoes, sanctions, or the denial of entitlements, or removal from jobs. Opposition forces may turn to slowdowns, work stoppages, strikes, or other initiatives to disrupt the economy. But a sure sign of the intensification of conflict is the political use of coercive force, such as in the imposition of curfews, and states of emergency, including martial law, the banning of opposition parties, imprisonment and torture, or exiling of opposition leaders and activists.

Nonviolent direct political actions have an accumulating effect on the escalation of conflict as they continue to challenge the system and its authorities. The inhibitions on the use of violence tend to breakdown when the relations between the authorities and the opposition are severely strained, or severed (Bond and Vogele 1995, 4). Often, such developments are indicated by the collapse of special talks, or negotiations. Some leaders may experience personal distress and threaten to, or in fact resign. They often do so warning of the impending crisis before the country, statements which are important kinds of signal flares to monitor for early warning.

In addition, the failure of the parties to use a stalemate to begin to build up better relations, and establish some institutional or ad hoc method for finding a solution can also contribute to the deterioration of relations. Amplified by a climate of psychological warfare, such developments open the way to the use of violence. Violent actions, especially spectacular events (assassinations, riots, destruction of property, bombings, mobilization of armed units, military blockades), accelerate conflict escalation immediately, and dramatically. Violent acts lead to outcomes which are not bound by the political system, and as such heighten fear and unpredictability in society by threatening chaos. The use of such means is highly destabilizing; the violent acts are like sparks that can set off a conflagration. By increasing the magnitude of the human and physical destruction of the conflict, the parties attempt to influence their opponents' calculations of the costs of continuing to prevail through confrontational strategies, and deferring a settlement to a later date.

Manipulating threat perceptions is an especially powerful tool for promoting group unity and legitimizing violence, especially when a group perceives that the conflict threatens core identity constructs. Control and manipulation of the media is often the key to creating a climate of psychological warfare. Ethnic ideologies and nationalisms provide the scripts. They can be threatening not only because they tend to exclude, but also because they are often based on the invalidation or victimization of the "other," especially through myths and ritual acts. Ritual acts are themselves a powerful means of promoting unity and legitimizing violence. They have special symbolic meanings, and are typically acted out in a highly structured, and standardized fashion, in particular places, and at special times, such as the marching season in Northern Ireland. During crises, rituals of solidarity, reassurance, and purification enable government leaders to be seen in control of the situation (staging press conferences, appearing on the scene of a disaster); responsive to the suffering of their people (laying wreaths); and committed to getting at the root of the problem. Of course, such rituals can also be used to de-escalate tense situations. Through dramatic acts in which leaders or individuals accept responsibility for past atrocities, or emphasize reconciliation, empathy, and solidarity by appealing to higher principles or moral cause, conflict can be transcended (Mack 1990).

Finally, it should be noted the parties may also have at their disposal various diplomatic means. The government may, for example, expel the diplomatic representatives from countries sympathizing with, or supporting opposition forces. Opposition forces may appeal to great powers, or regional powers to intervene on their behalf, or take other measures to support their cause. Both the government and opposition may appeal to international organizations, or non-governmental organizations for third party assistance, civilian monitoring, the deployment of peace keepers, the adjudication of a dispute, or mediation. These initiatives also tend to internationalize the conflict, and may have both intended as well as unintended effects. Indeed, the appeal by opposition forces to the international community may well be one means for it to gain legitimacy, draw the attention of the global media to its cause, and also to frame the issues at stake to its advantage.

Conclusion

Following Zartman's (1991) lead one can say that preventive action is most effective when the needs of the parties are still malleable, their internal unity is not so crystallized that the conflict has become hopelessly polarized, the goals have a sufficient degree of compatibility to permit resolution, and the means have not yet escalated to the large-scale use of violence. Thus, preventive action has a dual purpose: (1) to keep the conflict latent and, if possible, strengthen social stability; and, if this fails, (2) to restrict it to the non-coercive phase where options for peaceful solution still exist.

Preventive action should target actions or decisions which tend to accelerate the escalation of conflict, and early warning systems should monitor conflicts for evidence of conflict accelerators in particular. Signal flares may be indications that the conflict is moving beyond its latent stage, and thus early warning on the need to launch preventive actions is in order. Conflict triggers are clear evidence that the situation has reached crisis proportions and violence may be imminent.

Thus, early warning systems have as their primary objective the activation of mechanisms that can lead to preventive action to permit constructive conflict management and avoid the slide into the destructive one. In other words, preventive action should create a stalemate which either keeps the conflict contained or, at a minimum, non-coercive. Stalemates should be used to help buy time and develop new constructive solutions to the conflict. This may be important not only to provide opportunities for the parties to the conflict to reconsider their options, but also to permit third parties more time to devise appropriate interventions, and gain consensus on the principles on which the conflict can be further de-escalated and solutions sought. As the example of the EU intervention in the Former Yugoslavia illustrates, public pressures on international institutions to "do something" can lead to poorly timed interventions, the wrong (or competing) application of principles, and ill-targeted, and inappropriate intervention strategies. Thus, third parties, too, can benefit from stalemates and more time to work out appropriate methods of intervention.

The early warning and prevention of conflicts requires explicit indicators not only of background conditions in terms of their impact on conflict escalation, but also the escalatory dynamics of conflicts. Conflicts take place in specific contexts. Consequently, we reject generalized indicators for the early warning of all conflict. Case studies, more than correlational studies which are culture blind, are likely to be sensitive to the nuances of meanings, symbols, identification, and political context that are vital aspects of the background to and dynamics of conflict escalation. Such understanding is essential for monitors and policymakers to judge the deterioration of a conflict situation, and to devise appropriate intervention strategies.

From this vantage point we have developed a set of indicators which can be used to analyze individual cases of conflict. This approach ensures certain elements of comparability, and yet is sensitive enough to the circumstances and individual characteristics of cases to be politically viable. We emphasize the latter, especially in light of the "politics" of early warning and conflict prevention. Indeed, early warning and conflict prevention activities themselves introduce new elements into the conflict. Their potential impact, intended and otherwise, must be part of the political considerations taken into account.

While different combinations of background conditions and escalatory dynamics are likely to present themselves in different cases, we suggest that certain patterns to these developments can be discerned. This is especially evident in the dynamic view of conflict we have adopted. Even though different societies may have very different breaking points, the intensification of conflict is likely to share similar features across cases. An important consideration in further research is how the escalation of conflicts is fueled by certain combinations of background conditions, and whether these patterns vary regionally.

Conflicts also develop at different speeds along different dimensions, which dictate there are no panaceas in the early identification and prevention of conflict. Different types of early warning and preventive strategies are required depending on both the phase of conflict and the way it intensifies across the multiple conflict dimensions. In Chapter 5 we will look at the military, economic, and political means of influence that international organizations, governments, and NGOs can bring to the early warning and prevention of conflicts. Both top down and bottom up strategies are often critical to contain and find durable solutions to conflict. Supporting stakeholders in the peace process at the mid-level of society is especially critical (Lederach 1997). This is often stressed in the post-conflict peace-building phase, but the strengthening of civil society can also help avert the slide to conflict, and the collapse of the state in the pre-conflict phase, too.

5

KEEPING CLOSED THE GATES OF WAR: THE PEACE POTENTIAL OF PREVENTIVE ACTION

Aims and Types of Preventive Action

THE PREVENTION OF UNWANTED CONTINGENCIES IS A CENTRAL OBJECTIVE IN all international relations. The nature and objectives of multilateral preventive diplomacy were first systematically developed in the United Nations in the late 1950s and the early 1960s. The main aim was to keep great powers out of regional conflicts and thus forestall their horizontal escalation. This trend came gradually to an end in the 1960s when the improving relations between the great powers gave rise to mutual agreements on spheres of influence and the management of regional crises to prevent their escalation. The United Nations was pushed aside in preventive actions to avoid the involvement of third parties in the great power relations.

The situation has significantly changed after the end of the Cold War as the leading powers have become reluctant to unilaterally intervene in regional crises and the opportunities and incentives to manage them jointly have evaporated. Therefore, third parties are needed again to prevent the outbreak and escalation of deadly conflicts. At the same time the rationale of this intervention has changed; instead of safeguarding the stability of relations between major powers, external preventive involvement occurs mostly on humanitarian grounds. In this involvement NGOs are increasingly complementing the role of governments as they can enter a conflict zone more quickly and with greater flexibility.

Multilateral preventive diplomacy is a half-way house between the peaceful settlement of disputes, as spelled out in Chapter VI of the UN Charter, and the enforcement measures specified in Chapter VII. Preventive diplomacy combines elements of both of these approaches. Its basic rationale is that a successful prevention of the outbreak of violence, or if it fails, the subsequent prevention of escalation, saves human lives, economic burdens, and political costs. Moreover, the emphasis on prevention is due to the diminishing effectiveness of the traditional foreign policy tools of deterrence and intervention and the scarcity of economic resources to back them up (Lund 1996, 24–26).

The attractiveness of preventive diplomacy must be contrasted with its feasibility and effectiveness. On the one hand, there appears to be a rather widespread consensus that preventive diplomacy is not only necessary, but also possible, though difficult. The Carnegie Commission on Preventing Deadly Conflict (1997, xvii) argues at length that the "potential for violence can be defused through the early, skillful, and integrated application of political, diplomatic, economic, and military measures." On the other hand, it has been pointed out that there has been some naivete in welcoming the promise of preventive action and underestimating its risks and costs (Stedman 1996). Obviously, there are no easy answers to the problems of appropriateness and effectiveness in preventive actions and they depend, at any rate, on the criteria by which the success of prevention is measured. In addition, any assessment requires a benchmark against which the effectiveness of preventive actions can be compared.

Thus, the question is: What would have happened in the absence of those actions? Would the conflict have escalated into a more destructive confrontation or would the status quo have continued to prevail? Or would the conflict have even been abated? A simple answer is that the success of preventive actions can be measured by "the absence of conflict and, therefore, the absence of CNN coverage" (Perry 1996, 57). Deeper answers to these queries can be gained only by a counter factual reasoning contrasting the actual course of events with the alternative in which no preventive actions would have been carried out (on the methodology, see Fearon 1991). It also matters from whose perspective the success of prevention is evaluated; the government, opposition, third parties, or their mutual relations. It is conceivable that conclusions on the success and failure would differ from one actor to another (cf. Conflict Management Group 1994, 6–8). Finally, the conclusion also depends on whether the impact of preventive strategies is scrutinized in a short-, medium-, or long-term perspective.

An Agenda for Peace defines preventive diplomacy as "action to prevent disputes between parties, to prevent existing disputes from escalating into conflicts and to limit the spread of the latter when they occur" (Boutros-Ghali 1992, 11). A main feature of this definition is its focus on the objectives of preventive action and the neglect of its implementation strategies that can be both ethically problematic and politically contested.[1] Boutros-Ghali heeds the observation by George (1983, 369–70) that crisis prevention is a political objective which must be pursued by a repertoire of strategies. This repertoire is, in turn, an integral part of the general means by which foreign policy is conducted.

Foreign policy is not, however, any unalterable collection of means and ends, but they both change over time. This change has been especially pronounced in the last few years when the Cold War structure of international relations has been transformed into a more complex and malleable system. The coexistence of old and new elements in that structure has resulted in the bifurcation of foreign policies. Traditional, state-centric foreign policies aim to attain goals defined by governments by various political, economic, and military strategies. Foreign policy amounts, then, to problem-solving and advocacy by diplomatic means and, should they turn out to be ineffective, by intervention and enforcement, either coercive or noncoercive. Especially coercive interventions are prohibited by international law except for in special circumstances.

This "settlement-and-enforcement-centered model for international intermediation" and intervention can be contrasted with a more cooperative and flexible management of international problems. The latter approach relies more on a dialogue and "ripening" of the moment to resolve a dispute or other problem (Chigas et al. 1996, 28–32). This alternative image of foreign policy stresses more transformative actions to mold the complex environment than on the attainment of specific goals. Third-party intervention into and mediation of internal conflicts is an example of transformative politics. Third parties make efforts to expand and redefine the political space and thus encourage new actors, coalitions, and issues to enter the conflict stage. Transformative politics calls for different types of leadership. While in traditional foreign policy, the leader's position and capabilities are crucial, the "new" foreign policy has more use for "directional leadership" in which cognitive resources and persuasive skills are relevant (Malnes 1995, 95–99). The distinction between these two types of policies has fundamental implications for preventive actions as will be shown later on.

Elements of Preventive Actions

Preventive actions can focus either on: (a) short-term political actions to defuse a confrontation; (b) institutional arrangements to share power and build confidence between antagonists; and (c) structural economic and social reforms, sometimes called "preventive development." In making a choice between these different strategies, the decision-maker faces the problem of validity of preventive actions, that is, whether actions undertaken are a proper and effective way to address the causes of conflicts and their escalatory processes.

The validity problem has two aspects: the proper targeting and credibility of actions. The targeting problem appears, for instance, when preventive efforts rely primarily on short-term diplomatic moves, while the deterioration of conflict results in effect from much deeper economic and institutional failures. The credibility problem exists, in turn, when the threat of punitive actions is not adequate to forestall aggression either because the strength of threats is inadequate or they do not address the right actors and issues. Moreover, the fungibility of such status quo strategies as deterrence, balance of power, and collective security can be limited. If they have failed to discourage aggression in the first place, their utility in curtailing its escalation would obviously also be restricted.

Ultimately, the structural strategies of prevention are the most effective ones in a world in which violence is often fueled by deep-seated grievances caused by economic inequities and social injustices. Therefore, the prevention of deadly conflicts requires the thwarting of economic failures, social breakdowns, and environmental degradation. According to this view, "a comprehensive preventive strategy must first focus on the underlying political, social, economic, and environmental causes of conflict" (Commission on Global Governance 1995, 93–98). The ameliorating effects of these measures of conflict prevention are, however, often too delayed and, therefore, ineffective. Thus, they suffer from the targeting problem. For this reason more direct and tangible political strategies are needed. While deterrence, balance of power, and collective security have general preventive functions as they add caution to the calculations of a potential aggressor, they are not appropriate means to cope with complex communal and other intrastate conflicts.

Structural ills can be addressed by "developmentalist diplomacy," to use Jentleson's (1996, 7) concept. Such diplomacy involves actions to prevent the deterioration of socio-economic crises and structural cleavages into violence. As a rule, preventive actions are situated in the conflict spectrum between peacetime diplomacy and crisis or war diplomacy. Preventive actions are needed when peace is unstable and threatens to erupt into violence (Lund 1996, 37–44). In the pre-conflict phase preventive diplomacy can assume different forms in the efforts to bloc violent acts ("crisis prevention"), engage parties to cooperation ("pre-emptive engagement"), and promote dispute resolution ("pre-conflict peace building") (see Lund 1996, 46–48).

Our approach differs from this solution in at least one significant respect: preventive actions are located along the entire spectrum of conflict, from latent tensions through the culmination and resolution of conflict to the post-conflict peace-building (cf. Doom 1995, 16–24). In making this choice, one faces a trade-off between the conceptual clarity and the relevance of the approach. To our judgement, the loss in clarity is smaller than the gain in comprehension and relevance. In our solution preventive diplomacy is contextualized; its basic objective, namely, the forestalling and reduction of violence, is elaborated in different stages of the conflict.

Thus, in our approach the key phases of preventive diplomacy are:

1. *conflict prevention:* preventing violent disputes from arising between parties either by structural, institutional, economic, or cultural remedies

2. *escalation prevention:* preventing both the vertical and horizontal escalation of hostilities to more destructive means of warfare and to involve additional actors

3. *post-conflict prevention:* preventing the re-emergence of disputes by reintegrating and reconstructing the war-torn society

One benefit of adopting a comprehensive definition is that it helps to cover the four dimensions of the conflict background and processes and their early warning—that is, structural cleavages, institutional legitimacy, cultural tensions, and escalation dynamics—developed earlier. Both the means and goals of preventive actions are multiple and can, therefore, be combined in a number of different ways. Furthermore, actions are transformative; they both shape and are shaped by the environment.

Preventive actions can be initiated by and targeted at different actors. The targets are usually the key parties to the conflict: governments, opposition groups, ethnic and religious communities, or military organizations. The agents of preventive actions can be governments, international organizations, or national and international NGOs. Agents can be involved in preventive actions on all four dimensions of the conflict field. An important aspect of preventive actions is how their agents and targets form mutual coalitions and networks to promote their objectives.

As mentioned, the concept of preventive action adopted here is more comprehensive than that used by most other authors. Gareth Evans (1993, 65–70) observes that the United Nations has been typically involved in "late prevention" in which preventive actions are undertaken by the UN or other bodies only after the outbreak of violence seems imminent. In such a late phase of the conflict, preventive action may be either a non-starter or at least fail to extinguish the dispute. Therefore, "early prevention" of conflicts is preferable because it is more feasible; at this stage issues are still specific and more amenable to transformation, the number of parties to the conflict is limited, thus reducing its complexity, and early measures are cost-effective. Against this backdrop one may think that our definition is reminiscent of the "late prevention." This is not the case, however, because preventive actions during and after the conflict do not exclude them in its earlier phases.

Thus, while not disputing the importance of the early diplomatic actions to forestall violent conflicts, we want to expand preventive diplomacy to deal also with the intra- and post-conflict phases by both non-coercive and coercive means. The reasons for these choices are obvious; early prevention may not be resorted to at all, or it may fail, and non-coercive, diplomatic means are not always adequate to the task. Therefore, to assure the efficacy of preventive actions, diplomacy should cover all major phases of conflict, and rely on several types of actors and means to stop it. By conceptually and politically expanding the arsenal of preventive diplomacy, we want to avoid the situation in which the non-use or outright failure of preventive actions opens the gates of war (as happened in recent wars in the Gulf and in the Former Yugoslavia).

Conflict prevention measures are usually activated by the early warning information concerning whether the political and humanitarian situation in a country threatens to deteriorate in an unacceptable manner. As discussed above, the relationship between early warning and prevention is complicated; warnings may lead to appropriate and adequate answers, they may be ignored (as happened in Pearl Harbor and in the Soviet response to the information on the imminence of the German attack in 1941), or the responses may be botched. To gauge the likelihood of these alternatives, one has to conduct a detailed analysis of the policymaking style, organization, and history of the responding actor.

There are three main means by which third parties can try to prevent conflict: military coercion, economic instruments, and political influence. External coercion aims to deter the parties to a dispute from resorting to arms by threats of military or economic punishments, whereas diplomatic and positive economic instruments rely on non-coercive resources and can thus be more remunerative and persuasive. The earlier emphasis on the political dialogue and directional leadership results in the assumption that non-coercive and persuasive tools of influence are more effective in preventive action than material punishments and their threat.

The relevance of different external means of prevention and actors in addressing the main dimensions of conflict can be summarized as shown in Table 5.1.

This assessment of the validity of different preventive instruments is in many ways tentative. It considers only the direct impact of various policy instruments on the success of prevention and thus neglects indirect effects such as the use of economic tools to alleviate cultural tensions through structural reforms in society. Neither does this summary consider unintended effects of preventive actions such as the negative impact that the institutional rebuilding might have on the escalation dynamics by legitimizing the status of extremist groups. Indirect and delayed effects, and unintended consequences are, however, an inseparable part of international political dynamics (Jervis 1993, 31–33).

TABLE 5.1   **Goals and Means of Preventive Action**

	Structural Cleavages	*Institutional Legitimacy*	*Cultural Tensions*	*Escalation Dynamics*
Military Instruments	Not valid	Not valid	Not valid	Threats and use of force
Economic Instruments	Support to reforms	Not valid	Not valid	Economic sanctions
Political Instruments	Not valid	Rebuilding institutions	Reconciliation	Mediation

The above summary suggests that political means are the most versatile in addressing various causes of violence and its escalation. Economic and in particular military means have a more limited validity, even though they may have to be availed when political tools fail to achieve desired results. This is, in fact, a central political dilemma: Should transformative politics be ready to give way to enforcement actions if they are needed to ensure compliance with international norms? In other words, what is more important in the long-term perspective: compliance achieved by coercive actions or the continuation of the political dialogue? One possible answer is that the adjustment of interests and positions should be the main priority, but enforcement should be accepted if the violation of norms by the target exceeds a certain threshold and the prospects for a diplomatic solution seem remote (as happened in the Gulf in 1990–91 and in the Former Yugoslavia in 1992–95).

Table 5.1 also suggests that the escalatory dynamics are more malleable to external actions than problems rooted in the structure, institutions, and identities of society. Naturally, the escalation dynamics hinge also on them and not only on specific actions undertaken by the parties to the conflict; therefore, preventive actions focusing solely on escalatory moves, although more feasible than other measures, have only a limited chance of success. Coercive measures are a prerogative of states, or sometimes international organizations, while economic and political means can also be used by non-governmental actors.

Preventing Escalation: Top Down Versus Bottom Up Approaches

When expanding the scope of preventive diplomacy, the concept of escalation becomes relevant. This concept has multiple meanings depending on whether it, for instance, refers to change from a non-violent to a violent crisis or change in the extent and nature of violence (Brecher 1996, 215–16). We argue the key characteristics of the escalation process are the steps parties take that cross salient limits or thresholds.

If the escalation process is gradual, preventive actions should be exercised constantly and vigilantly to stop the increase in the intensity and magnitude of violence. However, from the point of view of preventive diplomacy, the idea of escalation as a series of strategic moves is more appropriate both as a description of reality and a basis for policy prescriptions. If salient limits, such as involving new states into the dispute or the use of especially lethal weapons, are stressed, then the policy should focus to prevent the crossing of these limits. Preventive deployment, for instance, aims to prevent the crossing of one salient limit, such as the territorial spread of the dispute.

In our working definition escalation is conceived to have essentially two dimensions: vertical and horizontal. *Vertical escalation* means the increase in the magnitude or intensity of dispute in terms of the number of its victims and the extent of their suffering. Thus, the control of vertical escalation aims to limit the human suffering and physical destruction caused by the use of military force.

Horizontal escalation expands, in turn, the geographical scope of conflict and brings into the sphere of violence new groups, communities, or states as well as increasing the number and size of issues and actors' goals. Both vertical and horizontal escalation can embody salient limits whose crossing third parties can try to prevent. Averting the spillover of conflict in regional contexts is also an important task in controlling horizontal escalation. It has been specifically suggested that the prevention and limitation of secessionist violence requires that neighboring states and other third parties are not permitted to assist the opposing parties (Levine 1996, 330, 338). The significance of this goal is enhanced by the fact that historically states have become regularly involved in intrastate conflicts in neighboring countries. This is reflected, among other things, in the ties the factions of an internal war have concluded with external powers (Heraclides 1990; Hammarström 1994).

In trying to prevent vertical escalation the international community can stress, for instance, legal restraints embedded in the laws of warfare, ban the supply of arms, especially more lethal weapons, and convey in no uncertain terms the message that the resort to more destructive methods of warfare will lead to the use of punitive measures. Horizontal escalation can be stemmed, among other things, by the preventive deployment of third-party troops as well as establishing demilitarized zones and safe areas.

Conflict prevention can be exercised "bottom up," although it is more often a method of "top-down conflict control" (Brown 1994, 236). The "bottom up" strategy is evident in efforts to foster local reconciliation and forgiveness by bringing hostile groups into mutual dialogue. This can happen by establishing common institutions and channels of two-way communication, promoting mutual learning, and enhancing material interdependencies. A moot point is whether these local efforts to prevent the escalation of disputes by peace-building should be assisted from outside either by non-governmental or governmental international organizations.

NGOs may become involved in conflict resolution in their own right or it may be connected with their humanitarian role. In the latter case a basic question is whether the political efforts of conflict prevention by NGOs will compromise other roles such as their ability to deliver humanitarian aid or whether they can really strengthen the positive role of grass-roots organizations. Both conflict resolution and humanitarian aid require access to the theater of conflict. This often requires striking a deal with local warring parties, which may be a precondition for any constructive role in conflict resolution (DeMars 1994). The negotiated humanitarian access to crises may become, however, a slippery slope for the NGOs as their aid creates local constituencies which may work both for peace and war. Thus, the humanitarian imperative is seldom neutral (de Waal 1997, 133–58).

The "top down" strategy of conflict prevention is usually conducted by governments and their mutual organizations. It relies on various political, economic and military methods to contain the intensification and spread of the dispute. Governments can use both active and passive means in preventive action. Passive methods tend to be "hands off" and rely on deterrence and other signals of contingent action, while active methods call for local engagement. Both passive and active approaches can focus either on ad hoc actions to prevent a particular event from occurring or a more systematic strategy of, for example, capacity-building (Nicolaïdis 1996).

In addition to choice of instruments in stemming the escalation of conflict, the timing of action is all important. The inertia of international relations, due to the tendency of governments to avoid costs and take care of their own interests, means that usually the preventive intervention takes place too late. It is a commonplace argument that an earlier and more forceful intervention by the international community would have saved Bosnia and maybe other parts of the Former Yugoslavia from extensive bloodletting that occurred in 1994–95. This view is shared by Secretary Perry (1996, 59) who points out that "in my opinion, the correct approach in 1992 would have been for the United Nations to give the task to NATO to perform peace enforcement operations."

Similar views have been expressed in the Rwandan and Liberian crises. In Rwanda there were several external interventions and intermediations in 1990–94. Therefore, it is not justified to say that the international community did not try in any way to prevent the genocide of 1994. It did, but the interventions were ineffective and failed to stop the slide towards the catastrophe. Their results might have been counterproductive and helped pave the way to the genocide. "The more fundamental lessons of Rwanda are that we can, and do, intervene early in conflicts, that we already engage in a form of preventive diplomacy, and that when we do the consequences of our interventions can sometimes be catastrophic" (Jones 1995, 247). Thus, preventive measures must be judged not only by their motives, but also by their consequences. However, there can never be full knowledge of the consequences of an intervention which must, as a result, be decided under imperfect information. In the Rwandan case, the verdict is that the inaction of the major powers, especially the United States, made matters worse than what they would have been as a result of a UN intervention (Melvern 1997).

Intervention can have counterproductive consequences also in other respects. Adverse experiences can create a domestic backlash in the intervening countries making it too cautious to become involved at all in crises and the government concerned may even hamper the efforts of others to do so. This is what happened in the United States, whose policy toward Somalia resulted in the May 1994 Presidential Decision Directive (PDD) which delayed preventive international interventions into Rwanda and Bosnia and permitted their political and humanitarian crises to escalate (Weiss 1995). The reasons for the US reluctance to intervene to prevent the escalation of violence were almost entirely domestic by nature (Daalder 1996, 463–69).

Similarly, it has been suggested that the inability of the US to make up its mind on its role in the Liberian civil war has led to the deterioration of the situation. According to this view, the US decision to treat Liberia as a humanitarian crisis and delegate military responsibilities to the Economic Community of West African States (ECOWAS), and its leading power, Nigeria, has in reality hampered the necessary political solution that would have ended the war (Beinart 1996). That solution would have been Charles Taylor's victory which he finally achieved through elections in 1997.

Military Coercion

By preventive actions governments make an effort, either directly or through international organizations, to contain the causes and dynamics of local conflicts to avoid their outbreak and escalation. Preventive military actions range from a large-scale preventive war through limited military operations to the establishment of deterrence and the balance of power. These optional strategies can be placed on the active-passive dimension, deterrence being the most passive form of action, while preventive war to block a too preponderant or aggressive power is at the extreme activist end of the spectrum. The resort to a pre-emptive war is, of course, a sign of the failure of other preventive strategies.

During the Cold War deterrence had a preventive role, although nuclear deterrence was unable to extinguish local conflicts. The central position of the great powers in the international system meant that their reactions had to be taken into account by every actor contemplating the use of use military force. Now such "contextual" deterrence has lost much of its relevance. If deterrence is hoped to have a preventive impact in a potential crisis it has to be directed to actors having aggressive intentions. This involves a need to communicate a credible threat to use military force should the target deviate from the preferred behavior.

The reluctance of major powers to use force unilaterally in local crises has, however, deprived conventional deterrence of its credibility. The use of force is today both mandated and carried out through collective multilateral arrangements. Such arrangements have little deterrent value in preventing the outbreak of hostilities because they are set up only after the conflict has deteriorated into large-scale violence. For this reason the multilateral use of force has a role only in the efforts to prevent the further escalation of conflict or its re-emergence after the cease fire. Multilateral deterrence can have a preventive effect only if it is institutionalized into a collective security system which the potential aggressors have to take into account in their decisions to use force (Kupchan 1994).

It is questionable, though, whether the international security dilemma can ever be completely managed multilaterally. There will be space for unilateral military operations, especially in the Asia-Pacific region where security arrangements are poorly institutionalized. The Chinese decision in the spring of 1996 to militarily scare Taiwan and the US preventive response, mixing political and military moves, provides a pertinent example. In a larger context the question is how and to what extent coercive politics can be used for aggressive and preventive purposes.

Preventive military action is always politically conditioned. It can be mixed with politics in what George, Hall, and Simon (1971, 26–28, 215–16) call a "strong form for coercive diplomacy." It relies on a "tacit-ultimatum" and contains a specific demand on the opponent, a time limit for compliance, and a strong and credible threat of punishment. Operationally, this variant of coercive diplomacy can use troop mobilizations, naval operations, and air strikes to achieve its political objectives. The scope of preventive military actions can be limited by directing them, for example, at terrorist capabilities or facilities producing weapons of mass destruction. However, it is difficult to gain international acceptance for pre-emptive unilateral strikes unless there is inconvertible proof that the target is a genuine threat to international peace and security (Haass 1994, 24–25).

Coercive diplomacy is supposed to rely on the use of force which is selective, discriminating, demonstrative, and clearly informed by political objectives. To avoid further escalation, the use of force in coercive diplomacy should not be confused by the target with large-scale warfare or preparations for it. Therefore, the use of military force has to contain pauses and escalation controls which give an opportunity and time for the target to understand the preventive motivations of the measures used (George, Hall, and Simon 1971, 8–11). To underpin such a process, the user of force should point to those salient limits which the target is expected to honor in the course of the preventive political and military bargaining (Smoke 1977, 241–42).

In addition, while coercive diplomacy may use limited violent means once threats have been exhausted, its functions should always be defensive and persuasive. Coercive diplomacy tries to speak sense to the targeted actor by employing the stick, but without overlooking the possibility of carrots. In George's words, "whether coercive diplomacy will work in a particular case may depend on whether it relies solely on negative sanctions or combines threats with positive inducements and assurances" (George 1991, 11). In fact, economic and other incentives have been an underappreciated instrument of preventive and other strategic international actions (Cortright 1997).

A combination of carrots and sticks may achieve outcomes obtainable neither by rewards nor punishments alone. Even if carrots and sticks are combined, the terms of any settlement of the conflict must be clearly spelled out, including specific terms for ending a conflict, and provisions for their verification to ensure that both parties hold to their commitments. The fears of leaders about the consequences of conflict settlement may also need to be assuaged (George 1991, 80; Stedman 1996, 351–56).

Coercive diplomacy aims at influencing the political will of the opponent instead of destroying its military capabilities. Thus, "force is subordinated to what is essentially not a military strategy at all but rather a political-diplomatic strategy of resolving or reconciling the conflicts of interests with the opponent." For this reason, the principle of proportionality is an important element in coercive diplomacy. The amount of force used to persuade the opponent must be adequate but not excessive to accomplish the desired task. The amount and nature of force obviously depend on whether its use is intended merely to convince the opponent that it should stop unacceptable behavior, or whether it is expected also to undo its action (George, Hall, and Simon 1971, 18–19, 23–25). Coercive diplomacy has mostly been practiced unilaterally by major powers. The US policy in Laos in 1961–62, in the Cuban missile crisis, and against Libya and Nicaragua in the 1980s are examples of such diplomacy.

The type of coercive diplomacy described above is based on an active military policy of influence; it aims not only to prevent the target from doing something, as deterrence does, but also to compel it to behave in a particular manner. Compelling threats requires strong action, even black-mailing, to make them credible. "This is so because often the only way to become physically committed to an action is to initiate it" (Schelling 1980, 195–99). Threats create a situation in which the target country is demanded to change its behavior. This forces the target to search for more information on the threats and their credibility, estimate consequences of potential concessions, and create an internal consensus to back up the decision to yield (George 1991, 5; 12–14). These goals will probably be better achieved if military action is integrated in a multilateral strategy and used in conjunction with political and economic means (Carnegie Commission 1997, 62).

Compelling threats are supposed to have preventive functions, and they often do. However, threats also contain a risk of escalation which, if realized, may leave every party worse off in comparison to the original situation in which conflict was controlled. Therefore, active military diplomacy has its drawbacks; instead of preventing and containing conflict, coercion can fuel it. The role of perceptions is central here; an expansive move by one party and a coercive response by another alter the structure of expectations in a manner which is seldom constructive and is, therefore, prone to further escalation (Smoke 1977, 273–75).

The feasibility and success of coercive diplomacy are strongly dependent on the political context and also influenced by the skills of implementation. In sum, "coercive diplomacy is a sharp tool—at times useful, but difficult to employ successfully against a recalcitrant or unpredictable opponent" (George 1991, 84). A key factor in the success is the opponent's perceptions, especially whether it believes that the coercing power is genuinely motivated by what is at stake; that there is a compelling and urgent need to respond to the demands by the initiating actor; and, third, that the target takes seriously the possibility that the initiator will engage in escalation that would pose unacceptable costs. But even when coercive diplomacy meets these criteria, it can fail, as happened in the Gulf conflict, in which neither deterrence nor compulsion worked, and led to an all-out war (Stein 1992).

The risk of escalation in military coercion would speak for the use of less extreme military measures such as the preventive deployment of military forces and the establishment of demilitarized zones and safe areas. These measures can be undertaken either with or without the consent of the states concerned, though in the absence of consent the initiators should be ready to enforce their policy. The principle of sovereignty requires, however, that deployment does not take place against the expressed will of the state(s) concerned. In the multilateral mode, effective preventive deployment may require the establishment of an international volunteer force (Our Global Neighborhood 1995, 110–12).

Preventive deployment can be used both to protect a country that feels itself threatened and to hamper the intensification of an internal conflict (Boutros-Ghali 1992, 16–17). These options refer to two distinct strategies of preventive employment. Preventive deployment at the border has the purpose of either separating the warring states from each other or, in rare cases, to lend support to a threatened state. In fact, traditional peacekeeping, intended to monitor and enforce a cease fire between warring parties, results in the interposing of forces to prevent the re-emergence of hostilities. In that sense peacekeeping can have functions similar to preventive deployment.

The deployment of 1,300 US and Nordic troops, under the UN aegis, in Serbia (from which they were subsequently expelled), and in Macedonia, to prevent the hostilities from spilling over their mutual border, is the only concrete example of preventive deployment so far (Archer 1994). Without any doubt its lessons have been positive, partly because of the credibility due to the US participation. The Macedonian example shows that the mere existence of a military force, backed by sufficient political determination, can influence the policies of parties to a conflict. It also supports a general conclusion that the "most successful use of power occurs when the least violence takes place" (Watson 1982, 57). The relevance of this maxim is tested in 1998 in Kosovo where international forces are deployed to seal the border between Albania and Kosovo and prevent the spill-over of the crisis into Macedonia.

The lessons of safe havens in Bosnia are much more pessimistic, though; the lack of credible capabilities and commitment by the UN forces to their defense gave an opportunity for Bosnian Serbs to attack them with impunity. The UN Secretary-General requested 34,000 troops to defend the six safe havens, but got only 7,600 soldiers. The commander of the UN forces, General Philippe Morillon, vowed not to leave Srebrenica before its inhabitants were safe. In the absence of sufficient firepower and constrained by restrictive rules of engagement, the UN troops did not resist the Serb takeover of Srebrenica in July 1995. The attack resulted in the mass murder of over 8,000 Muslims (for details, see Honig and Both 1997). Safe havens as a strategy to prevent the horizontal escalation of conflict were badly discredited in Bosnia.

Preventive deployment in intrastate conflicts aims to maintain internal stability, secure the supply of humanitarian aid and essential services, and protect minorities and other exposed groups. A moot point is whether troops deployed in the preventive mode should have enough firepower to thwart off an aggression or whether they should be lightly armed and focus mostly on monitoring. If troops engaged in such tasks do not use force, they can be set up by the Security Council under Chapter VI of the Charter. Then their functions would not differ much from the mandate given to peacekeepers and humanitarian assistance teams. Due to the lack of experience, the modes of operation, mandates, and objectives of multilateral preventive deployment continue to be ill defined. To be viable, preventive deployment has to be linked with a comprehensive plan to settle the underlying dispute (Evans 1993, 81–85).

The interstate and intrastate strategies of preventive deployment address different aspects of escalation. Intrastate deployment tries to prevent the vertical escalation of dispute, while deployment at the interstate border aims to forestall the conflict from spilling over the border. The involvement of great powers in the crisis creates a special problem of horizontal escalation. In such a case preventive deployment aims to neutralize the conflict zone. In fact, the prevention of great-power involvement in a crisis has traditionally been at the core of preventive diplomacy. Its failure would mean that several salient limits would be crossed in the escalation process.

Claude, Jr. defines preventive diplomacy primarily as the horizontal control of violent conflicts, hindering the involvement of great powers in a crisis and thus keeping the use of force local (1964, 317–25). Obviously, no collective international body can ultimately keep great powers at bay if they decide to embark upon an expansionist policy. Therefore, the neutralization of the conflict zone requires decisions by great powers not to act. The international community may demand that great powers formalize their commitments in a treaty and agree on enforcement mechanisms (Black, Falk, Knorr, and Young 1968).

With the abatement of the Cold War, unilateral military interventions by major powers have, except for Russian military operations in the post-Soviet space, become rare. This has altered the nature of preventive diplomacy in which the involvement of great powers does not loom as large as before. Paradoxically, the problem is often that major powers refuse to take part in peacekeeping and peace enforcement that would be needed to control the intensification and spread of violence.

Luttwak (1994) traces this "current unreality of the great power concept" to their "refusal to tolerate combat casualties" and proposes, rather incredibly, either the "Ghurka model" or the "foreign legion model" as remedies. A more important reason is that the military is, for professional reasons, unwilling to intervene in complex local conflicts which cannot be easily managed by outside force. The "decisive force" concept wants to limit its role to situations in which force can be overwhelming, serve a clear-cut political purpose, and have a specific exit strategy. Few if any internal conflicts meet these criteria (Daalder 1996, 469–76). Therefore, a richer array of means of intervention, combining peaceful and military elements, is needed to prevent the escalation of conflicts (Jones 1995, 236–37).

Economic Instruments

Economic means of influence in foreign policy can be either negative or positive, that is, punishments or incentives, and they can focus on a variety of transactions such as aid, trade, capital, and technology flows (in general, see Baldwin 1985). Economic sanctions are usually considered instrumental methods to enforce international norms and decisions, that is, punishments for deviating behavior. In that sense they are a half-way house between the "soft" diplomatic means and "hard" coercive military instruments (Damrosch 1994). To put it otherwise, economic sanctions are intended to convey the image of both restraint and resolve. Various types of sanctions are specifically mentioned in Article 41 of the UN Charter as a method for the Security Council "to give effect to its decisions without resorting to the use of force."

The standard instrumental theory of economic sanctions presupposes that they are initiated to punish the target for wrongful policies and force it to abandon them. In addition, sanctions are used to pass judgement on the mode of governance or specific policies by the targeted country. The success of economic sanctions cannot, of course, be taken for granted, but it varies from one case to another and depends on such factors as the severity of sanctions, the nature of the target, and the goals pursued (Eland 1995). According to common wisdom, instrumental sanctions are more effective than expressive ones because they contribute to conflict resolution.

However, case studies of economic sanctions used by middle powers suggest that the instrumental, rational theory of economic sanctions may not be a very valid description of reality. On the contrary, the decision to launch economic sanctions may not have been really motivated by the willingness to punish the target or bring about a change in its policies. Sanctions may have been more inspired by need to collaborate with allies and the push and pull of domestic politics. For this reason, sanctions have been compared with the rain dance; it has been important to organize a political spectacle to give an impression that something significant is happening (Nossal 1994).

Against this backdrop it is not surprising that discussion on the potential preventive functions of economic and other sanctions has been almost non-existent (for example Evans 1993, 133–42 examines the preventive role of sanctions). In addition to retributive punishment, economic sanctions have been used as instruments of both compulsion and deterrence, of which the latter comes closer to preventive action. Baldwin (1985, 263–66) has shown that the primary goal of the US sanctions against the Soviet Union after its invasion of Afghanistan in 1979 was to send an unmistakable message that while Washington wanted to retain the cooperative framework of East-West relations, the Soviet expansion beyond Afghanistan was totally unacceptable. In other words, sanctions were used, and successfully so, as a tool to prevent the horizontal escalation of conflict. This is consistent with the general conclusion that economic sanctions can be modestly successful, but usually only in carefully specified conditions (Baldwin 1985; Rogers 1996; Pape 1997).

Greater attention to the preventive functions of economic sanctions is justified by the need to develop intermediate instruments of conflict prevention. In combining coercive and non-coercive elements, they should signal both resolve and restraint. The search for non-violent alternatives to military coercion should be tempered, however, by the growing recognition that, quoting the UN Secretary-General, sanctions are too "blunt an instrument" which should be replaced by "smarter" and targeted acts of prevention and punishment. Sanctions often hurt the wrong targets; instead of punishing political, economic, and military elites, their adverse social and humanitarian effects hit the socially marginalized groups, including women and children (Damrosch 1994; Nossal 1994, 264–67; Boutros-Ghali 1995, 16–18; Carnegie Commission 1997, 52–57).

Briefly stated, while economic punishments have had a modicum of success, they do not seem to be an effective method of preventing the outbreak of latent conflicts into hostilities. For this purpose, they simply do not have sufficient short-term impact to compel the target to give up its plans. To be effective, economic sanctions require patience. In addition, economic punishment may not help in conflict resolution, especially if the crisis has economic roots as in the Former Yugoslavia. In such a situation, they can further fragment the social fabric and may strengthen the role of extremist leaders (Woodward 1995).

It is quite conceivable, however, that economic punishments can prevent the targeted actor from escalating the conflict further, beyond certain limits. This suggests that sanctions are more effective in preventing the escalation than the outbreak of conflict or to help resolve it. This concerns the prevention of both horizontal and vertical escalation (cf. Rogers 1996, 412, 429–31). For instance, the cases of Haiti and Serbia suggest that economic punishments have preventive value, although their humanitarian toll may be excessive in comparison to political results. A separate issue is the use of economic punishments in post-conflict demilitarization and political management of a country such as Iraq (Dowty 1994).

Economic incentives may well be more effective than punishments to persuade a party to the conflict to give up a course of action or change its orientation. This is especially the case if the supplier of rewards has in relation to the target sufficient material prowess and political credibility, its communications with the recipient are precise, and their relations are not clouded by major suspicions or grievances (Rothgeb 1993, 110–17). Obviously the impact of economic incentives depends on how they are contextualized, composed, targeted, and implemented (Crumm 1995; Cortright 1997).

The US "bribes" to the Ukraine, and the US and Japanese ones to North Korea are examples of successful economic rewards prompting these countries either to give up nuclear weapons or efforts to manufacture them. There is also evidence on arms transactions that rewards have been more effective than punishments to alter the recipient's behavior. On the other hand, the gains may be offset by the increased propensity and intensity of conflicts brought about by the arms transferred (Sislin 1994). Both sides of this issue are reflected by the US "train-and-equip" program in its relations with the Muslim government of Bosnia.

Generally, the effectiveness of sanctions depends on the choice of principles and the clarity of objectives that inform the policy. Another determinant is the comprehensiveness of the sanctions regime, and thus the costs that can be used to impose on the target state for attaining the objectives. Like in the use of military coercion, the objective of economic instruments is to induce or compel changes in behavior by getting the opponent to reassess the consequences of its policies. Furthermore, sanctions aim to shape domestic consensus in favor of an approach that is more responsive to international expectations.

These expectations are shaped, to a large degree, by non-governmental forces. Without their influence, governments or business would not necessarily initiate sanctions at all. Nossal (1994) provides evidence from Australia and Canada that domestic politics influence in an important way the sanctions decisions. Economic sanctions against South Africa are an even more vivid reminder of the importance of the national and transnational anti-apartheid movements. They pushed governments to punish the apartheid regime economically and forced many transnational companies to comply with a code of conduct and, later on, divest their investments from South

Africa. Corporations complied with the investment ban not so much for political sympathy, but because their business at home would have suffered from continued presence in South Africa, whose economy had started to decline in any case (Rodman 1994; Klotz 1995).

The South African case suggests that non-governmental actors and their coalitions have an important role in forcing the governments to implement punitive sanctions against misbehaving states. The impact of these actors is probably weaker in the preventive use of economic sanctions and in decisions to use incentives rather than punishments. Incentives require resources which non-governmental actors do not possess, while they can generate political pressures that lead to the denial of resource transfers, or, in other words, punishments. Both of these uses of economic instruments also require foresight and strategic planning, neither of which are a comparative advantage of social movements, geared to crystallize and articulate social criticism.

Although an effective approach in some cases, the "carrot-and-stick" logic may entirely fail in intractable conflicts in which the issues of power and identity are at stake. Carefully crafted carrots and sticks in the 1985 Anglo-Irish Agreement on Northern Ireland failed to produce desired results because the Unionists considered the entire initiative a threat to their power and identity. More generally, one can say that if "a regulating institution appears to take away local autonomy on an issue where community identity has been aroused, the regulator had better be a very strong institution. . . . Otherwise, the conflict will escalate to deny the legitimacy of the regulating institution, and obstructing that institution will become the primary objective, perhaps eclipsing all others, including economic ones" (Smyth 1994, 317–18).[2] This observation helps us to understand the backlash effect which negative sanctions and other external interventions often elicit.

In the end, economic rewards may be more effective as preventive tools at an early phase of the conflict. They convey a promise of future benefits to the decision makers of the targeted unit and also emphasize the basic political choice they are facing: either they become isolated pariahs or full-fledged members of the international community. Obviously economic engagement should be conditional and depend on the commitment of the target to cooperate. The policy to engage China economically can be thought to have preventive functions as it tries to make sure that this rising power will avoid aggressive or otherwise detrimental policies in the future (Shinn 1996, 31–62).

If the target chooses not to accept engagement and its non-conforming policies continue, then indifference and punishments remain the only options. At the later stages of conflict the role of punishments as instruments of influence is restricted to prevent the further escalation of hostilities. If sanctions are effective, then the promise to discontinue them becomes an economic incentive to agree to settle the conflict.

In the Yugoslavian conflict it was widely thought in 1990–91 that the federation could be kept together by helping it get over the economic crisis providing economic aid and other financial carrots (Maull 1995–96, 100–101). This was, however, an unwarranted view as the parties were rather preparing for war; therefore, economic instruments of prevention lacked validity. In effect, economic sanctions against Serbia strengthened the role of state and hardships created by them provided a fertile ground for the nationalist propaganda. The idea that sanctions encourage democratic pressure from below to alter the governmental policies did not work (Woodward 1995, 148–49).

Economic sanctions against Serbia had an impact, though, but only in 1994–95. Then they were a factor in the reorientation of the Belgrade leadership to accept and even push for peace in Bosnia. Thus sanctions can help in conflict termination, but only after they have been applied for years to have an accumulated economic and political impact. Economic tools can also be an essential component in post-conflict reconstruction and thus in the prevention of the re-emergence of hostilities (Ball and Halevy 1996). The Bosnian record suggests, though, that the international community uses the instruments of reconstruction in a politically haphazard manner (Väyrynen 1997).

The case of El Salvador suggests, nevertheless, that the world community is all too slow to provide necessary assistance and that the policies of different international institutions may be at cross-purposes. While a war-torn country would badly need additional resources for reconstruction, structural adjustment and other similar programs may choke the national economy and thus fuel tensions and hostilities anew (de Soto and del Castillo 1994). Another problem, witnessed in the economic and humanitarian rebuilding of Mozambique's war-torn society, is that the international donor community and its representatives operating on the spot fail to coordinate their actions. Instead, they may resort to unilateral actions resulting in acrimonious political relations and substandard performance (Alden 1995, 121–23). This undermines, in turn, the ability of economic tools to prevent the potential re-emergence of violence which fortunately has not happened in Mozambique.

Political Instruments

According to current usage, preventive diplomacy refers to political actions undertaken by states to prevent the outbreak or the escalation of a crisis. As noted earlier, preventive action is usually understood as targeted, pre-crisis diplomacy to forestall the outbreak or escalation of violent, high-intensity conflicts. Such a preventive diplomacy is different from "normal" diplomacy; its time-frame is medium- or short-term, and it operates in an environment where the intensity of conflict is still moderate (Lund 1996, 39–44). Thus, risks managed by preventive diplomacy are smaller and less pressing than in crisis or war diplomacy. Therefore, preventive action can rely primarily on political means of influence which are occasionally complemented by the resort to economic and military instruments.

As most other forms of diplomacy, preventive political action is expected to be sophisticated and avoid media visibility. This "elitist" conception of preventive diplomacy has been elaborated by Gareth Evans who suggests that "preventive diplomacy missions should in general be informal, low-key, non-binding, non-judgmental, non-coercive, and confidential" (Evans 1994, 14–17). His approach is almost diametrically opposed to the principles of forceful diplomacy in which the demonstration of the vitality of interests involved, backed up by the limited use of military force, has a key role (George 1991).

Part of this difference can be accounted for by the fact that Evans speaks primarily about third-party actions, while George focuses on the prevention of war in bilateral interstate relations. In this analysis, however, the focus is on multilateral political operations to prevent deadly conflicts.

Political instruments of multilateral preventive action vary considerably. For instance, the UN Secretary-General mentions confidence-building measures, including risk reduction centers, fact-finding, early warning, preventive deployment, and demilitarized zones as means of preventive diplomacy (Boutros-Ghali 1992, 13–19). Lund proposes an even bigger "preventive diplomacy toolbox" containing the use of armed forces and restraints on it, the threat or use of military force, coercive and non-coercive diplomatic measures, policies to promote economic development, and stable political governance as well as the enforcement of human rights (Lund 1996, 203–205).

The political instruments of preventive action can be classified on the basis of their degree of institutionalization. Ad hoc visits by fact-finding and monitoring teams as well as special missions to gather information and suggest guidelines for further action are at one end of the spectrum.[3] At its other end are institutional mechanisms that systematically try to contain the potential conflict from erupting into violence: arms control agreements, demilitarized and nuclear-weapon-free zones, and permanent field missions. Recently, the idea of preventive arms control, based on bilateral or multilateral regimes, has been put forward. Such arrangements should help to intervene in decisions to develop or transfer new nuclear and conventional military technologies that could have destabilizing or otherwise harmful effects (Darilek 1995; Neuneck and Wallner 1996).

There seems to be a general agreement that ad hoc preventive diplomacy has clear-cut limits. According to Evans, preventive diplomacy units instead require "adequate resources and infrastructure, with appropriate back-up personnel and equipment." These preventive teams should visit the conflict spots "on a regular and routine basis. . . . to identify emerging disputes, to track developments in existing disputes, to gain an in-depth understanding of these disputes, to develop a sense of trust and a reputation for fairness, to urge the parties to come to the negotiating table and to offer a range of dispute resolution options." He also suggests the establishment of regional peace and security resource centers in different parts of the world (Evans 1993, 71–76).[4]

Seen from the state-centric perspective, effective preventive diplomacy without adequate material and organizational capabilities and political clout, that is, without power to shape events, is hardly possible (Watson 1982, 52–68). Such capabilities are difficult to mobilize, however. Major governments are reluctant to both commit themselves to strong preventive actions and give multilateral organizations such a role. Effective preventive action is also undermined by the emphasis on sovereignty which is used on all sides as an argument against any early preventive involvement.

If one waits until conflicts escalate into acute crises, then the opportunity for effective preventive action is obviously missed. This leads easily to a pessimistic conclusion: preventive diplomacy is almost always either a non-starter or, if attempted, doomed to fail. Even if the international community had a clear indication of coming crises and recognized their escalation potential, several questions remain: How can they determine which of the crises needs the most urgent attention? How can reasonable schemes be devised to pool national contributions and use them for collective purposes? In particular, how one can establish what Maresca (1995, 63–64) calls a "credible process" of negotiations by which the outbreak and escalation of the crisis can be averted?

Whatever the organizational arrangement, the preventive involvement of third parties in civil wars faces tremendous difficulties. This is so for several reasons: timing is difficult to decide and gaining control of the situation may be even more difficult. As to timing, it is not easy to determine whether an early involvement is more effective than the intervention after the conflict has reached a stalemate persuading the parties to negotiate seriously. If an early intervention fails to prevent the outbreak of violence, third parties may not have power to enforce a peaceful solution. They may be at the mercy of the conflict dynamics (Princen 1992, 51–55). Rather than preventing the conflict they become its prisoners and, as the Yugoslavian crisis shows, unwittingly worsen the situation.

It is possible that third-party initiatives have more promise in conflicts which threaten to escalate horizontally to involve other countries than in cases involving the risk of vertical escalation. Also military and political deterrence seem to have a greater impact in the case of the horizontal escalation risk. If major powers have contending interests in the region, impartial third parties can try to stabilize the situation and prevent its further escalation by keeping these powers out of conflict (George 1983, 372).

The effectiveness of a third party depends both on its identity and the way its role is defined, as well as on its approach to getting involved. Especially relevant are non-judgmental approaches based on the confidence acquired by the third party. This is an approach which Jimmy Carter has perfected and applied to a variety of conflicts ranging from Sudan through Haiti and Bosnia to North Korea. Despite occasional efforts by the incumbent US administrations to rein him in, Carter has been able to operate in these crises in a flexible manner. In general, it has been suggested that flexibility has two dimensions: the lack of constraints and the capacity to influence (Botes and Mitchell 1995). Carter obviously has few constraints on his actions, but his capabilities are limited (although his status as a past US president is a political capability factor).

Flexibility should not be viewed, however, only as a property of the actors involved in the prevention and resolution of conflicts. The success of third-party approaches also depends on the independence and flexibility of the mechanism itself. If no single party can block its action, the multilateral mechanism may permit early responses in situations in which the lack of international consensus or reluctance of individual states to become involved would otherwise impede it. Such a flexible international mechanism can compensate for the lack of governmental leadership.

When the third party's role is non-binding but credible, it can help to create a kind of low risk environment in which opponents find it easier to temporarily suspend escalatory actions and consider cooperative alternatives. So far, the mandate and mode of operation by the OSCE High Commissioner on National Minorities (HCNM) provides probably the best example of a flexible multilateral arrangement to prevent the outbreak and escalation of ethnic crises (Zaagman 1994; Chigas et al. 1996, 51–63; Foundation on Inter-Ethnic Relations 1997). As pointed out earlier, such a preventive action by impartial mediation can be contrasted with muscular prevention in which political resolve and threats of coercive measures are used to forestall the escalation of the conflict.

In many cases regional organizations have failed to undertake effective preventive actions; this has happened most notably in Former Yugoslavia (Väyrynen 1996). The work of established regional or global organizations is also complemented, albeit often under their auspices, by new actors coming to the stage of preventive diplomacy. An example of this is the role of the Minsk Group and the High Level Planning Group in efforts to solve the conflict in Nagorno-Karabakh and prepare for the peacekeeping operation there (Vilén 1996). Another example is the pivotal role of the five-power Contact Group in coordinating the political processes connected with the Bosnian crisis both before and after the Dayton Accord (Boidevaix 1997).

Organizations in other regions than Europe have also started to develop their capabilities in conflict prevention and resolution. Thus, the Organization of African Unity established in its Cairo meeting in June 1993 the OAU Mechanism for the Prevention, Management, and Resolution of Conflicts. To make the Mechanism more effective (its record has been mixed so far), a number of new instruments for preventive diplomacy as well as the establishment of subregional "areas of cooperative security" have been suggested (Ayissi 1994; van der Donckt 1995). The Southern African Development Community (SADC) adopted in 1994 the Windhoek Declaration establishing a Ministerial Workshop on Democracy, Peace, and Security in the subregion. One may also mention the establishment of the ASEAN Regional Forum in 1994.

In general, one possible solution to the dilemma of initiating timely, effective, and collective international actions to prevent violent conflicts may be what Miles Kahler (1993, 299–305) has called "minilateralism." In the absence of a hegemonic power or an effective international organization, cooperation has to be organized by a small core group of countries either in the global or regional contexts. The UN Charter assigns, through Article 52, a special role to regional organizations in keeping international peace. They are not entitled, however, to carry out independent enforcement actions in accordance with Chapter VII as they are a monopoly of the Security Council. Therefore, regional organizations have to concentrate on conflict prevention by various means of peaceful settlement.

Political approaches to conflict prevention generally are process-oriented. Their success thus depends on consulting a wide range of groups in society in order to establish the facts and assess the situation from multiple perspectives and ultimately develop recommendations. The third party's focus on process helps it to gain the confidence and trust of the parties and, in that way, to transform the conflict. While third-party involvement in conflict prevention is by no means a panacea, it is often a necessary precondition to start narrowing the gaps between the parties to the conflict and initiate the process of reconciliation.

Conclusion

As stated at the outset, conflict prevention can be either bilateral or multilateral. It can use military, economic and political means to accomplish its goals. By the help of these two variables one can develop a classification of various measures to prevent deadly conflicts (see Table 5.2).

By using these instruments governments and international organizations can occasionally succeed in averting the outbreak and escalation of violence. Preventive action is an up-hill struggle, however. The failure of most governmental efforts at forestalling conflicts in their early phases calls for prudence in assessing the feasibility of preventive actions. It seems that specific, directed actions to prevent latent conflicts from erupting into violence are difficult to organize and sustain. Therefore, prevention should be an aspect in all policies by governments and international organizations. Risky countries should be engaged early on in transnational economic, political, and cultural networks. International isolation fosters crises in societies, integration helps to avert them. The transformative capacity of integration can strengthened by involving multiple actors in the networks. The involvement of NGOs especially enhances the transformative capacity of third-party interventions as they usually work at the grassroots of the society.

Of course, any assessment of the effectiveness of preventive actions is necessarily tentative. Obviously, political instruments are most versatile and flexible and can be used for prevention during all phases of the conflict cycle. While they are not often adequate to alter the interests of the targeted actor, political tools permit continuous contacts between the actors involved. They also are a creative instrument permitting the transformation of the conflict in a manner so that its resolution becomes possible or, at a minimum, further escalation is avoided. The transformative aspect of conflict prevention should gain more attention in the future.

Economic means of influence are only partially successful, although material incentives can be helpful in preventing the outbreak of conflict. In the control of escalation, economic punishments may be effective, although their impact is felt only over a long term. Economic tools have intended preventive effects only if their use is informed by political objectives. For this to be the case, the actors undertaking preventive measures must coordinate their actions in a comprehensive manner. Otherwise the targeted actors can play those exercising preventive diplomacy against each other.

Military coercion as an instrument of prevention is in most circumstances too rough a tool to have desired effects. On the contrary, it may elicit military countermoves and thus escalate the crisis. In intractable crises, political and economic means may not be adequate, however. Military enforcement actions and their threat may, as a last resort, be necessary to

TABLE 5.2 **Instruments of Preventive Action**

	Political Influence	Economic Sanctions	Military Coercion
Bilateral Prevention	Negotiations, confidence building, conciliation, etc.	Dyadic economic and other material rewards and punishments	Deterrence, military threats, shows of force, interventions, etc.
Third-party Prevention	Mediation, arbitration, fact-finding, monitoring, good offices, etc.	Multilateral economic and other material rewards and punishments	Third-party intervention, military enforcement, arms embargoes, etc.

back up the political efforts at the escalation, prevention and resolution of deadly conflicts. In sum, one may conclude that potentially the most effective combination of preventive actions relies on political mediation and economic incentives backed up by a credible threat to enforce peace, should the conflict be escalated by the parties to it.

Notes

1. A broader definition of preventive diplomacy has been adopted by Lund (1996, 37): "Action undertaken in vulnerable places and times to avoid the threat or use of armed force and related forms of coercion by states or groups to settle the political disputes that can arise from the destabilizing effects of economic, social, political, and international change." In this definition preventive diplomacy is a form of politics providing an alternative to the use of force which signifies its failure. A similar mainstream view is stated by Perry (1996, 56): "Well, the best approach to conflict management is preventive. The next best approach is deterrence using the threat of military conflict. And, if deterrence fails, we must finally be prepared to use that military force."

2. This conclusion is consistent with the notion that the efficacy of the preventive and enforcing use of sanctions is dependent on the credibility of commitments by the key senders of sanctions. This, in turn, is dependent on cooperation which the leading state can elicit from other states in implementing sanctions (see Martin 1993). Thus, a US motive in initiating sanctions against Afghanistan was to show leadership to its European allies, and its purpose in confronting Poland in 1982 was to underline dangers of a soft approach against Communists (Baldwin 1985, 267, 283–84). On the other hand, US sanctions against Iran in the 1990s have largely been a failure as European states have refused to support what they consider a unilateral policy.

3. Fact-finding missions as an element of preventive diplomacy have mushroomed in recent years. For example, in 1991–94 about 20 fact-finding reports on human-rights and citizenship issues were prepared on the Estonian situation by the United Nations, the OSCE, the Council of Europe, and the European Bank for Reconstruction and Development (for an assessment of these missions, see Birkenbach 1994).

4. In a similar vein Boutros-Ghali (1995, 7–8) urges the "establishment and financing of small field missions for preventive diplomacy and peacemaking" to complement the work of special envoys. According to him, qualified envoys are difficult to find and their work suffers from the lack of support on the spot. One may also add that the effectiveness of special envoys and supporting field missions suffers also from inter-agency disputes and other bureaucratic and political obstacles in the UN headquarters (cf. Sahnoun 1994).

2

CASE STUDIES

6

THE SHOCK OF THE FAMILIAR:
DISCERNING PATTERNS IN BURUNDI'S
CYCLES OF ETHNIC VIOLENCE

WHEN MAJOR PIERRE BUYOYA SEIZED POWER IN BURUNDI IN LATE JULY 1996, he claimed authority over a society at war with itself and a government that was collapsing, or had collapsed, by any standard definition of the modern state. The national institutions expected to provide public services and oversee official business had suffered so severely as a result of worsening political confrontations and increasing violence that apart from Bujumbura, the capital, and a few other areas, largely "ethnically cleansed," little remained except the army that had not become decimated, damaged, intimidated, or paralyzed to the point that routine operations had ceased or were reduced to damage control and token performance. Most foreign diplomatic posts and international relief organizations had already seen to the evacuation of non-essential personnel while some aid agencies had departed citing risks to their staff (Braeckman 1995; 1996a; 1996b, 195–20).

Many experts had been predicting this military takeover for some time and as the signs became clearer that it was imminent, specific warnings against it were issued in the top echelons of the international community (Buckley 1996b). But when the putsch came there was nothing to stop it. The remarkable concentration of global attention that had recently made Burundi the focus of a long train of distinguished visitors, high-level delegations, special rapporteurs, and formal inquiries had sought to shield it through "preventive diplomacy" from a possible recurrence in Burundi of the genocide against the Tutsi in Rwanda two years before. A wide assortment of officials, scholars, and commentators dreading "The Next Rwanda" (Friedman 1996) and asking "Is Burundi Next" (Gourevitch 1996) had been sounding alarms and recalling how the world had responded too late with too little. In January 1995, the prestigious Council on Foreign Relations in New York had set up the Burundi Policy Forum (later expanded and renamed the Great Lakes Policy Forum) "for the coordination and evaluation of NGO activities to prevent genocide in Burundi," while also noting that Burundi had "become one of the chief focuses of the international community's attempt to elaborate methods of conflict prevention in the post–Cold War world." In fact, however, for most close observers, the major risk in Burundi did not lay in the threat of the numerically superior Hutu slaughtering Tutsi but in the historically more likely possibility of a renewal of massacres of Hutu by Tutsi as had occurred at several junctures, the most devastating of which was the "selective genocide" of 1972, which the wider world had at the time ignored, which resulted in some 200,000–300,000 Hutu victims (Lemarchand 1973; Kuper 1982; Weinstein 1975).

But by the middle of 1996 conditions on the ground in Burundi, made a replay of Rwanda extremely unlikely, nor did they favor predictions of a cataclysmic "double genocide" spoken of by some, including Burundi's president, Sylvestre Ntibantunganya. The Tutsi population was effectively insulated in guarded enclaves, with Bujumbura, as "Tutsiville" a besieged virtually mono-ethnic city. Most probable in the short term was a general descent into chaos with the multiplication of armed bands on all sides caught up in a prolonged and bloody stalemate. Thus when the moderate Buyoya took power, he preferred to speak of "*le changement*" rather than a coup d'état. He quickly announced a cabinet which included eight Hutu, including his Prime Minister, and there followed a tempering in the tone of some international condemnations. Having averted a takeover by Lieutenant Colonel Jean-Baptiste Bagaza, the more radical candidate, whose followers included the extremist Tutsi militia groups with their high visibility on the streets of the capital, many inside and outside Burundi were relieved and encouraged in their hope that Buyoya, if given a chance, might be able to advance security in the countryside and promote an eventual settlement.

Nevertheless, in the eyes of others, notably Hutu opposition leaders, this return of the military to power intimated a fatal blow to the blossoming of multiparty democracy after three decades of military dictatorship. In a sense, Burundi had reverted to the past, as though the sweeping liberalizations launched at the end of the 1980s, the period mourned as "Africa's lost decade," had made the 1990s an era of still far greater loss still. Despite Buyoya's immediate promises of a quick return to "the democratic process" and to "restore discipline in the military," the depth of the mutual apprehension left little room to hope for an easy exit. Rather, interpretations of the Tutsi strategy since 1993 as a "creeping coup" now seemed vindicated (Des Forges 1994). However, in time and assisted by such external developments as the ascendence of Laurent-Désiré Kabila in the Congo which forced the evacuation of Hutu rebel bases in the former Zaire, the overall toll of death and destruction in the countryside seems to have gradually diminished. However, this relative lowering did not come without serious international objections to a number of the tactics employed by the Burundi military, including the forced repatriation of refugees and the coerced containment of Hutu peasants throughout the north of the country into "regroupment" camps where they lack sufficient shelter, food and good water. Also, UN observers reported the Burundi army engaged in both spontaneous and in some cases systematic killing of returnees, most of them young men suspected of being potential recruits for the *Forces pour la défense de la démocratie* (FDD), one of the major Hutu resistance groups (Prunier 1996; 1997).

Furthermore, it bears noting that while news reports referred to Buyoya's takeover as a "bloodless coup," alluding to the fact that leading figures of the previous regime escaped potential harm by taking refuge in various Western embassies, this shift of rule did not occur without a wave of killings of the sort that typify the entire conflict. The immediate pretext for the seizure of power came on July 20, 1996, when Hutu guerrillas attacked a displaced persons camp inhabited by Tutsi, in the central province of Gitega, killing about 330 of its civilian inhabitants. The coup d'état was announced a few days later, after the army had set up road blocks around the capital and moved in to occupy the national television and radio broadcasting building. Then, the Burundi military, which consists almost entirely of Tutsi, mounted an operation, conforming to a familiar pattern. According to Amnesty International, at least 4,050 unarmed civilians, essentially all Hutu, residing in the Giheta district of Gitega province were "extrajudicially executed between 27 July and 10 August 1996 by Burundi government forces." Most victims were killed when the army came to their villages, assembled the residents and shot them apparently after they denied knowledge of the whereabouts of rebels (Amnesty International 1996).

Dead End or New Beginning?

Major Buyoya was himself the driving force of the reforms that led to the adoption of a new Constitution for Burundi in 1992, paving the way for the re-establishment of a National Assembly and the first free elections in almost thirty years. Although he came to power through a coup d'état in September 1987, he had surrendered the presidency in 1993 after losing the election. Nevertheless, the Burundi that Buyoya had guided, not without difficulty, toward a transition to democracy and for which, at the same time, his government had negotiated the implementation of a World Bank sponsored structural adjustment program starting in the late 1980s, had changed altogether from the nation he was again seeking to lead in the late 1990s. The experience of successive failures at finding an acceptable framework for power-sharing had been punctuated by frequent assassinations and an escalation of fighting to the point of civil war. The drift toward a radicalization of positions inside both camps and virulent street violence in the capital had produced a climate in which it was increasingly hard for moderates to survive much less to advance toward common ground (McKinley 1996).

One major precipitating factor in the timing of the coup arose in response to an evolving convergence of views between Burundi's leadership and the international community regarding the prospect of introducing a multinational force into Burundi to restore order. In February 1996, the Secretary-General of the United Nations had called upon members of the Security Council to authorize contingency planning for such a force which could be stationed across the border in Zaire standing by if and when an intervention was judged necessary, especially in the event of genocide. Dissension had followed in the Security Council over whether such a force would contribute to a reduction of the bloodshed or would incite panic and only make matters worse.

Ahmedou Ould Abdallah who served actively and inventively from November 1993 until October 1995 as the Secretary-General's Special Representative to Burundi and who is widely credited with having helped to defuse an explosive situation that periodically threatened to erupt again into unreckonable ethnic violence, was one who shared the latter view. "Foreign troops," he argued, "are perceived, in Rwanda as well as Burundi, as favoring one group and disfavoring the other. Given that premise, their arrival risks unleashing massacres on an enormous scale. The very fact of organizing such an operation, calling up the different national contingents that would serve under the United Nations flag, would already be enough to provoke killings." He added that if foreign troops did intervene in Burundi, one only hopes that they would be able to stay for fifty years (Abdallah 1996, 78–79).

In addition, the practical complexities of a multinational force, its composition, who would pay for it, the details of its mandate, and its command structure also remained unresolved in the Security Council, leading to a postponement of the decision. Later, in the middle of May, the question was raised again after an Observer Mission established jointly a month before by the United States and the European Union had begun to deliver its findings and after Paulo Sérgio Pinheiro, Special Rapporteur for Burundi by the United Nations Commission on Human Rights had submitted the second in a series of deeply disturbing reports outlining the nature and extent of the violence. At that point, in view of the persistent deterioration of the situation in Burundi, the Security Council expressed approval of an eventual military intervention (Pinheiro 1995; 1996a). The United States was joined, among the donor states, by France, England, and Belgium, when it announced that bilateral aid to Burundi was to be suspended until security had been re-established. Further support for an intervention force came from the Organization of African Unity and the European Parliament. At a summit meeting held in Arusha in late June, the President of Burundi, Sylvestre Ntibantunganya, a Hutu representing the majority party FRODEBU (*Front pour la démocratie au Burundi*) and the Prime Minister, Antoine Nduwayo, a Tutsi of the minority UPRONA (*Parti de l'union et du progrès national*), although spurred by different motives, jointly requested the assistance of a regional multinational military intervention. Certain other Tutsi politicians and some extremist Hutu factions quickly declared their opposition to the request for an international force while the military reiterated its longstanding position, both rejecting any such intervention and warning aggressively against it. A month later, however, movement toward bringing such a force together was suspended and effectively abandoned when Buyoya's takeover made it plain that the sending of any external force would be treated as an invasion and would be openly resisted.

Thus not only had the internal realities of Burundi changed dramatically during the eight years separating Buyoya's first and his second ascent to power, but the region and the wider world had likewise undergone a striking conversion of attitude. The sum of these differences would make the settlement of what had once been technically ignored or muted as a localized conflict (Weinstein 1975) into a matter of substantial weight and urgency for the neighboring countries and a global consortium of leading transnational agencies and non-governmental organizations, as well as the major Western donor states. These vastly changed conditions would make it all but impossible for Burundi's old-guard Tutsi leadership to reverse the clock, as it were. No longer could they scorn or deflect external pressure in pursuit of a domestic strategy that refused equal treatment to an overwhelming majority of the society on the basis of officially denied structures of ethnic discrimination referred to by Tanzania's founding president Julius Nyerere as a form of "black apartheid."

Indigenous Patterns of Perception and Action

Given this background, addressing early warning and preventive diplomacy in the current context of Burundi does not allow for an easy distinction between a pre-crisis and a post-crisis threshold. Instead, as the situation has evolved, a series of related crises have occurred, indeed, accumulated, presenting a double challenge which requires an articulation of how these incremental or episodic phases are linked and an appreciation of how external influences may assist in averting them. First, therefore, attention should be paid to certain particularities of this society reflecting its habitual political culture, produced and reproduced through various institutions which help shape collective experience informing the way events are seen, recalled, and explained. Only through this indigenous lens is it possible to gain an appreciation for the local or native perspectives that underlie perceived behavior. An effort to understand the specificity of circumstances in Burundi belongs to an assessment of interactions that might otherwise be described in merely formal terms as the pronouncements of a political party, the conduct of the judiciary, or the structure of the education system. Similarly a basic awareness of recent key events, and of their chronological succession, provides valuable assistance in recognizing the overall direction and momentum of societal relationships. Such knowledge assists, for instance, in elucidating crucial distinctions between the ambiguously presented boundaries of "then" and "now." Information of this sort can also clarify distorting confusions and rectify inversions between "action" and "reaction" or "cause" and "effect."

Secondly, an examination of early warning mechanisms relevant to Burundi calls for attention to the fluid nature of the situation both within the country and on the international scene. The changing assortment of actors and factors that come into play affect the availability as well as the relative usefulness of various combinations of carrots and sticks. For example, one of the most significant developments in this domain which has become increasingly lucid since Buyoya's takeover in 1996, has been the concentration of the process that is pressing for an end to the fighting and the attainment of a political settlement in the hands of regional African leaders. The Great Lakes summit facilitated by Jimmy Carter and Archbishop Desmond Tutu, which met in Cairo in November 1995, signaled the public overture of what soon developed into an intermittent series of high-level gatherings usually under the patronage of Tanzania's eminent senior statesman, Julius Nyerere (Carter Center 1995).

Thus by virtue of several recent and intensifying cross-border involvements by African leaders intent on handling this crisis at a regional level, roughly inspired by the performance of ECOMOG in Liberia and Sierra Leone, a new set of coalitions has begun to emerge within the shifting interplay of East and Central Africa that is unavoidably reflected in the mechanisms for monitoring, analyzing, assessing, and responding to this conflict. As a result, the situation surrounding Burundi, like that touching on Macedonia, can be viewed with an eye sensitive to the experimental, as a privileged instance where key elements of post–Cold War, post-Kuwait, and post-Somalia approaches to early warning can be noted for their urgency if not always for their clarity. Thus, the bleak outlook for a rapid or a smooth end to the misery and violence of Burundi, is also related to such larger issues as the ample flow of arms and fragments of armies throughout the region and increasing polarization around categories of ethnicity, and the prominence of the Great Lakes Region as a site of contention for newly emerging African spheres of influence, not only touching on the projection of South African interest, but the changing divide between a Francophone west and an Anglophone east of the continent (International Crisis Group 1998).

Furthermore, one must not lose sight of the impact upon the entire region of the catastrophic violence against Tutsi and moderate Hutu unleashed in Rwanda less than a month after Nelson Mandela triumphed at the polls, followed by the colossal refugee crisis that continues to destabilize wide tracts throughout the area (Mazrui 1995; Cohen and Deng 1998). These events constitute a watershed that have left what can be described as an indelible mark bearing with it a traumatizing effect. To be sure, the core of the intractable problems facing Buyoya or any leader in his place, do not derive from external sources. Burundi as a nation has yet to reckon with the consequences of generations of abuse of power at the hands of a military oligarchy defined by region and ethnicity which maintained its position only through massive intimidation and systematic repression. Helping Burundi break out of this cycle presents formidable obstacles. On the one hand, the Tutsi community, including the military, possessed by fear continues to flaunt basic rights, has again forcefully reclaimed power, and shows little real inclination to surrender it. Hutu opponents, on the other hand, seeing this restoration as the palpable threat of a return to the dark and desperate past are no less determined to resist, having in the meantime, beginning in exile communities, cultivated an alternate nationalist ideology that delegitimizes the Tutsi as citizens and regards Burundi as a Hutu nation by right (Malkki 1995). Meanwhile, behind, before, and between both groups the living specter of genocide whether *en masse* or as Pinheiro put it "by slow drip" never ceases to loom (Chrétien 1994; Pinheiro 1996b).

The Origins and Makings of a Polarized Society

Burundi is located near the geographic center of tropical Africa, although in most other respects the treatment it has received from the start of its colonial history has relegated it to marginal if not negligible significance. From the beginning of this century it has fondly claimed for itself the sobriquet *au coeur de l'Afrique*, an image enhanced when its cartographic shape is exploited for its resemblance to a heart but, in fact, until recently, the course of its overall development has been characterized by political isolation, economical insularity, and social introversion. Set in the verdant highlands at the east of the northern tip of Lake Tanganyika and just to the southwest of Lake Victoria, Burundi is blessed with a pleasing climate and an abundance of fertile soil where coffee, its principle export, flourishes as well as a rich assortment of tropical food crops that have long enabled it to produce enough to make it agriculturally self-sufficient. Its landscape, like that of Rwanda and of the adjoining Kivu region in the eastern Congo, formerly Zaire, consists largely of a broad expanse of steep rounded hills and fecund valleys which define this area as a distinct geographic and ecological zone, set apart from what surrounds it. In ethnological terms, Burundi's population reflects a complicated mix that has emerged out of a layering of migrations in the distant past. The result was a relatively homogenous cultural community, sharing a single language, with its own cohesive political identity, characterized by a central ruler and related practices of hierarchical social stratification (Newman 1995, 162–169). Many of the structural elements of these ranking systems were similar across this region although their actual workings involved important differences.

One of the most conspicuous common features of these peoples involved the superior status of a minority group, the Tutsi (known by various names), who kept cattle, were warriors, and monopolized chiefly office, over the rest consisting of the Hutu who tended to be cultivators and the Twa, who were hunters and gatherers. This system of dominance was maintained through a number of diffuse and often sophisticated mechanisms based on bonds of clientage, tribute, ritual exchange and royal favor which many, especially during the colonial period, called a form of "feudalism" (Richards 1959, 378–394). As might be expected, frequent scholarly debates and a deluge of propagandistic polemics have arisen surrounding efforts to describe, characterize, explain, and otherwise account for the actual nature of the relationships between Hutu and Tutsi, using and abusing history as well as drawing on a wealth of racial and cultural theories to support or refute contending accounts of them (de Heusch 1966; Vansina 1998). But interestingly, most parties seem to agree on the relative demographic proportions that specify the comparative size of each group. For decades, with few exceptions, scholars, district officers, and the nation's own citizens have repeated very similar figures, claiming for Burundi approximately 84 percent Hutu; 15 percent Tutsi; and 1 percent Twa (Lemarchand 1994a, 6–16). Often, overviews tend to omit reference to the Twa altogether, but it is important to include them despite their very small numbers and general "pariah" status, since as pygmies, they clearly represent a distinct group regarded explicitly on the grounds of their putative "ethnic" or "tribal" difference whereas physiological stereotypes of Hutu and Tutsi, although widely mentioned, are by no means consistent indicators of actual differences.

The extraordinary degree of centralized order, prosperity, and integration in Burundi under a traditional monarch greatly impressed late nineteenth century Germans whose subsequent writings, emphasizing the so-called "three Ks," namely, *Könige, Kasten und Kühe* (kings, castes, and cows) were instrumental in the way Burundi together with Rwanda, were defined as a distinct administrative unit. Administered by a version of "indirect rule" (the European administrative staff in 1936 numbered less than 50), they represent the exception in sub-Saharan Africa, insofar as they maintained their unity throughout the colonial period and emerged at independence in 1962 as nation-states within the approximate indigenous boundaries that had defined them prior to this intrusion (Lemarchand 1970; 1977). After the Germans, with the help of Swahili mercenaries, completed their military campaigns in Burundi in 1905, the victors concluded a treaty with the *mwami* or "king," setting out the juridical basis of this kingdom and linking it as a pair to Rwanda, creating, first under Germany and, after World War I, under Belgium what was to be known for almost sixty years as Ruanda-Urundi, the Swahili version of their names.

Seen from below, the decisive transitions of this period were widely regarded as continuous with the past institutions. Local readings of the changes that followed after the arrival of the Europeans gave credit first to the recognized forces, such as princely rivalries, dynastic intrigue, successful alliances, military strength, or powerful magic, that were long familiar elements in indigenous power struggles. "If Western historians of the period envision Germans as the *Mwamis'* primary opponents, Burundian oral historians identify the primary actors as Burundian, with Germans as assistants" (Wagner 1991, 549). This inwardly oriented understanding appears to have been especially deeply rooted among Burundi's less privileged, whereas the ruling groups, which benefitted disproportionately from increasing European penetration, responded more quickly to new opportunities.

On the scale of European geography Burundi is small and its demographic profile is unremarkable. But in the African context, it is territorially minuscule whereas it ranks, along side Rwanda, as one of the most densely populated areas on the continent. Lesotho, for instance is slightly larger in size but has only 150 persons per square mile as contrasted with Burundi's figure of 590. Tanzania to the east is thirty-four times larger than Burundi with less than one seventh its population density while the Congo to the west is eighty-four times greater with less than thirteen times the population density ratio. Belgium, by contrast, which is only 10 percent larger than Burundi, has 840 residents per square mile. But Belgium's population is 96 percent urban while Burundi has an urban proportion of only 6 percent and virtually all the rest, are rural, primarily involved in agriculture, herding and related pursuits.

For decades, coffee has accounted for 75 to 80 percent or more of Burundi's foreign exchange earnings although recently, spurred by international investment incentives, successful tea cultivation has begun (Englebert and Hoffman 1994). According to recent World Bank figures, before the onset of the current troubles, Burundi was ranked as the twelfth poorest country in the world with an average per capita annual income of $220. In 1995, however, this figure had slipped to $150 which hovers close to Afghanistan as the world's lowest. On the scale of the Human Development Index, however, produced by the United Nations Development Program, Burundi fares slightly better, placing it at number 152 out of a total of 173 nations listed. Not surprisingly, Burundi's trade deficit has been consistently high. In 1990, while export earnings were figured at approximately $48 million, imports totaled about $160 million. The principal way the country managed to maintain itself, given this imbalance, has been through receipt of foreign assistance, which in 1992 amounted to just over one quarter of its gross national product. Debt servicing for the country's foreign loans had reached a cost that was equivalent to one third of its total import revenues (Laurent 1995).

The origin of the current impasse is usually dated from late October 1993, when elements within the nation's military staged a midnight assault on the presidential palace which soon led to their assassination of the newly elected president, Melchior Ndadaye as well the murders of several other high government officials, including all those in the line of succession according to its recently adopted Constitution. But this rebellion and slaughter also produced the spark which ignited a massive outburst of killings throughout the country that continued for some three weeks. Since Burundi's military consists almost entirely of Tutsi, whereas Ndadaye was a Hutu, these highly significant murders by the army were instantly perceived in the tragically familiar ethnic logic of the *dynamique globalisante*: "As the military had killed the president, therefore the entire army is guilty; as it was the Tutsi who killed the president, the Tutsi are responsible" (Reyntjens 1994, 268). It was understood, certainly by most Hutu, that this direct and brutal attack on the new government was intended precisely to eliminate the rule of law and restore the Tutsi dominance. The Kirundi proverb "the family/group will be blamed for the deeds of one of its members" then took on horrific meaning as Hutu fury over Tutsi lawlessness translated into a colossal slaughter of innocents throughout the countryside (Kadende-Kaiser and Kaiser 1997, 49).

This 1993 coup d'état which collapsed within days, was instigated, on the surface, by junior army officers. However, from all indications, including the composition and behavior of the quickly proclaimed "National Council of Public Safety," its real leadership reached to the highest military ranks (Reyntjens 1995, 14). It failed quickly in the face of widespread condemnation inside and outside the country because its initial declarations lacked credibility and seemed irrelevant as the extent of the bloodbath engulfing the nation became obvious (Chrétien 1994). What began following news of the coup with Hutu militants turning on their Tutsi neighbors was followed by the Tutsi military and related militia group replying by training their weapons, mostly indiscriminately, on masses of Hutu. This sudden eruption of mutual slaughter resulted in the deaths of an estimated 30,000–50,000 persons, believed to be roughly equivalent numbers of Hutu and Tutsi, while as many as a million more fled their homes, some crossing into neighboring countries while others remained displaced within Burundi (Nindorera 1995).

The Politics of Amnesia

Understanding the character of the conflict in Burundi requires recognizing that each group has forged its own view of the origins, the nature, and the ideal outcome of this struggle which subordinates or excludes the other. Each has constructed and constantly fortifies its own edifice of moral justification for their position, designed to defend their version against that of their rival. The result, as René Lemarchand has summarized it, writing shortly before the tragic collapse of order in October 1993, is that "out of two perfectly plausible and complementary lines of reasoning have emerged two radically different and incompatible 'mythologies' which, to this day, leave little room for compromise in so far as they have acquired the force of dogma among some groups on both sides of the ethnic divide" (Lemarchand 1993, 161). Furthermore, these two opposing "mythologies," elsewhere labeled "mythico-histories," are the products of a single national heritage characterized by two sets of collective recollections that have seldom been openly shared and even less often subjected to sustained critical examination within their own respective communities (Lemarchand 1994a, 19; Malkki 1995). On the contrary, due to the strained and lately highly volatile nature of relations, the gap between the Tutsi and the Hutu viewpoints has progressively widened to the point where meaningful dialogue on the level of leadership is barely possible.

Several common features of the value system of both Tutsi and Hutu, that is, fundamental elements of a shared cultural logic have permitted these contesting "mythologies" to arise apart but simultaneously, to mature separately although in unison and to persist in strained complementarity, with convincing force among members of each group. Among these traits, none is more disturbing than a pattern of socio-historical "amnesia." In a certain form, this habit of exercising a short and highly selective memory was already deeply rooted in the political traditions of pre-colonial Burundi. But in what might be called its neo-traditional version, this amnesia continues to manifest itself, despite the considerably changed circumstances where archaic attitudes collide with expectations bred of modern norms calling for consistency, accountability, transparency, and respect for objective evidence.

One potent version of this disjointed continuity can be found in the inclination toward what might be labeled "ethnic amnesia." Especially since independence, this trait has been widely displayed in outright denials of the relevance of Hutu and Tutsi identities, notably by the ruling elite which have insistently refused to acknowledge any role played by ethnicity in Burundi's national life and especially in any of the several crises that has so deeply divided Burundi precisely along these lines. With added emphasis after the massive killings of Hutu in 1972, any allusion to ethnic difference was likely deemed subversive or treasonous by Burundi's leaders, who never conceded it, strictly avoided mentioning it and lashed out at any such reference as hostile foreign interference (Weinstein and Schrire 1976). During the Bagaza regime from 1976 to 1987, coinciding with measures of draconian suppression toward Hutu aspirations, the repeated version seemed to assume that "by eliminating all public references to ethnic identities, ethnic discrimination will no longer matter either as a policy or a source of intergroup conflict." In elite diction they were stigmatized as "at best a figment of the colonial imagination, at worst a part of a neocolonial stratagem designed to play one group of citizens off again another" (Lemarchand 1992, 82).

In certain types of traditional African monarchies, of which Burundi was a prominent example, "there was," Jan Vansina writes, "a strong bias against history . . . It was in everybody's interest to forget about history, whether it were the chief in his province, the subchief who had been dismissed, or the king himself, who relied now upon one faction, and now upon another" (Vansina 1965, 166 ff). The *mwami's* authority rested on metaphysical convictions which endowed the office with an sacred aura, making him an effective symbol of unity for all. But unlike the case of Rwanda, where the king ruled with absolute authority through a strictly centralized and militarized organization of subordinates, the institution of kingship in Burundi, lacked clearly prescribed legitimating norms, nor was it surrounded by ornate aristocratic ritual. The practices which any incumbent undertook to obtain this high office and to defend it against other contenders inevitably involved an array of deft maneuvers and endless feuds between the crown and the princely clans from which every *mwami* came, collectively known as the *ganwa*. A high rate of turnover among court favorites and provincial office holders was normal, in such a system, accompanied by no small amount of intrigue and switching sides (Thibon 1995). In this setting, there were neither court historians such as the *abiru* found in Rwanda who were royal keepers of the oral tradition, nor memorial cults meant to preserve dynastic lore. "On the contrary," notes an anthropologist writing just prior to independence, "in Urundi it is said, each king makes custom anew, and the princes tended to assume the prerogative for themselves as well" (Albert 1960, 55). Or, as a political scientist put it, to the degree that such memories "tended to confirm the legitimacy of their rival's claims, the incumbents had indeed a vested interest in fostering oblivion" (Lemarchand 1977, 96).

What has been widely noted as the essential "orality" of Burundi's public life may also be mentioned as a concurring feature of this amnesia. In this society personal relationships rather than professional standing or institutional roles provide the primary grounds for opinion formation, association, and collective endeavor. "Information is passed on and variously subjected to commentary or distortion in order to satisfy the duties of hospitality and good cheer, as people converse, share a glass, or gather around the same table. The consequence is a mistrust of those who do not share the viewpoint of one's own circle, or who might respond in an accusatory manner to euphemistic statements. Cafés and bars are frequented by people who share the same regional origins, the same ethnicity or the same party . . . Burundian intellectuals develop in a climate where a culture of the spoken word has priority over what is written" (Ndarishikanye 1995, 165). In such a setting where proverbs are also privileged vehicles of cultural knowledge, it is not surprising that a considerable repertory of folk sayings reflect sharp ethnic suspicions and admonish accordingly (Crépeau 1981). Reflecting this tendency, it has likewise been pointed out that most Burundians tend to read seldom, perhaps scarcely at all, after finishing school, even for personal enjoyment. Reasons for this neglect must include the inadequacies of the primary schools where the language question of Kirundi versus French remains divisive in addition to deficient literacy rates which, in 1995, after decades of steady improvement were only at 35 percent. The limited availability of books and newspapers, which are hardly available outside of Bujumbura, is also a factor, plus the generally very poor journalistic quality marked by highly opinionated often inflammatory ethnic bias (Barnabé 1994).

Orality and amnesia also reappear in considering ways that implicit codes of conduct underlying traditional interactions have helped to produce social boundaries between Tutsi and Hutu, such as prohibitions against eating together or sharing the same drinking tube. While some of these old taboos dealing with sharing food may be more relaxed today given the advance of liberal thinking, observance of the same practices often remain and even gain extra strength due to the galvanizing effect of solidarity as a part of a primarily oral culture's response to cycles of ethnic violence (Turnbridge 1996). The circulation of stories, songs, and other expressive forms related to tragic events or touching on selectively recalled incidents of ethnic animosity, has tended to flow in separate channels within each community thereby contributing to increased cohesion and exclusivity of both, while at the same time, ultimately providing fertile ground for "political leaders using symbolism associated with these events to transform division and separation into antagonism and violence" (Kadende-Kaiser and Kaiser 1997, 46).

Warnings from the Making and Remaking of Rule

Burundi's passage from colonial status to independence illustrates several configurations of violence and ethnicity that reappear with enough regularity to merit examining their value as potential warning signals. This initial transition occurred under a troubled Belgian administration that had consistently treated Ruanda-Urundi as a marginal appendage to the Congo which had governed it in a manner "*toujours . . . très centralisatrice et très paternaliste*," and had behaved with such flagrant disregard for international standards in setting out the modalities for establishing Burundi's self-governance that the United Nations was twice required to intervene (Rossel 1992, 14). But it would be a mistake to view this transition to statehood in too narrow a time frame. The form of government which was to mold the shape of Burundi society today does not date from July 1962, when it took its place among the family of new African nations, but from November 1966, when the constitution was discarded, the monarchy deposed, provincial governors were replaced by army officers, and rule was assumed by a National Revolutionary Council consisting of twelve military officers headed by Colonel Michel Micombero. How Burundi arrived at this condition of domination under a military oligarchy, from which it would not depart until very briefly after the elections of 1993, covers a key episode of national history in which selective amnesia is plainly in evidence. Thus a brief sketch recalling the dynamics leading up to and immediately following the military takeover of 1966 adds helpful perspective to the current crisis and calls attention to several consistencies as well as important amplifications and modifications shedding light on the "transition anarchies" of the 1990s (Lemarchand 1994b).

This first transition, of thirty years ago, proved to be an experience that would divide the nation first at the level of the traditional elites. Only later did it stir division, in every widening rings, along Hutu/Tutsi ethnic lines. At first, Burundi's Tutsi had looked more with detachment and disdain than apprehension upon the tumult in Rwanda which brought with it, from 1959 onward, attacks on Tutsi as the prelude to a Hutu led social revolution that succeeded in overthrowing the monarchy in Kigali (Reyntjens 1994, 24–36). Only later would these events evolve to embody the pinnacle of horrors to be resisted at all costs in their own country. Burundi, in this preliminary phase, was spared openly ethnic political confrontations owing to a number of factors, the most important of which derives from a set of structural particularities affecting its traditions of rule, succession, and clan order.

Since Burundi, unlike Rwanda, did not draw its *mwami* or king from among the Tutsi but from a separate and distinctive classificatory group of clans known as the Ganwa, which had no parallel in Rwanda, many crucial practices involving the nature of kingship and dynastic rivalries functioned quite differently in each kingdom (Lemarchand 1977). One effect of these differences, for Burundi, in traditional terms, was a markedly more fluid, mobile, and porous system of access to and participation in the relative benefits of wealth, prestige, and power for both Hutu and Tutsi (Albert 1960). In mid-century, however, the Belgian authorities had inaugurated policies that sought to impose upon Burundi the narrower model of ethnic polarity native to Rwanda which the colonial office had made still more juridically rigid in a way that resulted in explicit and widespread bias against Hutu especially in such contexts as schooling, housing, jobs, availability of credit, and appointments to office (Laely 1992; 1995, 285–94).

In time, these discriminatory measures served to distort, confine, erode, and suppress many delicately balanced features of the complex webwork, linked to status and other kinds of relationships. These importations, unknowingly perhaps, worked to undermine familiar patterns of exchange, of precedence, and of authority creating in their place, unaccustomed pressures and unstable realms where the rules were in doubt (Rozier 1973). For example, the official assimilation of Tutsi and Ganwa into a single group in Burundi, has been seen as contributing substantially to the enlargement and the exacerbation of tensions in a veiled underworld where fierce intra-Tutsi rivalries, spawning baroque coalitions and gothic conspiracies, have lurked mightily behind a number of incidents of excessive violence by Tutsi regimes and related militia, including the great trauma of 1972 (Greenland 1976; Manirakiza 1992).

In Burundi, the first incidence of ethnic violence on a massive scale took place only in 1965. But to appreciate the significance as this prototype in a cycle that would be repeated in 1966, 1972, 1988, 1991, 1993, and has persisted intermittently since then, it is helpful to go back four years to a sort of dark founding moment of this turmoil, namely an assassination of which Lemarchand writes: "Perhaps no other event has weighed so heavily on the destinies of Burundi." (Lemarchand 1994a, 54) The victim was Prince Louis Rwagasore, son of the *mwami* and thus born to eminence, but more still, a charismatic figure with sympathetic personal qualities and populist opinions who appealed directly to a broad constituency embracing Hutu peasants as well as the growing coteries of urbanized youth and *evolués*. His tragic death in October 1961, came at the hands of a hit man in the hire of leaders of a political party heavily supported by the colonial administration that had been trounced in an election the month before by UPRONA, led by Rwagasore, which won 80 percent of the votes cast, taking fifty-eight seats out of total of sixty-four in the new legislative assembly. Credible evidence points to complicity in this plot and more than likely encouragement by certain Belgian functionaries but the two major instigators, subsequently publicly executed, were brothers who belonged to a rival Ganwa clan called the Batare. They were acting not only on the basis of personal and political ambition but they were settling "old scores" arising from "feelings of rage . . . in the face of a situation that had denied them once and for all the opportunity to make good their traditional claims to power" (Eggers 1997, 23).

Immediately following this fateful murder, a power struggle erupted over succession to the presidency of the triumphant UPRONA involving two contrasting figures who profoundly distrusted each other. Their animosity and mutual suspicion would not only eventually split the party but sow the seeds of the enduring ethnic divorce to come in a way that neither could foresee. André Muhirwa was one of the few Ganwa of Batare origins to have supported Rwagasore. His tall stature, aristocratic bearing, quick mind, and political shrewdness, together with "his ability to conceal his inner feelings behind a mask of indifference made Muhirwa something of a caricature of the Tutsi type." His opponent, Paul Mirerekana, was a Hutu agronomist and founder of a highly successful agricultural cooperative who had been one of Rwagasore's closest advisors. Said to be distinguished by his "sense of naive self-righteousness and his simplicity of manners . . . He retained all his life the sturdy outlook of Hutu peasant, qualities that his followers came to respect and appreciate but that drew only sarcasm from a man of Muhirwa's class" (Lemarchand 1994a, 64).

The personal characteristics of these men, so consistent with the racial stereotypes that were used to justify official bias during the colonial era and more subtly afterwards, foreshadowed the ultimate outcome of their rivalry. For Mirerekana and other Hutu leaders, the signal event that sent shock waves through their ranks, known as the Kamenge riots, occurred in January 1962, six months before the official handover of independence. At that time, an urban-based, violence-prone Tutsi youth movement, calling itself Jeunesse Nationaliste Rwagasore, instigated armed raids, engaging in arson and murder, aimed at prominent Hutu labor and political figures. This sudden and calculated display of unrestrained Tutsi aggression in the capital city infused a note of urgency into the atmosphere of dissention that was already spreading from the party to parliamentary and administrative domains.

Frustrated by the temporizing and lack of resolution, Mirerekana, just after independence, opted to take the matter to the rank and file of UPRONA at a mass meeting called in a stadium which the government, under Muhirwa as Prime Minister, sought unsuccessfully to halt. Next the *mwami* intervened, although exceeding his specified authority, by announcing a meeting of the party to elect a new executive committee to be held a few weeks later in Muramvya, in the interior. Numerous high-handed tactics surrounded this gathering, including the issuing to Hutu members only a small number of official passes which were needed to travel in order to vote. Nevertheless, Mirerekana, as well as Muhirwa, were elected as two of three vice presidents of UPRONA, although this compromise was doomed from the start and it failed to work. Some months later, when Muhirwa ordered the arrest of three Hutu ministers the National Assembly censured him and he was obliged to resign.

A moderate Hutu who had also been very close to Rwagasore, Pierre Ngendandumwe, was asked to form a new government, which he did although it was was soon brought down by manoeuvres described as "Byzantine practices," on the part of Tutsi extremists (Eggers 1997, 103). A Tutsi Prime Minister took over but lasted only a few months before he too was forced to step down after a no confidence vote. Once more, in January 1965, Pierre Ngendandumwe was appointed the head of government but a few days later he was shot and killed. The murder was committed by a Rwandan Tutsi refugee, in part, an emblem of the growing impact of some 50,000 Rwandan Tutsi residing in Burundi, but still more foreboding, an index of the rising stakes of ethnic cleavage for several leading Burundi Tutsi were also implicated in the killing, including Muhirwa and the head of the Jeunesse Nationaliste Rwagasore although the courts eventually acquitted these others for lack of evidence.

With the state in a quandary, at the *mwami's* initiative, new elections were called which brought the Hutu faction to power by a landslide, winning them twenty-three out of thirty-three seats. However, despite this mandate, the *mwami* refused to accept a Hutu nominee to form a new government. He appointed instead his cousin, a Ganwa protegé of the court. This politically reckless act marked the ignition of a fuse linking two explosive elements. One was the pellucid violation of democratic process by disregarding the vote which fanned Hutu exasperation into rage, and the other was the risk to stability brought on, first of all, by the *mwami's* conspicuous overstepping of the bounds of constitutional authority and secondly, by his physical absence, since he had fled and was residing in Switzerland. The unraveling began in October of that year with an ill-conceived coup attempt led by Hutu members of the army and gendarmerie which not only failed in its immediate objectives, but produced, by way of reaction, the first wave of massacres of Hutu, beginning with summary killings among members of the army and police. A year later, in 1966, after the successful takeover of the state by the army led by Colonel Michel Micombero, the process was accelerated still more mercilessly with "extensive purges of the army and gendarmerie and the physical elimination of every Hutu leader of any standing" (Lemarchand 1994a, 71). In the interior, especially in Muramvya, some Hutu bands reacted to this slaughter and attacked Tutsi families and burned their homes. These assaults then triggered rapid and brutal retaliation by the army and the *jeunesse,* that is Tutsi youth militia, as well as by civil defense groups killing thousands of Hutu outright and imprisoning thousands more under horrendous conditions that the Red Cross at the time declared to be "absolutely beyond belief." Here too, no legal actions were taken against Tutsi perpetrators, further establishing a precedent for selective impunity which has, in effect, remained a fixed component of these cycles of violence.

Provocative Extremism in the Service of Maintaining Domination

When Colonel Micombero seized power it meant not only an absolute closure on any prospect of power-sharing with Hutu, but a decisive re-alignment of Tutsi groups. Not only was Micombero not of Ganwa blood, thus disqualifying him from rule, but his origins were those of a Hima from Bururi in the south, a Tutsi group which was held to be inferior to the Ruguru Tutsi, concentrated in the center of the country, known as the "better stock" or *meilleure souche* (Reyntjens 1994, 36). This difference, given the importance of social status and the penchant for arcane political maneuvering against a backdrop of loyalties built upon kinship calcula-tions, led progressively to a consolidation of power through the concentration of southern Hima Tutsi in high positions. From this time on, the military and the regime leadership have largely overlapped as Micombero's successor, Lieutenant Colonel Bagaza and after him, Major Buyoya, have all been clan cousins. Furthermore, to maintain their grip on power, the Hima have seen the need not only to limit the role of Ruguru Tutsi in key positions, but at several junctures, to arrest, imprison, and even to liquidate groups of them, as occurred most dramatically during the devastation primarily leveled against Hutu in 1972 (Elias 1995, 42).

But recognizing the muted intensity and persistence of these intra-Tutsi hostilities not only corrects the faulty impression of a simple bi-polar confrontation in Burundi, it also points to a potential barometer for early warning. The phenomenon of extremist youth groups fronting for political operatives, familiar enough in many parts of Africa, has played an especially prominent role in Burundi as a major catalyst in the cycles of provocation and wholly disproportionate retaliation and the overall polarization of factions. For example, after the September 1994 "Convention of Government," signed by all except one tiny fringe party, had devised an agreement for restoring joint rule by parcelling out offices, in effect, along ethnic lines, the often violent protests and acts of intimidation carried out by such gangs in the streets of Bujumbura, including the declarations of *ville morte*, calculated to paralyze the city, became a major factor in the steady undermining of the truce and destroying the trust prerequisite for dialogue on which this agreement depended (Cervenka and Legum 1994). These strikes, in all senses of the word, were directly responsible for the pressure that forced the resignation of Anatole Kanyenkiko who had been chosen by the Forum of Political Parties for the post of Prime Minister. Although he was a Tutsi of UPRONA, he was not a Hima of Bururi as was Antoine Nduwayo, who the protesters demanded be appointed in his place (Abdallah 1996, 55).

To some extent, it might seem that the militancy of these Tutsi youth groups arose as a by-product of the instability and vendetta surrounding the failed coup d'état of 1993. But it might be more accurate to identify their prominence as the reappearance, in fragmented though familiar form, of the same *jeunesse* phenomenon that first fomented the Kemenge riots and after that lashed out against supporters of the *mwami* and eventually took its place in the vanguard of the carnage against Hutu in 1972 (Kay 1987, 5). In fact, the Jeunesse Nationaliste Rwagosore that had done so much to set the stage for the first explosions of ethnic violence was, in 1966, absorbed into UPRONA, now declared *le parti unique,* changing its name to Jeunesse Révolutionnaire Rwagasore. The two main leaders of the JRR at the time were included in Micombero's new government.

During the campaign leading up to the elections of 1993, youthful activists from both sides were fully engaged and numerous cases of harassment, assault and some deaths were reported, largely instigated by Tutsi, while arbitrary arrests of a general "demonization" of FRODEBU supporters also became a heated public issue (Reyntjens 1994, 228–29). But evidently, the Tutsi, including the youth, were convinced, with the help of published pre-election polls to support them, that Major Buyoya, the UPRONA candidate for presidency, would win and retain his office even if FRODEBU did manage to gain a majority in the Parliament. But even so, most were apparently also confident of a very strong showing for UPRONA in the legislative as well. The new constitution, ratified by referendum the year before, not only forbade political parties organized on the basis of ethnicity, but it put an assortment of blocking mechanisms in the parliamentary voting system requiring that "diverse component parts of the Burundian population," meaning ethnic groups, be reflected in party lists. The unstated rationale was clear: "while parties must propose a sufficient number of Tutsi for reasonably safe seats in application of the 'component parts' principle, ethnic voting by Hutu at their expense has no effect on the number of Tutsi eventually elected to the "*assemblée nationale*" (Reyntjens 1993, 566). It should also be noted that, undoubtedly as a safeguard against a possible cohabitation, with the President and the parliamentary majority being of different parties, the framers of the 1992 constitution had constructed a "zero sum governing structure" that located power primarily in the hands of a strong executive (McMahon 1996). When, therefore, clearly to their surprise, UPRONA, the old party of Tutsi hegemony, lost the presidency and then won less than 20 percent of the seats in the National Assembly, the shock was registered most dramatically by militant Tutsi youth and students who immediately took to the streets demanding a rejection of the polls calling it an ethnic census rather than a democratic election (Gahama 1995).

The steep and steady deterioration of the political process in Burundi in recent years has been advanced and prolonged in many important respects by the capacity of ethnic extremists, often representing minuscule elements, to dominate public discourse and subvert efforts at compromise. Frequently, the pressure such extremist groups bring to bear originates in forceful tactics which might otherwise be indulged as youthful excess although close behind the bigger bosses are lurking. In fact, many have seen in the conduct of the coup attempt in 1993, an advanced version of this arrangement with junior officers in the van with their seniors waiting to reap the benefits. Not surprisingly, two of these young officers directly leading the failed takeover bid, both now in Uganda, Lieutenant Jean-Paul Kanama and Commandant Hilaire Ntakiyica, have admitted their role but refuse to be made scapegoats, accusing Buyoya of being the mastermind behind the assault (*Africa Confidential*, 17 April, 1998).

A host of non-governmental organizations, United Nations agencies, and diplomatic observers who have assessed the situation in Burundi have with virtual unanimity pointed to the need for establishing and nurturing an atmosphere where a strong and vibrant civil society can thrive (Van Eck 1996). But the formidable difficulties encountered in efforts to realize this goal, including the persistent obstacles hindering the conduct of the genuinely all-inclusive "national debate," mandated in the 1994 "Convention of Government," are due in large part to the continuing gaps of amnesia that have come to displace accountability and fill in the space instead with increasingly strident "mytho-historical" versions of their relationship.

The warning signals that Burundi was already balancing near the razor's edge in 1993 were, one may discern in retrospect, just beneath the surface. The public account, which has been canonized in official histories, promulgated in school texts, and insistently defended by the ruling Tutsi elite that persists in refusing to acknowledge or even to decline discussion of events or structures exhibiting flagrant exclusion, repression, and, by normal standards, colossal violence against Hutu, has left a massive moral debt of impunity. And to it, more recent acts of ethnically motivated murder on a wide scale by Hutu militants has not evened the balance but only added to the reckoning (Abrams 1995). The opportunity to vote in an open contest in which UPRONA had early on sought to demonize FRODEBU as a Hutu front and to label any Tutsi who joined it as a traitor, had the effect, paradoxically, of bringing the ethnic test to the surface in a fashion that did seem to validate the allegation that the popular vote, at least for the Parliament, reflected roughly the demographic proportions of Hutu and Tutsi.

Certainly, the growing turmoil in Rwanda, following the invasion of the Rwandan Patriotic Front in 1990, had a multiplier effect that charged Burundi's tentative democratic experiment with devastating voltage. But the great catastrophe in Rwanda which followed six months after Burundi's army had slaughtered the leadership of the newly elected government only subsequently came to play its oddly determinative role in the struggle: "As in a game of mirrors, reflecting symmetrical images, the Rwanda genocide quickly entered the consciousness of the Tutsi community in Burundi in the form of a self-fulfilling fantasy, giving retrospective justification for Ndadaye's assassination" (Lemarchand 1997). But such distortions of memory, fused with obsessions to rule run very deep in Burundi, nor are they restricted to the Tutsi. Ahmedou Ould Abdallah, the UN Secretary-General's Special Representative, who took it as a central task to isolate extremists by encouraging contact and interaction among adversaries at all levels, spoke toward the end of his stay with growing frustration over the all but insurmountable levels of the mutual distrust: "What we need here are psychiatrists. I meet the politicians every day. They are all frightened of each other. When I shake their hands they are dripping with sweat. There is not one who would not murder another for the sake of an hour of political power" (Ignatieff 1995, 39).

Conclusion

Given all that Burundi has suffered, inflicted sadly by its own people upon each other, not only since 1993, but to frame the tragedy properly, since 1961, it is only reasonable to read the current situation as filled with risks for the future. What particular events might trigger a more precipitous decline and what preventive measures might be taken to forestall them or their likely consequences, not to mention the prospect of a hellish mobilization of hatred similar to that of Rwanda, a scenario which seems less plausible in Burundi, entail a wealth of speculations that have received enormous attention in recent years as the Great Lakes Region continues to occupy a place at the top of the world's docket of high risk sites (Evans 1997). What this case study has sought to address is not so much a reiteration of why conventional early warning approaches failed to predict the rapid collapse of Burundi, despite its longstanding profile as containing a "minority at risk" (Gurr 1993), but rather to emphasize the significance of certain less noted native socio-cultural dynamics that cause this crisis to resist standardized international assessments and responses.

While it is a bit awkward to leap from a conclusion that for Burundi remote warning techniques are of limited usefulness to an endorsement of alternatives that have yet to prove their effectiveness, one may nonetheless discern some positive lessons emerging from what is hoped corresponds to the late and perhaps the final phase of this crisis. The most promising of these innovations (which are more visible since the return of Buyoya in 1996) is the amount of initiative and stamina displayed by regional actors, especially Tanzania and Uganda, with the strong support of the Organization of African Unity, in efforts to reach a solution to the disastrous situation in Burundi (Salim 1996). This new diplomatic activism marks an impressive step forward in that it recognizes at close range the problematic anomaly of Buyoya's regime which represents an ailing authoritarian dinosaur that survives only at the cost of mounting ethnic violence which has caused repeated waves of refugees burdening its neighbors and of chronic instability which obstructs the overall economic development of the entire area (Ehrenreich 1996).

After two years of controversial application, questions about the continuing usefulness of the economic embargo against Burundi, which was initiated by states in the region and only later given United Nations approbation, have become, for many, more of a humanitarian imposition than a political sanction. The growing consensus seems to concur that while the embargo can be credited with some achievement, in pressing the government to take specific steps toward restoring democracy and bringing all the parties together for constructive negotiations, the preoccupations about retaining or lifting it have also introduced a detrimental distraction, drawing attention away from the central concerns (Hoskins and Nutt 1997). Nevertheless, talks held in Arusha in June 1998, once again under the patronage of Julius Nyerere, did manage to bring seventeen parties together seeking a "just and durable solution to the conflict" and the meeting ended with an agreement to implement a cease-fire the following month. Unfortunately, however, enthusiasm over this prospect was very short-lived. At the signing of the document, Burundi's government chose to issue an impromptu qualification claiming that the army did not consider itself to be an "armed party to the conflict" and therefore would not hold itself bound by the agreement (Fondational Hirondelle 1998). This eleventh hour reneging, citing a semantic exception, has, not unexpectedly, prompted the major Hutu rebel group, the *Conseil national pour la défense de la démocratie* (CNDD) and its military wing *Forces pour la défense de la démocratie* (FDD) to call the entire Arusha cease-fire agreement void blaming Buyoya's government with lacking the will for a peaceful settlement, if not lack of sincerity in entering the talks. Thus, an extraordinary accord which seemed at first to count as a major diplomatic breakthrough has been shattered by an apparent rhetorical afterthought which undoubtedly derives from substantial tensions between hardline and more accommodating elements among the Tutsi. Nevertheless, this greatly enhanced involvement of regional players, supported by a newly wakeful international community which has already signaled its readiness to intervene, if it would help end the internecine conflict and nurture the reconstruction of democracy in Burundi by some new formula of participation, seems to represent a turning point in its own right. It gives reason to hope that the next phase of the conflict in Burundi will be one in which subsequent warning signs will be increasingly integrated into a system of prompt regional multi-dimensional response that will break the spell of amnesia, isolation, and trauma which have made much of this nation's modern political development an epic of progressive division leading to ghastly bloodshed, spiraling disappointment, desperately seeking substance for its claim to unity.

7

PREVENTING CONFLICT IN MACEDONIA:
A LASTING PEACE OR A LINE IN THE SAND?

Important Test Case[1]

OF ALL THE SCARCITIES THE REPUBLIC OF MACEDONIA HAS FACED SINCE THE breakup of the Former Yugoslavia, time has been the most critical. The country had little opportunity to develop into a democracy and free market economy before it faced multiple challenges to its legitimacy and viability as a newly independent state. Macedonia faced hostile relations with its neighboring countries, including an illegal economic blockade by Greece and the refusal of Serbia to recognize their common border. Competing historical, cultural, and territorial claims to the new Republic left the Macedonian people feeling encircled and endangered. At the same time, inter-ethnic tensions within Macedonia have increased over the 1990s, to which the government has been slow to respond. The main problems have concerned the grievances of the ethnic Albanian community over what they perceive as a "second class citizenship," lack of power sharing arrangements, representation in administrative positions, and access to entitlements. But the lack of education in the Albanian language at the secondary and university level became a flashpoint for conflict.

The threat of the spillover of conflict into the Republic of Macedonia from other parts of the Former Yugoslavia, along with the dangers of conflict erupting within the country, prompted the first-ever preventive deployment of United Nations peacekeeping troops in 1993. Its arrival was preceded by a Spillover Mission dispatched by the Organization for Security and Cooperation in Europe (OSCE),[2] and a monitoring mission by the Council of Europe. Other international organizations have also served as intermediaries, including the OSCE High Commissioner on National Minorities, officials of the International Conference on the Former Yugoslavia, and a special envoy from the Clinton administration working with a UN official. A variety of non-governmental organizations have also launched programs in Macedonia, including Catholic Relief Services, the

Open Society Fund and Search for Common Ground. The unprecedented attention reflects the international community's concern that violent conflict in Macedonia could lead to a wider Balkan war that would bring in NATO allies Greece and Turkey on opposite sides.

The main challenge before the international community and the Republic of Macedonia has been to build a viable multi-ethnic and tolerant democratic society resilient to the spillover of conflict, and able to work out its own inter-ethnic relations peacefully. In many respects, efforts to provide early warning and conflict prevention in Macedonia have been successful. This chapter will explore several key reasons. First, international assistance has been tailored to the country's particular needs. The initiatives have been comprehensive: not only the dangers of conflict escalation, but to some extent the underlying sources of tension in the country have been targeted. For the most part, third parties have coordinated their intervention and worked together effectively to encourage moderate leadership and a commitment by all parties to find solutions through dialogue. Macedonian President Kiro Gligorov has played a central role in guiding the country to a peaceful transition to independence, in spite of pressures from radical nationalist parties.

However, third party intervention is a "stick with two ends." It changes the dynamics of the conflict, and not always as intended. Macedonia has been no exception. First, in some instances, third party involvement has helped the more extreme factions radicalize the domestic political environment, and gain international attention to their cause. Second, for some of the problems the third parties have helped control, they also may have had a role in exacerbating, however inadvertently. For example both the OSCE and the UN peacekeeping mission have dealt with these kinds of dilemmas while intervening in crisis situations. Third, the success of preventive action depends on the extent to which operations "cover the bases" as concerns both the domestic *and* regional context. However, the lack of an effective international response to the growing crisis in Kosovo, and outbreak of civil war there in 1998, risks debilitating, if not unraveling, efforts to prevent violent conflict in Macedonia.

Tinderbox of Underlying Tensions

Deeply Divided Society

The Republic of Macedonia is a multiethnic society with a total population of nearly two million, though the most salient social cleavage is between the majority Macedonian and minority Albanian community. According to the 1994 census, Macedonians constitute 65.6 percent of the population, and the Albanians 22.9 percent—the largest minority nationality in Macedonia. However, some Albanians contest the 1994 census, and still claim (as they did after 1991 census which produced similar results), that they represent as much as 40 percent of the population. The ethnic distribution of the rest of the population is 4 percent Turk, 2.3 percent Roma, 2 percent ethnic Serbs, and 0.4 percent Vlachs (Statistical Office of Macedonia 1994). According to the 1991 census, 2 percent identified as Macedonian Muslims (known as Torbeshes, Pomaks and Poturs) (see Human Rights Watch Helsinki 1994). While most Macedonians and Serbs are Eastern Orthodox Christians, most others are Muslim. (However, the Macedonians have their own autocephalous church, which the Serbian government, as well as most Macedonian Serbs do not recognize). The numbers of Macedonian Muslims has varied greatly over the last forty years, apparently due to their tendency to self-identify either as Turks, or Albanians (Poulton 1991, 55).

Relations between Macedonians and Albanians are characterized by sociopolitical, cultural, and religious differences reinforced by the territorial homogeneity of the Albanians, especially in the northwestern regions of Macedonia. While the 1991 census shows that the urban population predominates in Macedonia (with 57 percent of the entire population), 64.6 percent of the ethnic Macedonians live in urban settings, as compared with 52.7 percent of ethnic Turks, and only 32.8 percent of the Albanian population. The majority of Albanians are a rural community, devoted to agriculture and animal production. However, according to the 1991 census, around 50 percent of the employed Albanians are engaged in the private sector (23,313 out of 56,436 employed Albanians), where they represent a disproportionately high percentage of the work force (as compared to 33,009 Macedonians).

Ethnic Albanians faced socio-economic and cultural oppression during the communist era in the Republic of Macedonia. They were then under represented in most spheres of public life, a situation that has continued in the post-independence period (Macedonian Information Center, hereafter MIC, April 1994, 18). However, differences in access to educational entitlements have become one of the most salient aspects of inter-communal tensions. Studies have shown that the percentages of Albanians pursuing higher education drop off precipitously as they enter secondary education, and dramatically at the university level. Thus, whereas 23.4 percent of the graduates of primary schooling in the 1992–93 academic year were Albanians, only one in three of these continued to high school, representing only 7.7 percent of the high school student population. The percentage graduating from high school was even smaller: of the 26,150 students registered at the university in Skopje and Bitola in 1990–91, only 1.5 percent were Albanians, as compared to 87.9 percent

Macedonian (Macedonian Information and Liaison Service, hereafter MILS 1993, 17).

Several factors account for their under representation. Traditionally, Albanians have not sent women to school beyond primary schooling, a practice which predominates in rural areas (and is also observed among rural Macedonians) (MILS 1993, 17). In addition, there has been an in-sufficient number of Albanian language high schools, and Albanian parents have been reluctant to send their children to Macedonian language schools. This has limited the number of Albanian students prepared for university level instruction. Albanians also had a low level of enrollment at the uni-versity in Macedonia because many studied at the university in Pristina (Poulton 1991, 61), or elsewhere in the Former Yugoslavia, rather than in Skopje, where Macedonian was the primary language of instruction (MILS 1993, 11–12). However, the option to study in Pristina was cut off in the early 1990s, after President Slobodan Milosevic suspended Kosovo's au-tonomy, and turned the university into a Serbian language institution, in effect, driving the Albanians out.

Demographic trends also increased the salience of discrimination in the field of education, and struggle for political power and access to en-titlements. The Albanian community has had a much higher average birth rate (per 1,000) citizens than other ethnic communities in Macedonia, ranging as high as 25.5 percent in Debar, and 23.7 percent in Tetovo, as compared to 9–17 percent in communities where Albanians do not live (MIC April 1994, 18).

While cultural and social practices account to some extent for the low percentage of Albanians in higher education in Macedonia, these must be viewed in light of the political context. The decision to close down Skopje University's Pedagogical Academy in the Albanian language in 1985, was a key factor behind the shortage of adequately trained Albanian secondary educators. That decision was part of a wide-scale program of repression led by Macedonian communist party officials throughout the 1980s against Albanian nationalism and demands for their own republican status. Among the human rights abuses reported were arbitrary and extensive dismissals of Albanian teachers at the primary and secondary level in Macedonia (Poulton 1991, 63 and 80). Thus, education became the field which provoked the most opposition from the Albanian minority (Poulton 1991, 81; 1995).

There are some instances, however, where religious and ethnic identi-ties lend themselves to cross-cutting ties. This is apparent in the higher percentage of Muslim and Orthodox believers, than of Albanian and Macedonia nationalities represented in the country's entire population. For example, 30 percent of the population considers itself Muslim, 0.5 percent Catholic, and 66.6 percent Orthodox (MILS 1993, 19; Poulton 1991, 82).

There are also some Macedonian Muslims; however, they often self-identify as Albanians, or as Turks. In addition, there are some Albanians who are essentially Macedonian speakers. Thus, according to the 1991 census, only 21.4 percent of the population identifies as an Albanian speaker, whereas 69 percent do as Macedonian (MILS 1993, 19). These few ties remain, however, at the margin of prevailing trends.

Thus, ethnic, cultural, religious, language, demographics, and a compact settlement pattern have led to deep divisions between the two main ethnic communities, a separation reinforced by a recent history of political repression and the near total absence of social interaction. It might also be noted that religious differences may be even more salient than ethnic, as the great reluctance of the different communities to marry across confessions more so than nationalities demonstrates.

Competing Claims to Identity

The limited space for creating states, and the presence of numerous national communities fighting for it has created serious conflicts in the Balkans since the late 1800s. The "Macedonian Question," like all Balkan national problems, was born out of a multitude of forces, including Ottoman decline, Great Power rivalries, imperialism, political expediency, the rise of Balkan nationalism, a search for religious autonomy, and the spread of education. At the crux of the matter lie three main issues: (1) contention over the territorial demarcation of "Macedonia;" (2) questions about the state(s) to which Macedonia belongs; and (3) the nationality of the people of the region (Perry 1988, 2). Today, the Republic of Macedonia consists of about one third of the region historically known as Macedonia, with the rest divided among Greece, Bulgaria, Serbia, and Albania.

The survival of Macedonia in modern times has depended on guarantees from external powers, and more recently, a federal Yugoslavia. Although nationalism typically confers legitimacy on the state, Macedonia's neighboring states have contested its very essence. The Macedonian language, cultural symbols of the ancient Macedonian civilization, history and heroes, the Orthodox religion, and the land itself are each claimed by at least one other neighboring ethnic group. Bulgaria has refused to recognize Macedonia as a distinct language and instead treated it as a dialect of Bulgarian, holding up the signing of numerous bilateral cooperative agreements because the two countries cannot agree on the language(s) in which the agreements are to be signed. Serbia has contested the communist's reestablishment of the autocephalous Macedonian Orthodox Church, including the revival of the ancient archbishopric of Ohrid in 1958, which separation the Serbian Orthodox Church still refuses to recognize. (And Macedonia refuses to recognize the Serbian Orthodox Church within

Macedonia). Serbia has also refused to accept the internal administrative borders of the former Federal Republic of Yugoslavia as the international border, instead making claims on three strategic points that would take considerable bites out of the Macedonian territory. Greece has perceived Macedonian nationalism and any claims to a Macedonian state culture as the illegitimate appropriation of its own cultural heritage. It especially objected to the former Yugoslav republic calling itself Macedonia.

Within the Republic of Macedonia, invoking myths and framing the conflict between Macedonians and Albanians in terms of a clash of religious belief systems reinforced ethnocentrism, and deepened the main cleavage in Macedonian society (Simoska 1993, 96). Framing the conflict in confessional terms (an "endangered Orthodoxy" and a "Muslim conspiracy") plays on the history of Macedonians as victims of various interests, rather than as active participants in shaping their own destiny. The Albanian population's high rate of demographic growth and adherence to the Muslim faith are also used to back chauvinist arguments, and justify fears that "one day the Muslim population is going to outnumber the Orthodox." Simoska argues that defense of confessional unity is much easier to manipulate than of nationality because religious identification is subject to less differentiation than nationality. Confessional identification "produces an 'image of unity' without options, which people relate to more easily" (Simoska 1993, 97–98).

The sense of endangerment also has a regional context. One aspect relates to the history of Serbo-Albanian relations in Kosovo. The Kosovo region itself is of high symbolic importance for Serbian and Albanian ethnic communities, though it plays a different role in shaping the national consciousness of each. Kosovo was the cradle of Serbian cultural and religious civilization in the Middle Ages, and the region still holds many of their prime cultural and religious monuments. Kosovo plays a central role in Serbian mythohistory: in 1389, the Serbs lost the area to the Ottomans in the famous Kosovo Polje (Kosovo Field) battle. Mojzes (1994) describes this event as a "defining moment for Serbian self-awareness," giving rise to the Serbian myth of victimization, and resurrection. Milosevic played up these myths in his campaign to mobilize the Serbs along nationalist lines during the mid-to-late 1980s to counter the rise of Albanian nationalism (Janjic 1995). This campaign culminated in the Republic of Serbia's decision in 1989 to suspend Kosovo's status as an autonomous province, to which the Kosovo Albanians responded, in 1990, by proclaiming a Republic of Kosovo. The Serbs then dissolved the province's parliament, and removed local authorities to fill health services, the local administration, judicial system, and police force with Serbs.

In response, the Albanian parliamentarians adopted a new constitution and declared Kosovo independent in 1990. This led to the development of a system of parallel institutions and social structures (a virtual Apartheit situation), and inducing a political stand-off (CSCE 1992a). It was contained through 1997 by the Milosevic regime's highly repressive measures on the one hand, and a non-violent resistance movement led by the Kosovo Albanian leader, Ibrahim Rugova. With the international community remaining mostly on the sidelines, inter-ethnic tensions erupted into civil war in 1998, as rebel factions within the Albanian community challenged Rugova's leadership and began an armed campaign, to which Milosevic responded with increasing military force.

The long-standing fear of many Macedonians during the communist era and since, is that any efforts to create a separate Albanian republic out of Kosovo or to allow it to secede would lead to the absorption of the Albanian-inhabited western districts of Macedonia. This fear helps account for why the Macedonian communist party officials conducted their own anti-Albanian campaign in the field of education in the 1980s, paralleling, if not exceeding the Serbian oppression (Cviic 1990, 98–99). Many Macedonians fear that if Kosovo Albanian secessionist attempts succeed, this would also encourage Greeks, Bulgarians, and Serbs to act on their historic territorial claims to Macedonia (Poulton 1995, 127).

It also has to be remembered, however, that Macedonian communist officials were as repressive, if not more than their Serbian counterparts, against the Albanians in Kosovo. Thus, in addition to denying ethnic Albanians access to higher education in the Albanian language, there were many other forms of cultural repression, including prohibitions on the registering of nationalist Albanian names; the disbanding of cultural clubs; the dismissal of Albanian communist officers for attending Albanian weddings where nationalist songs were sung; a ban on the sale of property in the western part of the republic (intended to keep Albanians from buying out Macedonians and creating an ethnically pure region); and an amendment to the law on religious teaching—in order to prohibit youth up to the age of fifteen from attending organized religious instruction. Prison sentences handed down to ethnic Albanians were also reportedly harsher than those imposed by the Serbs on the Kosovars (Poulton 1995, 126, 128–29).

Challenges to Political Legitimacy

From the Macedonians' perspective, the disintegration of the Former Yugoslavia posed new opportunities but considerable risks for their identity and security as the Macedonian people. Among the poorest of the Yugoslav republics and most vulnerable from the perspective of inter-ethnic relations, Kiro Gligorov, president of Macedonia, along with Alija Izetbegovic, president of Bosnia-Herzegovina, "spared no effort" during

1990 and 1991 trying to find a settlement to Yugoslavia's constitutional crisis (Glenny 1995, 57; Cohen 1995, 201–202). They realized its breakup would leave both republics with internal and external threats to their security and legitimacy.

Nevertheless, in the first multiparty elections in Macedonia held in December 1990, the majority of the newly formed political parties competed—as in other republics—on the basis of ethnopolitical stakes. The electorate split into three tendencies. The first was a Macedonian nationalist, pro-independence right wing coalition of four parties, the Macedonian National Front—led by a political organization taking its name from the revolutionary terrorist organization of the first decades of the century (the VMRO-DPMNE). It alone won thirty-seven of 120 seats (31.7 percent) in the unicameral legislature (Woodward 1995, 121–22).

The second group, the pro-Yugoslav, but increasingly pro-independence, center-left League of Communist Party of Democratic Change, won thirty seats (25.8 percent). In contrast to the Macedonian coalition, the last group, the ethnic Albanians created and voted for separate ethnic parties. The largest of these, the Party of Democratic Prosperity (PDP), gained twenty-four seats. The pro-Yugoslav tendency within the center left was temporarily strengthened by the nineteen seats (eight in coalition) won by Markovic's Alliance of Reform Forces. Its leader, Kiro Gligorov, a prominent figure in Yugoslav federal politics (especially in financial and economic affairs), was chosen in January 1991 by parliament as the country's new president (Woodward 1995, 122).

The referendum for independence of the Republic was held in September 1991 and received widespread support. Although the PDP advised its members to boycott it, the majority of Albanians participated and voted overwhelmingly in favor of passage (CSCE 1992b). Late in 1991, the parliament drafted and approved a new constitution, although without the support of the Albanian parties, who did not vote for its adoption. They objected to the new Constitution's Preamble (which following the 1990 constitutional amendment), asserts "the historical fact that Macedonia is established as a national state of the Macedonian people, in which full equality as citizens and permanent co-existence with the Macedonian people is provided for Albanians, Turks, Vlachs, Romanies and other nationalities living in the Republic of Macedonia . . ." The Albanians (and other minorities) protested the exclusive treatment of Macedonians as a constituent nation, and their relegation to a nationality, which they considered "second class citizenship." But the country endorsed the new constitution in a 1992 national referendum.

Although the first government (formed in March 1991) consisted mostly of non-party experts, subsequently, there have been coalition governments which have included the more moderate Albanian nationalist party, the PDP, since 1992. The accessibility to, and participation of opposition groups in the Macedonian government and political institutions has helped to minimize ethnic tensions, fears, distrust, and insecurities. Internal disunity, and the radicalization of the main nationalist Albanian and Macedonian political parties has tended, however, to undermine the cooperation of the opposition with the government. These problems have been especially acute within VMRO-DPMNE, which since its early election success has not played a central role in government. One of the precipitating factors for the fragmentation of the party was opposition of the more radical elements to the government's agreement with the Serb Macedonian minority granting them certain cultural rights. Moreover, the decision of the VMRO-DPMNE party leaders, along with the Democratic Party to withdraw from the second round of the 1994 elections over dissatisfaction with what it claimed were irregularities in the electoral process, both weakened its national influence, and contributed to the splintering of the party. Consequently, an important opposition force remained outside the formal political process, a boycott that facilitated the Alliance for Macedonia (a coalition of the Social Democratic Alliance of Macedonia, the Liberal and the Socialist parties) overwhelming victory in the 1994 elections. But strong support for President Gligorov's moderate course came at the cost of a substantial portion of the electorate not being represented.

Challenges to the Republic of Macedonia's sovereignty and legitimacy also have come from the regional context, for which the government was ill-prepared. Militarily, the breakup of the Former Yugoslavia left Macedonia in an extremely vulnerable position. Although Gligorov's skillful diplomacy secured the withdrawal of the Yugoslav army, Macedonia was stripped of all military equipment. In addition to removing heavy weapons and aircraft, and stripping military barracks, the JNA also took away all border monitoring equipment, including x-ray machines, electronic and radar sensors, and even binoculars, sinks and sockets. Thus the republic had practically no means of national self-defense when the population voted favorably in a national referendum for independence (CSCE 1992b, 5–6).

Conflicts with neighboring states undermined the new state's legitimacy. For example, although Albania did recognize Macedonia as an independent and sovereign state, it blocked consensus for Macedonia's admission to the CSCE because of the failure of the Macedonian government to respect the human and national rights of the Albanian minority in conformity with CSCE standards. Because of Greek opposition to its name and appropriation of other "Greek" cultural symbols (for example, the use of the star of Vergina on the flag and other cultural symbols on the state money), the Republic of Macedonia gained admission to the

United Nations only under the provisional name of the Former Yugoslav Republic of Macedonia (FYROM). In addition, Greece not only blocked Macedonia's accession to European organizations, but the Greek lobby in the US, coupled with massive protests in Thessaloniki, succeeded in persuading the Clinton administration not to extend full diplomatic relations to the Republic of Macedonia, after the US had taken the initial steps to do so in February 1994.

Greece (along with Bulgaria) also objected to Article 49 of the 1991 Constitution as irredentist, which proclaimed that the Republic of Macedonia "cares for the status and rights of those persons belonging to the Macedonian people in neighboring countries, as well as Macedonian expatriates, assists their cultural development and promotes links with them," and also "cares for the cultural, economic and social rights of citizens of the Republic abroad." In protest, Greece imposed an illegal embargo on Macedonia (which included transport, trade and oil blockades). It was all the more onerous in the light of UN sanctions against Serbia. Both dealt severe blows to the country's economy, and eliminated its main export/import routes. By 1995, UN sanctions against the Former Yugoslavia were estimated to cost Macedonia US$3 billion, whereas the country's total budget for 1995 was $1.2 billion (Bonner 1995). The cost of the Greek embargo was estimated at over $330 million in lost exports during its first year (USAID 1995, 1).

UN sanctions and the war in Bosnia cut off the country's main trade route to the north, imposing substantial cost increases due to transportation through non-direct routes. Meanwhile the trade embargo from Greece also cut off its alternative transport links, as well as markets to the south. The East-West axis was hardly a viable alternative (lack of direct rail links, poor roads in Albania), but out of necessity, this is where Macedonia developed its strongest regional ties, especially with Turkey (Perry 1995, 1). The lack of diplomatic recognition of the independent Republic of Macedonia undermined its economic development during the period of transition to a market economy, blocking bilateral assistance from Western countries. Macedonia obtained access to international financial institutions only in 1994 (USAID 1995, 1; 3). Prior to this, the government overcame several financial crises with emergency loans from the international financier, George Soros.

Despite recognition of the Former Yugoslavia's administrative borders as international borders by acts of the international community (including the UN, European Union, the OSCE, and NATO), Serbia withheld recognition of Macedonia, continued to treat its border with Macedonia as an internal border, and refused to participate with Skopje in a joint commission to resolve border questions. Thus, despite the onerous embargo by

Greece, the Macedonian government considered Serbia its gravest threat to national security (Poulton 1995, 179).

Although the Serbian population in Macedonia is relatively small, there have been growing concerns about the possible demonstration effects of the separatist nationalist policies of Serb radicals in Croatia, Bosnia, and increasingly Kosovo. In addition, there have been reports that Macedonian Serbian radicals operating under the Serbian extremist Vojslav Seselj have talked of creating a Serbian Autonomous Region of the Kumanovo Valley and Skpska Crna Gora. Since the 1991 constitution did not list them as a minority, the Serbs also protested their status in post-independent Macedonia.[3]

Towards the Abyss

Throughout the 1990s, the ethnic Albanians have struggled for improved access to entitlements and political power within Macedonia, while the government has tended to do too little, too late. The Albanians see their demands to have an equal place in the new Macedonian state and society as fundamental—particularly their demand for greater access to secondary and university education (CSCE 1993, 6). Additional Albanian demands have included calls for better representation in public services and administration, and a law on local self government to provide a basis for cultural autonomy. They have aimed at decentralizing the Macedonian state (which continued to be highly centralized in the post-independence period). They also called for a law on the official use of national languages in addition to Macedonian in municipalities where they constitute a majority or substantial part of the population. They have insisted more time be allotted to TV and radio programs in Albanian. Many of these demands are echoed by the other nationalities, including the Turkish, Serb, Romani and Vlach minorities.

Key to the ethnic Albanians demand for constitutional and political accommodations is their claim to represent 40 percent or more of the Macedonian population. To back this up, they called for a new national census, having boycotted the 1991 census because they felt that it would not accurately reflect the real numbers of Albanians in the Republic of Macedonia. Part of the dispute concerned Macedonian policies towards new Albanian arrivals from Kosovo, whom authorities would not consider eligible for citizenship, unless they or their parents were born in Macedonia, or they had continuous residence in Macedonia for fifteen years; or they were married to a Macedonian citizen. The Albanians saw these criteria as onerous for a couple of reasons. First, the fifteen-year criteria for continuous residency ensured that the flood of Albanians into Macedonia in the aftermath of the 1981 riots in Kosovo would not be eligible—only the pre-1981 emigres. Second, over the years many intellectual Albanians, among others, had moved to Kosovo to avoid repression in Macedonia. The 1991 census criteria could have excluded some of them. In addition, many Albanians had returned to Macedonia from other parts of the Former Yugoslavia—as many as 130,000 were previously in Croatia alone, of which many came from Macedonia. Finally, under international standards for conducting censuses, a household member absent for one year or more is not counted. For Albanians, these policies negated their actual numbers in Macedonia, and undermined their claim to constitutional status as a constituent people (Poulton 1995, 183). This also jeopardized their demands for other special preferences, including a system of semi proportional representation, as well as affirmative action to increase their numbers in public administration.[4]

As part of its initial response to the ethnic Albanian demands, the government made a number of efforts to increase quotas for Albanian students in secondary education. The Ministry of Interior continued initiatives to increase the number of ethnic Albanians on the staff, and in the police. The government also undertook steps to increase the number of hours of TV and radio programs in Albanian, as well as Turkish, Vlach, and Roma languages. The government also indicated a willingness to set up a TV channel only for ethnic groups—though it argued it needed financial assistance to carry through with the project (CSCE 1993). The government agreed to hold a new census under international supervision in 1994, and it also reached an agreement with the Serbs on their status, following talks the CSCE facilitated between the government and representatives of the Serb minority. The arrangement allowed the Serbs to claim special rights under the constitution's "and others" category as a minority, including primary and secondary education in the Serbian language (Poulton 1995, 180).

But the ethnic Albanians contend the Macedonian government has been slow to realize its promises. For example, in May 1993, no less than seventy laws—a considerable number of them regarding provisions for non-Macedonian groups—were awaiting adoption (CSCE 1993, 7). The law on local self-government detailing the use of national languages at the local level, and rights of ethnic communities to use their national symbols, did not come to the parliament in draft form until March 1995.

The flashpoint of contention has focused on the ethnic Albanian demands for university instruction in Albanian, particularly the reestablishment of Skopje University's Pedagogical Academy in the Albanian language. By 1994, the Albanians started to set up their own university in Tetovo. The Macedonian government warned its establishment would be non-constitutional and illegal—that the constitution only provided for nationalities to have the right to instruction in their mother tongue at the primary and secondary levels, not the university level. A Skopje Commercial Court, which had jurisdiction for the request for registration of the ethnic Albanians' initiative to create the Tetovo University, also determined it did not meet legal conditions, and rejected the request. As Lazarov explains (1995, 36), "according to the rules, in order to form a university a former legal existence of two or more faculties is required, as well as the consent of the Assembly [Parliament] of the Republic of Macedonia."

Ljubomir Frckovski, then Minister of Internal Affairs, viewed the Albanians university demands as having little to do with education, and everything to do with a political agenda, including a first step towards the integration of ethnic Albanian political parties, and their mobilization to achieve a "single solution of the Albanian issue in the region" (as quoted in Lazarov 1995, 36). For the Macedonians, this would be the Albanian "Krajina-type solution," so the government was determined to preempt any Albanian moves which could lead to regional autonomy and secession.

Tetovo University Clash

In spite of the government ban, Albanian leaders proceeded with the establishment of the Albanian University in Tetovo. Its opening led to a clash between police and students in the village of Mala Rechitsa on February 17, 1995, resulting in the death of Abduselam Emini, an Albanian student, and injuries to twenty individuals, including six police—one of them seriously. Later Dr. Suleimani, Rector of the University, and Mr. Nevzet Halili, president of the (then) recently formed People's Unity Party, were arrested, along with four other ethnic Albanians.

Many members of the ethnic Albanian community immediately took steps to inhibit further violence. Delegations of the major Albanian political parties came to Mala Rechitsa in the afternoon of February 17 to persuade the crowd to go home. PDP President Abdurahman Haliti appealed on the Albanian-language program of Macedonian television for Albanians especially in Tetovo, and throughout Macedonia to stay calm. While he blamed President Gligorov and the government for the crisis because of their unjustifiably delayed action on Albanians' education demands, he also disassociated himself from statements made by Suleimani, including the latter's call to Albanians to defend the University (Panov 1995, 7).

But actions taken by other Albanians activists increased tensions. For example, the "Committee of Albanian Political Subjects in Macedonia" collected signatures supporting its "Petition for Equality Against Violence." It reiterated the Albanian community's complaints about Macedonia being a "one-nation" state, described Macedonia as a " 'police state,' " where the legal system is degenerating into a 'police system,' " and called for resistance by all Albanians (CSCE 1995, 2).

There were many signs the crisis had exceeded salient limits the government and the Albanian community had respected in their on-going disputes.[5] Many Albanian deputies suspended their participation in the parliament; others participating in government did as well (Lazarov 1995, 37). Their walkout had the effect of delegitimizing the political process, and cutting off channels of communication between the government and the opposition group. Moreover, the deputies demanded certain conditions be filled before they would resume their duties, including the right to make speeches in Albanian in the Parliament, and the convening of special preliminary consultations with ethnic Macedonian deputies on draft laws affecting ethnic Albanians. They were seeking a mechanism to reach a consensus on legislation before its provisions were officially discussed in parliament (CSCE 1995, 2–3). Thus, the number of issues to be resolved increased as the conflict escalated.

In the aftermath of the clash, there also were symbolic violent acts, including (for the first time in Macedonia) the desecration of Muslim graves in Kumanovo by radical Slav Macedonians, and also some revenge desecration. In addition, the symbol of Serbian unity was reportedly found inscribed over the threshold of the university building which police had charged in Mala Rechitsa, leading to suspicions of either Serbian, or Serbophile involvement among the officers. The Skopje students' Alliance organized a protest against the Tetovo initiative with the slogan, "let the Albanians not become sheep, but let them show individuality and intellect." The demonstration was in turn depicted as nationalistic, xenophobic, prejudiced and egotistical in an article written by L. Jusufi, "Students against Students," that appeared February 24, 1995, in the Albanian newspaper *Flaka e Vëllazërimit.* Much of the local media coverage of the Tetovo crisis contained provocative and even dehumanizing rhetoric, and played a role in heightening the sense of endangerment and injustice among the different ethnic communities. Social pressures forcing individuals "to choose sides" reduced safe space in society for moderates, and delegitimized efforts to find mutually acceptable accommodations.

The crisis heightened the profile of the radical Albanians, and helped to put their demands on the international agenda in three ways: (1) through the involvement of the Albanian president; (2) presence of international monitors; and (3) coverage by the international press. The clash intensified the polarization of inter-ethnic relations in the country, and increased concerns the radical Albanian leadership would succeed in "homogenizing" the ethnonationalist agenda of the Albanian community, and integrating its various political parties.

Macedonian Government's Response to the Tetovo Crisis

The government was unyielding on the founding of the Tetovo University. Throughout fall 1994 and early winter 1995 the government warned that it would take all legal actions at its disposal to put an end to these illegal actions, and that "the responsibility for the consequences which will arise from these illegal activities of the initiators, particularly because of the possible aggravation of the international relations, lies with the movers of this unconstitutional and illegal initiative" (as quoted in Lazarov 1995, 35).

One aspect of the impasse was the fact the existing law on education dated from 1985. There needed to be new legislation to take into account the country's new political realities. The government's focus on the illegality of the Tetovo initiative, rather than on opening a dialogue to shape new legislation also masked its concerns university education in Albanian could become a center for Albanian radicalism. Hence it treated Albanian demands for the university as a first step leading to the establishment of parallel institutions as in Kosovo, and eventually separatism (Woodward 1995, 41, 43). Macedonians also pointed to the fact that some members of the Albanian community exploited ties with potential allies in Kosovo as well as Albania to gain leverage in the internal bargaining process, and argued this lent legitimacy to suspicions about Albanian loyalty.

However, President Gligorov acted quickly to help diffuse the crisis. He immediately offered condolences to the family of the slain student, stating in a telegram that "such unnecessary deaths once again warn that, in these times of wars, conflicts and hatred, it is essential for the peace and security of all our citizens and the future of the country, to have all sides ready to resolve even the most complicated problems through dialogue and within the system and its institutions. This is the only way to promise a better common future" (as cited in Panov 1995, 7).

A tacit agreement emerged: the government would take no further action against the Tetovo University initiative and its leaders, as long as they would not meet in any public buildings. And despite the opposition of strident Macedonian nationalists, the government made some concessions—most notably agreeing to initiate instruction in Albanian at the University of Skopje. The ethnic Albanians were dismayed, nevertheless, that the Government simply appointed faculty to such positions, rather than hold an open competition. However, the introduction of these measures spawned counter-protests. In spring 1997, high school and college students, apparently at the instigation of the right wing Macedonian political forces, demonstrated in the streets of Skopje and other cities, against allowing Albanians to study at the Skopje's Teacher College. And while the government has not shut down Tetovo University, it has refused to recognize the diplomas of the first group of graduating students.

Keeping Violence at Bay

Macedonia is a unique and important case in the study of the early warning and prevention of conflict for at least two reasons. The international community became involved at a relatively early stage, and the response was multifaceted. The main reason for the quick action was the growing concern in 1992 that conflict elsewhere in the Former Yugoslavia could spillover into Macedonia and destabilize the south Balkans. In response to an initiative by the Co-Chairman of the Steering Committee of the International Conference on the Former Yugoslavia, Lord Owen (representing the European Union) and Thorvald Stoltenberg (representing the UN Secretary-General), the UN Secretary-General dispatched a fact finding team of military, police and civilians to the region to prepare a report for the deployment of a preventive peacekeeping operation, which the Macedonian government had already requested.[6]

The security situation in Macedonia was acute in late 1992. Strict enforcement along the entire border presented both philosophical and technical problems. It would place the weak army, which had to call on Ministry of Interior units for assistance, in an inherently unpopular enforcement role. The entire Serbian border had always been an open border. Its closure (due to UN sanctions)—particularly in the Kosovo region—resulted in significant economic and personal hardships, cutting existing commercial links, and separating (mostly ethnic Albanian) families. Because this situation had much more impact on the Albanian minority than on any other group, enforcement of the border by an army representing the Slavic majority of the population could be a formula for trouble (CSCE 1992b).

Authorities also kept an uneasy eye on Kosovo, convinced an outbreak of war there would quickly spillover into the Republic, as Macedonian Albanians came to the assistance of their kinfolk (Andreev, et., al. 1995, 61). They also feared this could provide Belgrade with a pretext for entering Macedonia. Moreover, the border region in northwestern Macedonia had already presented a number of potentially destabilizing incidents, including seven confirmed killings of Albanians in border incidents. Smuggling was a serious problem as well, stemming from extensive black market operations. These problems would worsen with increased refugee flows and economic challenges, possibly resulting in the alienation of the armed forces by one third of the population (CSCE 1992b, 5–6).

On December 11, 1992, the Security Council passed Resolution 795, authorizing the deployment of a UN Protection Force to the Former

Yugoslav Republic of Macedonia, or UNPROFOR (which was renamed UN Preventive Deployment Force, or UNPREDEP after a separate Macedonia command was established in March 1995). The Nordic countries made the initial contribution of troops (with 700 Swedish, Norwegian, and Finnish troops). The US agreed June 18, 1993, to add 520 US troops for deployment to the northeast sector of the country, bringing the total number to 1,032 troops (Archer 1994). The commitment of US troops, in particular, was intended to send a military and political message to the Serbs "to keep their hands off" Macedonia.

The essentially preventive mandate of the military mission called for UNPROFOR to establish a presence on the Macedonian side of the Republic's 240 kilometer-long border with Serbia and along part of the border with Albania (no troops were deployed along the Greek or Bulgarian border) to: (1) to observe, monitor and report all activities that could undermine confidence in and stability of Macedonia or threaten its territory; (2) to liaise between FYROM Commander and Macedonian civil and military authorities, as well as with UN humanitarian agencies; and finally (3) to liaise and coordinate with United Nations Civil Police, OSCE, the Macedonian Sanctions Monitoring Mission, and other agencies in the area. To these ends, the peacekeeping mission has conducted community patrols and investigated incidents along the border, including those involving the Macedonian military. It has also contributed to the monitoring and collection of information to facilitate international humanitarian assistance.

The Macedonian UN peacekeeping operation has consisted of an integrated parallel military/political command. Its civil affairs mandate issued by the Security Council Resolution 908 of March 31, 1994, called for Mr. Hugo Anson, deputy of Mr. Yarushi Akashi (Special Representative of the Secretary-General for the Former Yugoslavia), to work in cooperation with political and civilian authorities of the Republic of Macedonia and to use his good offices to contribute to the maintenance of peace and stability in the republic. In accord with its mandate, the Civilian Command has focused its efforts on three main issue areas: (1) internal political and ethnic problems, such as the demands of the ethnic Albanians, VMRO's self-imposed absence from the Parliament, the census, elections, and such incidents as the Tetovo University clash; (2) economic problems, including the collection and dissemination of economic facts and studies, review of the need for external assistance, and sanctions against Serbia; and (3) external political factors, such as the trade embargo and tensions in Kosovo, and relations with Bulgaria.

In addition to the peacekeeping force, Macedonia has hosted a OSCE Spillover Mission since September 1992, while receiving the good offices of Max van der Stoel, OSCE High Commissioner on National Minorities, and Ambassador Ahrens of the ICFY. The latter's mandate was to help the parties find solutions to the outstanding issues stemming from the break up of Yugoslavia as a whole, as well as to some more specific regional issues, such as Macedonia's conflicts with its neighbors, including Greece. Many aspects of the Macedonian dispute with Greece, however, have been mediated by Cyrus Vance (under the auspices of the UN Secretary-General) and Matthew Nimetz, special envoy from the Clinton White House.

The OSCE Spillover Mission to Macedonia was established at the 16th meeting of the Council of Senior Officials on September 18, 1992. The decision was taken in the context of the European Community's efforts to extend its Monitoring Mission to the neighboring countries of Serbia and Montenegro in order to avoid the spillover of tensions into these areas, and in response to the request of the Macedonian Government. The Mission's original objective was to monitor developments along the Macedonian Republic's borders with Serbia and other areas vulnerable to the spillover of conflict from the Former Yugoslavia, to promote respect for territorial integrity and the maintenance of peace, stability and security, and to help prevent possible conflict in the region.

The military-security responsibilities were assumed by the UN peace-keeping force on its arrival, but the CSCE mission continued its operations in Macedonia, focusing on the political tasks in its mandate. These included: (1) dialoguing with governmental authorities; (2) establishing contacts with representatives of political parties and other organizations and with ordinary citizens; (3) conducting trips to assess the level of stability and the possibility of conflict and unrest; and (4) in case of incidents, assisting in establishing the facts (CSCE 1994a, 37).

Because the key flashpoint in Macedonia's internal conflicts concerns inter-ethnic issues, in many ways it is the High Commissioner on National Minorities who "mediates where the rubber hits the road." Van der Stoel has focused many of his efforts on issues concerning education, as well as the broader participation of ethnic Albanians in Macedonian society. In addition, the High Commissioner has supported and reinforced recommendations by Ambassador Ahrens, including his proposal for the Council of Europe to monitor the preparations of the 1994 census, supervise its execution, as well as ensure that appeals for a progressive staffing of the military and police at all levels, by adequately reflecting recognized nationalities, be the subject of annual progress reports by the Macedonian Parliament's Council for Inter-ethnic Relations.

The Republic of Macedonia has also hosted numerous international nongovernmental organizations. Some have been engaged in preventive actions as part of their overall humanitarian and development assistance mission (Catholic Relief Services), while for others it has been their main goal (Search for Common Ground). A third category consists of organizations such as the Soros Society or the National Endowment for Democracy (see Samuels 1995), whose programs are aimed at strengthening democracy and civil society. Organizations of a governmental nature have also been represented, such as the United States Agency for International Development, which has helped to facilitate networking among non-governmental organizations and international aid agencies and organizations, including the European Union and the UN High Commissioner on Refugees. USAID has channeled economic aid to projects aimed at enhancing democracy and civil society as well as inter-ethnic tolerance, including the Parent Teacher Association (PTA) program launched by Catholic Relief Services.

Search for Common Ground has promoted cultural sensitivity training among journalists, and inter-ethnic reporting, as well as conflict resolution skills training, which have led to some positive results. The Soros Foundation has operated a large-scale program in Macedonia, with its massive resources impacting much of the country's public life, including the development of a variety of independent television and radio stations, print media, and support of educational initiatives. While CRS's main mission was to provide humanitarian assistance and promote development, it also established an innovative program to support the formation of local chapters and a national parent teacher association. The PTA project responded to CRS's mandate to identify and meet basic needs, since the practical side of the project was to repair dilapidated school facilities. Yet the PTA program also increased society's capacity to withstand inter-ethnic tensions, particularly by giving local people skills to reframe and depoliticize solutions to problems that had become "ethnicized" (Leatherman 1999).

Evaluating the Impact of Early Warning and Conflict Prevention

The success of early warning and conflict prevention depends in large measure on the capacity of the international community to tailor assistance to the particular needs of the country in question. This means creating an effective international coalition that can deploy the right resources to deal with the immediate potential for the eruption of violent conflict, while also giving attention over the long term to addressing the underlying sources of tensions. Both the OSCE and the UN peacekeeping missions have dealt with the immediate risk of spillover of conflict into Macedonia. While the OSCE continued to intervene as a third party to help diffuse crises, its members also promoted dialogue among different ethnic communities, and worked to clarify problems that created political impasses.

Over the short term, the main concern of the UN peacekeeping mission was to diffuse tensions along the Serbian border. It assisted in the arrangement of a zone of demarcation between Macedonia and Serbia, a significant step in the absence of any formally agreed and recognized international border between Serbia and Macedonia. The peacekeeping force reported regularly on Serbian border patrols, showing in 1994 an average of five to ten incursions a month by Serb soldiers. Typically, these incidents involved between three to fifteen Serb soldiers crossing the border into Macedonia for a few hours, and then returning (Atanasov 1994, 23). Throughout spring 1994, however, Serbian incursions were deeper and more frequent. This escalated into a crisis over the period mid-June to mid-July 1994 involving a military build-up along the border zone at "Hilltop 1703." The mountain which lies opposite Kosovo and is known as Cupino Brdo, is highly strategic because it overlooks not only Serbia, but also Bulgaria and Macedonia (as well as smuggling routes used to circumvent UN sanctions on Serbia).

The incident began when Serbian forces detained a Macedonian Lieutenant at the border for interrogation. The Macedonian government requested UN assistance to secure his release. With both sides engaged in a military build up at this strategic point, the crisis escalated. On June 19 Macedonia threatened military action. One factor apparently precipitating the Serb build up were concerns the US troops in the UN peacekeeping forces were preparing to assume an offensive posture, in conjunction with NATO enforcement of UN resolutions regarding the conflict in Bosnia. Rumors and allegations were circulating among the Serbs that the US was bringing in various types of enhanced fire power, including rockets and anti-aircraft, and deploying White Hawks outfitted for offensive operations. However, as part of the UNPROFOR mediation efforts to defuse the crisis, the Serbs were invited to inspect the UN peacekeeping forces equipment, which in fact allowed them to verify their non-offensive posture.[7] With both Serbia and Macedonia refusing to negotiate with each other directly, UNPROFOR Commander Tefelson mediated through "shuttle diplomacy" the withdrawal of the Serb and Macedonian forces from this strategic position, and the placement of a Nordic Battalion and UN flag on the top of the mountain.

The incident at Hilltop 1703 is an important example of the difficulties third parties can face in executing their mandates. In this case it underscores the adage that "more (that is, military capacity) is not always better," if it leads one of the parties to take punitive actions to counter perceived threats. Then "success" amounts to little more than minimizing the deteriorating effects of the peacekeeping mission's own presence. On the other hand, it is essential that third parties be capable of managing not only the intended, but also unexpected consequences of their involvement.

For the most part, the evidence suggests the UN peacekeepers have had a stabilizing influence on Macedonian-Serbian relations. Atanasov argues that "its strong defensive character . . . has had a calming effect," while providing a base for building up a larger contingent of blue helmets, should the need arise. President Gligorov judged that politically, the UN mission was "the most important stabilizing factor inside the country," an opinion all parties shared. A survey of public opinion in Skopje conducted by the Center for Ethnic Relations found that of the 1,200 respondents (of all nationalities), more than 50 percent were satisfied with the results of the peacekeeping operation, and supported its continued presence (Atanasov 1994, 23).

In addition,"the UN presence has been seen as an important indication of general political support, especially when Macedonia was not recognized as an independent state, and has opened the way for many other international organizations and institutions to work" in the country (Atanasov 1994, 23). For example, an initiative undertaken by Anson, with Akashi's support, in summer 1994 led to the opening of the UN Development Program office in Skopje, and the establishment of a liaison between the government and donors, and international financial assistance.[8]

For its part, the Macedonian government has been reluctant to face directly the possibility of the spillover of conflict from Serbia. The worsening situation in Bosnia and concern about the renegotiation of the UNPROFOR mandate for Croatia during spring 1995 raised new uncertainties to the North, and brought again to the fore concern about the possibility of an influx of refugees from Kosovo should another front open up in this area. Discussions among officials from international humanitarian assistance organizations, the UNHCR, and UNPROFOR in Macedonia underscored the operational challenges of such a situation, especially should refugees seek direct protection from peacekeeping forces in their small observation posts.[9] These fears materialized in the spring of 1998, as fighting intensified in Kosovo. However, the estimated 70,000 refugees have either remained internally displaced, or fled across the border to Albania and Montenegro. The Macedonian government has indicated it would receive refugees in accord with its international obligations, but only as a transition station onto third countries.

In addition to its military-security functions, the UN peacekeeping operation in Macedonia has encompassed a civilian command with a political mandate aimed at socializing the conflict parties into constructive conflict management approaches. Akashi, together with Anson, has sought to impress moderate elements working within the government and within the Albanian community of the need to negotiate and sustain dialogue.

Their role has thus supplied one channel of communication across the main fault line in society, with the objective of helping to mitigate and find solutions to the international and intranational dimensions of conflict.

In addition, through regular consultations among the UNPROFOR officers, representatives of international humanitarian assistance organizations and other NGOs, and assistance programs (such as USAID), UNPROFOR officials determined the mission could play a significant role in identifying villages with acute humanitarian assistance needs. The objective was to help people falling through other safety nets provided by the Macedonian government.[10] These considerations led to the development of a systematic reporting procedure, organized through UNPROFOR's village visitation program. UNPROFOR and UNCIVPOL also assisted with the delivery of humanitarian supplies in conjunction with its routine patrolling (during winter 1994–95, UNPROFOR channeled assistance to some 6,000 villages).[11] Such activities ensured the peacekeeping mission would have non-military contact with the local population, which may have helped build trust and confidence between UNPROFOR and the local population, while also helping stabilize the vulnerable population in the country's northern/northwestern rural districts.

In general, the complementarity of the different mediation efforts has been an important factor in helping promote dialogue on, and some solutions to, inter-ethnic tensions in Macedonia. The OSCE Spillover Mission has helped by serving as a bridgehead. In addition to holding regular consultations with officials from UNPROFOR/UNPREDEP, NGOs, and other international organizations, the Mission has acted as a "multinational embassy," or liaison for other third party initiatives in Macedonia, though especially the OSCE HCNM, van der Stoel, and Ambassador Ahrens. In many instances these different third parties have intervened on the same issues. This was case with the 1994 census, over which ethnic Albanians expressed grievances concerning the ethnicity of the enumerators used for conducting the census, and its data processing. The efforts by the HCNM and Ambassador Ahrens helped the parties identify acceptable modalities for conducting the census, and also secured the appointment of a Council of Europe expert to oversee the data processing.

The OSCE Mission's efforts also contributed to the compromises that paved the way for ethnic Albanians to participate in the census. It helped settle claims by an ethnic Albanian member of parliament that 1,200 people in his village had not yet received papers to get citizenship, and that as many as 140,000 ethnic Albanians in Macedonia were lacking theirs. When the Mission examined this situation in the MP's village, only five hundred cases were actually presented, of which half had already received their papers. The OSCE officials were able to clarify the facts and assist in resolving remaining cases, thus helping to diffuse these tensions.[12] The matter of citizenship papers would not have affected the enumeration of the Albanian population in Macedonia. However, attention by the OSCE to this matter, coupled with the government's commitment to hold the 1994 census, helped speed up the distribution of citizenship papers. This also helped pave the way for more ethnic Albanians to participate in the 1994 elections.[13]

Evidence from the Macedonian case suggests that the generally good coordination of third party efforts has averted the problem of "forum shopping." The conflicting parties have thus had fewer opportunities to play international organizations off each other in order to get a deal that suits them better. At the same time, the presence of international monitors may have had some unintended consequences on the conflict, precipitating its escalation. For example, whether or not the presence of OSCE monitors at the opening of the Tetovo University, along with the Civil Police from the UNPROFOR Civil Command actually inhibited greater violence on the part of the Macedonian police is not clear. Some of these international officials expressed concern their presence may have encouraged the ethnic Albanian leadership to take their protests to the street: the presence of monitors and international media attention would thrust the ethnic Albanians' agenda into the international spotlight. On the other hand, the efforts of the OSCE mission to help determine the facts of the clash and, along with other third parties, to encourage the government to respond moderately to the crisis, helped to diffuse a potentially dangerous situation.

Monitoring and reporting on host country developments by the OSCE mission also has provided other international authorities with important information and analysis from trained observers familiar with the political and cultural terrain. These functions are critical to promote the international community's awareness of the potential eruption of violent conflict, and understanding on the issues involved. But the activity of reporting itself is not neutral. As Ambassador Bøgh acknowledged, the OSCE mission has been accused of being biased in its assessments.[14] Perceptions of bias have also arisen in connection with the Mission's advocacy role. In an attempt to invite moderation, the Mission has often emphasized the special difficulties the Macedonian government faced with the embargo imposed by Greece, and the Serbian sanctions. And in the aftermath of the Tetovo crisis, the OSCE Mission sought to exert influence by granting interviews to the media, and trying to encourage moderation. It tried to redirect the focus on inter-ethnic relations from the issues in contention, to the opportunities and need for cooperation on a variety of pressing economic, social and ecological concerns facing the country as whole. On the other hand, the ethnic Albanians have sought OSCE advocacy of their positions, and protested when these were not forthcoming from the OSCE, including when the High Commissioner did not criticize the Macedonian government in 1998 for refusing to recognize student diplomas from the Tetovo University.

The Macedonian case also illustrates that international incentives can aid in the effectiveness of third party intervention. Awaiting the decision of the European Union on Macedonia's international recognition, and in order to refute the accusation that the name itself, Macedonia, implied expansionist aims and aspirations, on January 6, 1992, the Parliament set forth Amendment I. Replacing a paragraph in Article 3 of the Constitution, Amendment I states that: (1) the Republic of Macedonia has no territorial pretensions towards any neighboring state; and (2) the borders of the Republic of Macedonia can only be changed in accordance with the constitution and on the principle of free will, as well as in accordance with generally accepted international norms. Amendment II complements the reference in Article 49 to the Republic of Macedonia's concerns with the status and rights of Macedonian people in neighboring countries. It states that in the exercise of this concern the Republic will not interfere in the sovereign rights of other states or in their internal affairs. These amendments demonstrated the readiness of the Republic of Macedonia to cooperate with the European Union and also to contribute to building constructive relations with its Balkan neighbors. Although they gave some reassurance about Macedonia's respect for international borders, these changes did not sufficiently meet Greek objections.[15]

The availability of a variety of third parties also allowed for a more efficient division of labor, and with it, the disaggregation of the issues at stake in the Greek-Macedonian conflict. The successful conclusion of the Macedonian-Greek Interim Accord on September 18, 1995, is a notable contribution to conflict mitigation and confidence building in the regional context. Opening the way for Greek recognition of the former Republic of Macedonia, and the lifting of the Greek embargo, the agreement was expedited in the final stage by US Assistant Secretary of State Richard Holbrooke, who met in Athens with both the Greek Foreign Minister and Prime Minister. Employing shuttle diplomacy throughout the whole exercise (the parties refused to meet each other face to face until the actual signing), the mediation efforts of UN negotiator Cyrus Vance and US envoy Matthew Nimetz helped the two countries find solutions to a number of critical issues at stake in their relationship.

The 1995 agreement between the two countries only partially resolves the outstanding issues in dispute.[16] The crux of the dispute over the name itself "Macedonia" was not solved, but the parties agreed to disagree on this issue for the time being, in the interest of making progress on other matters.

Article 6 of the Accord provides solemn assurances that addressed Greek concerns about those Macedonian constitutional provisions it perceived as implying a right to interference in internal affairs of Greece, or as claims to its territory. The Macedonians also agreed to change the country's flag, thus helping to meet Greek objections about the appropriation of cultural symbols. Greece committed itself not to block Macedonia's accession to international organizations. This quickly opened the way for Macedonia to join the OSCE, the Council of Europe, and Partnership for Peace. Much of the agreement also committed the parties to strengthen their economic relations, to cooperate in a variety of scientific and technical fields, and promote the free flow of people across the borders—although as concerns the latter in particular, implementation continues to be hampered on the Greek side. Nevertheless, the agreement specifically encourages contacts at all appropriate levels and in accord with relevant international agreements and instruments, including the Helsinki Final Act and other OSCE documents.

The international non-governmental organizations working in Macedonia, often in partnership with local organizations and leaders, have been able to bring resources to bear on some of the key background conditions fueling and accelerating tensions between the country's ethnic communities. Search for Common Ground's work training journalists in cross-cultural reporting and helping to build bridges across the language divide where the media is concerned has had both short-term and long-term impacts. Over the short-term, the news articles themselves helped bridge different communities' perspectives of the difficult situation they have faced in the post-independence period, thus de-ethnicizing many aspects of it. Inter-ethnic cooperation among journalists laid the foundation for more culturally sensitive and responsible reporting, and modeled new behaviors and professional practices.

Catholic Relief Services' PTA program has also brought ethnically diverse communities together to deal with educational issues as a common concern, rather than on the basis of competing communal objectives at a time when educational issues have been among the most highly ethnicized in the country. The project has helped communities identify and prioritize the needs of the local school system. The process relies on self-motivated and experiential learning, as well as socialization to new ways of accomplishing common goals. The PTA participants—both its leadership and rank and file members—become an important village resource. They represent a third stream—a group of stake holders that cuts across the divisions in society. The participants share a common interest in finding mutually satisfying solutions to their community's problems, and are empowered to interact in society and express their opinions based on their roles in this organization, and not merely as a member of an ethnic group.

International support for moderate leadership, especially of President Gligorov, has been one of the most important aspects of the success of preventive diplomacy in Macedonia. Known for his great analytic abilities and experience in politics, Gligorov has also enjoyed wide popular support in the country, even among many of the ethnic Albanians.[17] A moderating influence on political developments and inter-communal relations, President Gligorov guided the country through grave economic crises, and numerous domestic tensions. During his tenure in office, he has gained a reputation for his openness for contacts and meetings with various government and non-government structures in the state, and with large numbers of individuals with formal or informal competence. Consistent with his efforts to encourage dialogue and to help build consensus on key policies, in 1998 he inaugurated a series of inter-party consultations.

President Gligorov's national strategy has been to act cautiously, seldom taking radical steps in either foreign or domestic affairs. Domestically, he has promoted the development of rule of law and civil society; and worked for more stable inter-ethnic relations. One of the most important of these steps involved the drafting and adoption of a 1991 constitution. He also managed to turn adversity into advantage. Some would argue that he used the Greek embargo to strengthen national resolve. Yet his leadership was crucial in reaching the 1995 agreement with Greece.

There has been some progress in bringing the levels of national minorities in the military, and to some extent also among the police to represent their proportion of the population, but the government has continued its slow approach to other recommendations. This proved most critical in its reluctance to begin instruction in Albanian at the Pedagogical Academy, which the HCNM had repeatedly urged.[18] However, by discouraging a hardline approach, the presence of the international community in Macedonia probably helped the government diffuse tensions over the 1994 census, the 1994 elections, as well as the 1995 clash over the opening of the Tetovo University. The continued participation of moderate Albanian leaders in a national coalition government has also been an important means of maintaining the legitimacy of the political process.

In spite of the multifaceted efforts to avert the outbreak of conflict in Macedonia, there have been missed opportunities. The most critical of these to regional peace and stability within Macedonia concerns the destabilization of Albania in 1997 and the outbreak of civil war in Kosovo in 1998. Albanian arms have been smuggled into both Macedonia and Kosovo. In the meantime, the international community has continued to exhibit a weak and inconsistent approach to the problems there. The key aim of the five nation Contact Group (US, Russia, Great Britain, France, Germany) has been to get the Albanian Leader Ibrahim Rugova to negotiate an agreement with Yugoslav President Slobodan Milosevic for the restoration of autonomy. This is linked with the aim of getting the Kosovo Liberation Army (KLA) to sit down at the negotiating table with Rugova. This policy ignores the fact that Rugova has been espousing independence since the early 1990s. His inability to achieve it through a campaign of non-violence discredited his leadership, and led to the radicalization of the movement. Although the Western allies considered NATO intervention in the summer of 1998, they turned away from this option as the KLA gained numbers and with nearly 40 percent of Kosovo's territory in their control.

The West's policy of pressuring Milosevic to accept a cease fire and withdraw his military was also full of contradictions. This would inevitably create a vacuum the KLA would quickly move to fill. This could only take them closer toward de facto independence, and also risk raising the specter of the creation of a greater Albania. On the other hand, by allowing a protracted civil war to unfold in Kosovo, there will only be greater dangers of the conflict spilling over into Macedonia. Already there are indications of increasing radicalization of the Albanians in Macedonia. The instability in Albania itself complicates matters, too. Although President Fatos Nano has not advocated a greater Albania, his political rival, the ousted Sali Berisha does. He is operating out of northern Albania and facilitating the KLA movement.

Conclusion

The international community has made a considerable investment in the prevention of conflict in Macedonia. The efforts have produced some important results over the short term. UN peacekeepers' presence has helped stabilize the country, while giving the political leadership time to find solutions to regional conflicts, including the illegal Greek embargo that exacerbated its economic crisis, blocked recognition, and accession to international institutions. In addition, the deployment of the UN peacekeeping forces and the UN civil command has helped channel international assistance into Macedonia, and into the hands of individuals falling through the government's safety net. These initiatives and resources helped to avert a more serious social crisis among the population at large during a period of tremendous social, political and economic transformation, which displaced much of the working population. The outbreak of war in Kosovo in 1998 makes the peacekeeping mission all the more crucial for preserving regional peace. But in reality, its presence is symbolic. It will have little meaning as a trip wire if the international community is not prepared to bring additional resources into play to prevent the spillover and/or outbreak of conflict in Macedonia.

Preventive diplomacy in Macedonia has enhanced the transparency of inter-ethnic relations in a regional context, as well as within the country. This was accomplished through the monitoring and patrolling by peace-keeping forces, as well as by the OSCE mission and other international monitors, brought in to assist in specific tasks, such as the conduct of the census, or the 1994 elections. Their presence, and the generation of trusted information and analysis of conflict events, also helped to minimize fears and conspiracy theories, while building up confidence and understanding. Certainly international mediation between Greece and Macedonia has helped to remove a series of potentially explosive issues, and has led to an open border for trade between them. But the minority Macedonian communities in neighboring states, and especially those of Aegean descent, still face repression.

There is some evidence that the mediation of inter-ethnic disputes within Macedonia has led to the adoption of new cultural norms and the institutionalization of new practices. For example the fact that moderate ethnic Albanians have continued to collaborate in coalition governments has been an important factor in the stability of the country, as well as legitimacy of its political institutions and leadership. However, the crisis in Kosovo is leading to the radicalization of the Albanians in Macedonia. In the absence of any solution to the problems in Kosovo, there will need to be even more concerted efforts to find solutions to the demands of the ethnic Albanians. With the regional crisis mounting, the Macedonian government is likely to find it more difficult, not less, to be responsive to the Albanians concerns. The international community needs to take measures to minimize the sense of threat and endangerment that the crisis in Kosovo portends for Macedonia.

Over the long term, the constructive management of inter-ethnic conflicts requires more than ad hoc solutions to crises. It calls for a viable political process, and with it a set of mechanisms and tools that ensure open channels of communication and methods of reaching accommodations between majority and minority communities. Non-governmental organizations have been helpful in creating some of these kinds of mechanisms in society, as the work of Search for Common Ground among journalists, and Catholic Relief Services with communities developing PTAs illustrates. These approaches are important because they help target the material and cultural tensions that fuel identity conflicts.

The Macedonian experience suggests it may be more productive to help different communities find ways to live together, rather than to separate. But the international community needs to work systematically from the outset to promote solutions to not just to the crises at hand, but also to the underlying causes of conflict, rather than wait for problems to escalate to the point that international resources and capabilities are no longer a match for the dimensions and complexities of the problems. The fighting in Kosovo has, unfortunately, seemed to reach this point, and it bodes ill for the success of preventive action in Macedonia.

Finally, this case study points to the importance of promoting multi-faceted, well coordinated, and multilevel solutions to inter-communal conflicts. Along with other international actors and organizations, NGOs, both international and domestic, also play vital roles, and even more so in former socialist states like Yugoslavia, where they strengthen civil society. It is crucial, however, that the work of third parties contribute to building cross-cutting ties in order to minimize, rather than duplicate and reinforce, the structural and cultural divisions within society. And finally, these efforts must be complemented by attention to the regional context of tensions and conflict dynamics. Otherwise preventive diplomacy may have little more staying power than a line drawn in the sand.

Notes

1. The Author expresses her appreciation for the assistance of OSCE officials of the Office of the High Commissioner on National Minorities; OSCE Mission members in Skopje; officials of the Macedonian Government; the US Liaison Office in Skopje; Brigadier General Juha Engstrom, GOC UNPROFOR, Macedonia; Catholic Relief Services; Search for Common Ground; and faculty of the Balkans Peace Center, Kiril and Metodji University, Skopje.
2. The OSCE was known until January 1, 1995, as the Conference on Security and Cooperation in Europe (CSCE). The acronym CSCE is used for all references preceding that date.
3. Because the Serbs were a nation of Yugoslavia, they did not have minority status in the Socialist Republic of Yugoslavia under the communist's federal system.
4. Author's Notes: Interview with Member of the OSCE Spillover Mission, Skopje, Macedonia, March 1995. See also CSCE (1994, 3).
5. This was the first such incident that led to loss of life since the November 6, 1992, riot at the open market of Skopje, known as the "Bitpazar." While attempting to quell that riot, police killed three Albanian men and one Macedonian woman. Quick government action to frame this as a street brawl helped to keep it an isolated incident. There was a high degree of awareness that such confrontations could be framed as "inter-ethnic" and lead to civil war, as had happened in Bosnia.
6. President Gligorov's request for a UN preventive force was supported by all the political parties except the PDP (Atanasov 1994, 22).
7. Author's Notes: Interview, UN Civil Affairs Officer, UNPROFOR Headquarters, Skopje, Macedonia, March 1995.

8. Author's Notes: Interview with UNPROFOR Civil Affairs Officer, UNPROFOR Headquarters, Skopje, Macedonia, March 1995.

9. UNPROFOR began, in spring 1995, to revise the August 16, 1994, "OPLAN Black Refugee," its refugee response plan, in consultation with international humanitarian assistance organizations, based on planning figures for up to 150,000 refugees, including the arrival of as many as 60,000 on a weekly basis. But this plan envisioned a minimal role for the UNPROFOR military command in initial reception and management of refugees—despite the possibly threatening circumstances under which they might be fleeing.

10. UNPROFOR, FYROM Command Skopje, Minutes of 05 November Liaison Conference. November 8, 1993, p. 2.

11. Author's Notes: Interview with UNPROFOR Civil Affairs Officer, UNPROFOR Headquarters, Skopje, Macedonia, March 1995.

12. Author's Notes: Interview with OSCE Mission Member, OSCE Spillover Mission Office, Skopje, Macedonia, March 1995.

13. Author's Notes: Interview with OSCE Mission Member, OSCE Spillover Mission Office, Skopje, Macedonia, March 1995.

14. Author's Notes: Interview with Ambassador Tore Bøgh, OSCE Spillover Mission Office, Skopje, Macedonia, March 1995.

15. Note, however, that Article 108 of the Greek Constitution specifies that the Greek government shall care for Greeks residing abroad and for the maintenance of their ties with the fatherland. See CSCE (1993a).

16. See the (Macedonian-Greek) Interim Accord, October 18, 1995; see also Foreign Press Center Briefing with Ambassador Matthew Nimetz, Special White House Envoy. Subject: Macedonia-Greek Agreements, Monday, September 18, 1995. Transcript of Press Center Briefing.

17. Author's Notes: Interview with Official of the OSCE Office of the High Commissioner on National Minorities, The Hague, The Netherlands, March 1995.

18. HCNM Recommendations Concerning Inter-Ethnic Relations in the Republic of Macedonia. CSCE Communication No. 35, Prague, p.t. Rome, November 24, 1993.

3

POLICY RECOMMENDATIONS

8

INVENTIVE DIPLOMACY:
POLICY RECOMMENDATIONS FOR EARLY
WARNING AND CONFLICT PREVENTION

Bridging Concept, Case, and Policy

OUR ASPIRATION, IN THIS VOLUME, TO MOVE FROM A CONCEPTUAL FRAMEWORK and case studies to specific policy recommendations confronts a set of gaps between three poles. At the first pole, social scientific approaches tend to seek general explanations for the causes of conflict, and to promise relevance to policymakers at some point in the future when the crucial pressure points for policy manipulation are identified. Such promises of policy control through general scientific theory have proven to be illusory, and will continue to do so, we argue, because they ignore the particularity of conflict processes.

At the second pole of the three-way gap stands the case-study approach, whose advocates emphasize the unique interaction of multiple variables in particular cases. In order to apply policy conclusions to divergent cases, it is conventional to draw "lessons" that rarely amount to more than broad exhortations. Policymakers either apply such lessons blindly, or, more often, take them with a grain of salt and proceed to confront the next unique conflict in an ad hoc manner. Either option leaves the gap between analysis and practice unbridged.

Indeed, policymakers themselves are part of the gap between concept, case, and policy. They constitute the third pole, often eschewing explanation altogether in favor of action. Causal analysis that portrays events as the inevitable result of unique conjunctures of historical forces may be the enemy of policymakers, who seek to cut the deep historical roots of conflict in societies and to cultivate the seedlings of peace. Policymakers committed to conflict prevention have a professional responsibility to reject or ignore explanations that reify conflict processes.

Spanning the gaps between concept, case, and policy is a task for many workers in the field of conflict resolution. In this chapter we cast several lines in the hope that they may be useful to others for hauling across the gaps the makings of a useful bridge. Our conclusions are framed as four interim insights, proceeding from the conceptual analysis and case studies in this volume, and leading toward fruitful ways of thinking about conflict and its resolution. Each conclusion is expressed as a *hypothesis* for discovering the causal processes by which conflict either escalates or is prevented in each particular case, and also as a *criterion* for designing and evaluating policies for early warning and conflict prevention. By pairing hypotheses with criteria, we make explicit the normative commitments of conflict prevention and the standards of excellence for its pursuit. In previous chapters, we argue, the hypotheses find confirmation and the criteria find exemplification. But their greater value is the light they shed on future challenges of conflict prevention. We promise illumination of political processes rather than control over political outcomes. These conclusions, if successful, will draw the attention of policymakers and analysts toward inventive diplomacy that can generate peace.

We conclude, in sum, that successful conflict prevention requires policy actors to *cover the bases* by engaging key societal players, *monitor through engagement* to discover the causes of conflict, *cultivate networks* as a source of power, and *build coalitions* of national and international stakeholders for peace.

Cover the Bases

Hypothesis of Multi-dimensionality

Conflict, and its prevention or resolution, are multidimensional and multi-level in their causal structure, incorporating structural, cultural, and institutional dimensions, as well as societal, elite, and international levels. An adequate explanation of conflict (or its resolution) must account for this multidimensionality as expressed in each particular context. Single-factor theories are misleading explanations for conflict escalation and unreliable guides for preventive policy.

Criterion of Comprehensiveness

In effective early warning and conflict prevention policy, international actors collectively *cover the bases* through a division of labor that puts them in a position to monitor and influence all important dimensions and levels of a society. If any important segment is neglected, the effort is likely to fail.

We offer a simple framework for policy analysis, summarized in Table 8.1, that captures the general features of the early warning and preventive action project while leaving room for the wide variations between particular conflicts. The specific policy proposals in Table 8.1 are for illustration. In practice, there is a much larger menu of options from which to choose, and the most important task is to tailor the actions to the dynamics of each particular conflict.

Conflict and its escalation can be understood analytically as growing out of three dimensions. Structural cleavages entail the broad social distinctions demarcated by categories such as economic class, racial group, and urban/rural division, and the way the distribution of wealth and privilege is mapped onto these distinctions. Structural cleavages are not necessarily static, but may remain stable for long periods. Whether or not they are politicized in a particular period, they provide the potential for mobilizing populations in support of political projects.

Culture is a real, though elusive and dynamic, variable in generating conflict. Cultural difference does not necessarily lead to cultural tension or outright conflict, but it is a fertile field for the politically ambitious, particularly when cultural divisions coincide with economic cleavages or carry memories of past victimization. Political language and symbolic politics are significant elements of conflict, whose contextual and shifting meanings can be discerned best by observers who are deeply engaged and intimately familiar with the cultural context.

The legitimacy and effectiveness of political institutions is a critical factor influencing whether structural cleavages and cultural differences generate conflict escalation. Institutional legitimacy can be threatened when state administrative capacity erodes or during a fragile transition from authoritarian to democratic institutions.

These four dimensions can be understood as background conditions that create the potential for conflict and peace, and can be shaped either to leverage escalation to violent conflict, or to support non-violent political processes.

As summarized in Table 8.1, the critical actors who escalate or prevent conflict are national elites, intergovernmental actors, and non-governmental organizations. The most important of these are national elites, including the leaders of rival political parties and military groups, and also prominent leaders in civil society such as journalists, lawyers, business people, and representatives of unions, popular organizations and local NGOs. It is these national elites who ultimately choose to escalate a conflict or move toward resolution. Early warning and conflict prevention, however, is an *international* policy project designed to influence national elites to choose non-violent processes of political contention. It is always, therefore, a form of international intervention, whether or not it includes coercive force. Such intervention is legitimate when it allies with and bolsters national elites who are committed to peace. It is also legitimate, at least in principle,

TABLE 8.1 Policy Framework for Early Warning and Prevention of Intrastate Conflict

Actors	Structural Cleavages	Institutions	Cultural Tensions	Escalation Dynamics
National, Political, and Societal Elites	• Promote affirmative action policies • Transform systemic sources of discrimination and exclusion • Promote cross-cutting ties through civic initiatives	• Create multi-ethnic political coalitions • Ombudsman • National roundtables • Power sharing arrangements	• Promote civic conceptions of identity/citizenship • National reconciliation • Conflict resolution training • Cultural awareness/tolerance through media • Cultural autonomy	• Monitor for early warning • Keep open channels of communication with opposition • Call for international assistance or mediation
Third-party Governments and IOs	• Use economic incentives • Alter reward structure • Provide economic aid or aid conditionality • Develop smart sanctions • Coordinate international policies and monitor for unintended effects	• Advocate civic conceptions of citizenship • Support development of independent judiciary • Develop political incentives for elites to use legitimate institutions for non-violent contention	• Use international norms to socialize political elites to adopt moderate policies • Support national efforts at reconciliation/conflict resolution programs • Develop political incentives for elites to use legitimate institutions for non-violent contention	• Use third-party mediation • Deploy preventive peacekeeping forces and international civilian monitors • Use humanitarian assistance for peacebuilding • Monitor, report on human rights
International NGOs	• Enhance communication across ethnic lines • Reduce poverty effects of structural adjustment • Provide humanitarian assistance to all conflicting parties as symbolic gesture	• Support development of democratic institutions • Assist demobilization of soldiers and reintegration into civic life • Help rebuild civil society • Support and legitimize peace entrepreneurs • Report on human rights abuses	• Catalyze initiatives for conflict resolution through media, schools, civic organizations, women's organizations, and professional groups	• Give early warning of escalation through engaged monitoring • Coordinate monitoring and reporting with IOs and other third parties

because international forces and actors have set the historical stage for many of the conflicts that afflict the post–Cold War world. The United States and the Soviet Union played out much of their rivalry by sponsoring weak state elites through transfers of military and economic aid, strategies for political control, and ideologies for state legitimation. As a consequence, many Third World state elites depended for their power and survival more on international sponsors than on their own people and economy. The inevitable result was state neglect and violence toward their own populations, which became fertile ground for anti-government political/military movements. In addition, the legacy of colonialism, particularly in Africa, left behind oppressive state structures and practices that post-colonial leaders often simply made their own rather than replacing. And colonial policies of divide and rule pitted against each other groups who often had little previous history of conflict.

Groups and identities channeled toward violent contention over decades of colonialism and Cold War do not easily change course. However, it is simplistic and self-serving for Western observers to attribute conflict in the Third World to "primordial ethnic identities" without acknowledging the international role in shaping those identities. For this reason, we do not designate the object of analysis as "ethnic conflict." By signaling an assumption that the ethnic component is a constant rather than a variable in the explanation, this nomenclature fails to account for how collective political actors construct their very identities through the process of conflict, and how such identities carry forward in time when the political context changes. A traditional cultural distinction, constructed and rigidified through a historical process and manipulated as a lever for allocating security and wealth, can even create structural cleavages that coincide with itself. In Rwanda and Burundi, the Hutu and Tutsi who are killing each other by the hundreds of thousands speak the same language, eat the same foods, and often grew up in the same villages. They share the remnants of a single traditional culture in which they were distinguished socially and economically as cultivators and animal herders who depended on each other for survival. To attribute their current conflict solely to historical ethnic rivalries is to distort history and discount the role of political choice in fomenting conflict, and, potentially, in restraining it.

Early warning and conflict prevention can succeed, in spite of the weight of history, if only because violence benefits a narrow elite at the expense of the vast majority of the population. The possibility of redirecting political processes in weak states by placing international actors on the side of non-violent forms of contention is the basis of early warning and preventive action. It is a broad normative imperative for refocusing all aspects of international diplomacy rather than a distinctive set of policies or tools.

One key to the success of conflict prevention is a comprehensive international response. As the structure of Table 8.1 suggests, all three categories of actors can act on all four dimensions of the conflict. All actors collect and analyze information that can contribute to early warning of incipient conflict. All actors also bring to bear some form of influence that can fuel conflict escalation or support resolution. The first criterion for effective early warning and conflict prevention policy is comprehensiveness. International actors cover the bases through a division of labor in which some actor in the international community is in dialogue with, and in a position to both monitor and influence, all important dimensions and levels of a society. Comprehensiveness as understood here does not set the impossible standard of knowing everything about a society; neither is it satisfied by collecting identical generalized indicators for early warning in all conflicts. What must be monitored is not the same across different conflicts, but must be discovered through a deep knowledge of each one. The criterion of comprehensiveness simply defines the necessary but not sufficient first step in coming to such an understanding.

The cases of Macedonia and Burundi illustrate the necessity for comprehensive international engagement. The policy framework for international involvement in Macedonia has been a model of excellence on the criterion of comprehensiveness. In each of the structural, cultural, and institutional dimensions of the society, international actors have struck a sound balance between NGO engagement with the broad population, and third-party state and IO engagement with political elites. Burundi presents a clear contrast, with a bottom-heavy international response that relies excessively on NGOs and UN diplomats unarmed with coercive or material incentives. Specifically, no international actor is directly engaged to monitor and influence the Burundi military. The government has rebuffed all proposals to send UN peacekeeping troops, and the UN Security Council resisted Secretary-General Boutros-Ghali's call for a rapid deployment force to be deployed in the region to respond to sudden escalations of violence. Consequently, the elements of the Burundi military responsible for permitting or committing the ongoing violence against Hutu can reasonably conclude that they have a free hand. The odds are against the success of conflict prevention in Burundi, if this gaping hole in a comprehensive international response is not filled. At the same time, the persistence, courage and remarkable success of many NGO personnel, diplomats, and policymakers who are deeply engaged in promoting peace in Burundi is highlighted by contrast with the timidity of the major power response.

International actors can exercise influence through some combination of resources, socialization, and political incentives (both coercive and noncoercive). These three currencies of international power correspond roughly to the three dimensions of conflict. The inflow of international resources can shape the structural cleavages of the society. International socialization seeks to influence the way that cultural differences are expressed in politics. To prevent conflict, international actors advocate inclusive, civic conceptions of national identity rather than exclusive, ethnic conceptions. Coercive and non-coercive political incentives are designed to influence national elites to use and legitimate institutions for non-violent political contention.

The three currencies of power are most effective when used in combination with each other. For example, international resources that pass through the hands of national elites (such as foreign aid) can also serve as incentives for them to take a political path toward either conflict escalation or resolution. Coercive incentives work best when they are legitimated through socialization and sweetened with resources. Finally, whether a civic or ethnic conception of national identity gains ascendancy can also influence the interpretation that political leaders will put on structural cleavages.

At stake for national political elites is how to define citizenship for the long term in a way that helps them gain and keep power in the short term. Those who opt for "playing the communal card," can manipulate structural cleavages, cultural tensions and political institutions to ride the ethnic whirlwind for several years while consuming their own societies (Human Rights Watch 1995). Yet politicians respond not only to material incentives; they are also susceptible to persuasion, at least at some times and on some issues. This is why international socialization is so important in the formation of post–Cold War national elites. In Africa, a powerful force for socializing democratic leaders is the example of South African President Nelson Mandela. In Eastern Europe, leaders such as Vaclav Havel play an analogous role.

A fundamental contribution of the United Nations is also to socialize leaders. Secretary-General Boutros Boutros-Ghali understood this, as exemplified by his performance at a meeting with Hutu and Tutsi leaders in Bujumbura, Burundi in July 1995. As reported by Michael Ignatieff, Boutros-Ghali first listens to the accusations and counter-accusations of both sides.

Boutros-Ghali says nothing until everyone has finished speaking. He then tells them that they make him ashamed to call himself an African. You seem to assume, he says, staring along the two rows of eyes that will not meet each other, that the international community will save you. You are deceived. Remember Beirut. Many good friends of mine died there, deceived by the same assumption. The international community is quite content to let you massacre each other to the last man. The donor community is fatigued. It is tired of having to save societies that seem incapable of saving themselves. He brings the flat of his palm down upon the baize table. "You are mature— *majeurs et vaccinés,*" he says. "God helps those who help themselves. Your enemy is not each other but fear and coward-ice. You must have the courage to accept compromises. That is what a political class is for. You must assume your responsibilities. If you don't, nobody will save you." He then sweeps up his papers and strides out (Ignatieff 1995, 39).

Clearly, conflict prevention is much more than averting catastrophic events. It includes admonishing elites on "what a political class is for." It is the active reconstruction—in the moral, material, and epistemological senses of the word—of states and societies. This is the task set before governments, intergovernmental organizations, and nongovernmental organizations.

Conflict prevention relies heavily on political socialization and persua-sion because it requires little political will and expense to send volleys of diplomats, UN officials, NGO representatives, and academics to monitor events and to show political elites that the world is watching them in coun-tries like Macedonia or Burundi. This strength of conflict prevention is also its weakness, however, because, while socialization can be a powerful tool when used in combination with appropriate resources and coercive incentives, socialization alone is a weak reed.

A useful way to organize an analysis of policy alternatives is to consider how third-party governments and intergovernmental organizations can address each of the three dimensions of conflict. In the 1990s, northern governments and IOs are largely indifferent to *structural cleavages.* Indeed, the International Monetary Fund and World Bank are administering struc-tural adjustment programs that often widen the gap between rich and poor. The imperative to reduce the size of government in order to spur the mar-ket through export-led growth exacerbates structural cleavages in societies of the North as well as the South. Nevertheless, this pattern strains effec-tive conflict resolution and prevention. In the Salvadoran conflict, while a UN team worked with the warring parties to negotiate the peace and tran-sition agreement, the IMF negotiated a structural adjustment plan with the Salvadoran government. The two agreements were hatched in com-plete isolation from each other, and their substantive policies worked at cross-purposes (de Soto and del Castillo 1994). With few exceptions, this example is not an anomaly that will be alleviated through effective policy coordination in the future. It more probably illustrates the new norm— that conflict resolution will have to be conducted in a context of shrinking state resources and international economic conditions that exacerbate long term structural cleavages.

Within this new norm there is still room for maneuver, and policies that alter the economic environment on the margin can have important consequences for conflict prevention. The efforts of European countries and the United States to persuade Greece to lift its economic embargo of Macedonia were an essential contribution to stabilizing the economy and easing tensions over competition for resources. Relatively small sums of economic aid can go a long way to stabilize weak governments that are committed to peace. The United States contributed $2.5 million in 1995 to pay the Rwandan government's World Bank arrears, and $4 million to rebuild government ministries. This aid was dwarfed by the $274 million spent by the US on humanitarian assistance in Rwanda.

The *cultural differences* in a society can be managed in ways that either escalate or contain potential conflict. Certain international policies exert considerable leverage on this process. The timing and conditionality for recognition of national independence, international assistance in establishing judicial systems, and aid to strengthen a free press all carry significant impact. Such policies can encourage democratic management of cultural tensions by promoting a civic definition of citizenship rights that is an explicit cultural alternative to an exclusive, ethnic definition of such rights. This is an unconventional line of analysis. It claims that neutrality in both its diplomatic and humanitarian forms says to elites who are playing the communal card, "We are neutral concerning the conflict between your ethnic groups, and seek to facilitate a non-violent solution to the conflict." At the same time, the unarticulated message is, "We are not neutral concerning the definition of citizenship. We oppose the tight linkage of citizenship rights to particular ethnic identities; while we support a civic definition of nation and citizenship." Such neutrality seeks to influence the political choices of elites and groups at a fundamental level.

The international community has sent signals to state-building elites concerning whether restrictive, communal definitions of citizenship and nationhood can lead to successful bids for power. Those signals, however, have been at best ambiguous and at worst pernicious in both the Former Yugoslavia and Rwanda/Burundi. International signals that inflamed violence included the premature recognition of Slovenia and Croatia by Germany on the basis of an ethnic claim to national self-determination, and also the lack of international response to earlier episodes of genocide and near-genocide in Burundi and Rwanda. The International Tribunals for both the Former Yugoslavia and Rwanda indicate a belated but welcome effort to promote the rule of law. Both Tribunals are the products of mixed motives by major power governments, and Britain and France have acted to hinder their effectiveness (Forsythe 1994). This is yet another arena in which very small resources can produce significant results. The United States committed $8 million toward promoting justice in Rwanda in 1995, divided between the Rwanda War Crimes Tribunal, the UN Human Rights office in Rwanda, and the administration of justice by the Rwandan government (Shattuck 1995). In mid-1996, in the absence of political will for a UN military response to restrain violence by the Burundi military, the US State Department is promoting an extension of the mandate of the Ad Hoc Tribunal for Rwanda to also prosecute perpetrators of the 1993 massacres in Burundi.

Third-party governments and intergovernmental organizations can play a role in the *institutional legitimacy* of non-violent channels for conflict resolution. Diplomatic intervention requires the assignment of highly skilled and committed persons to the task, but it can be effective at very low cost. The UN Secretary-General's Special Representative to Burundi during 1994 and 1995, Mauritanian diplomat Ahmed Ould Abdallah, has been effective against heavy odds. On April 6, 1994, when the plane carrying the Presidents of Rwanda and Burundi was shot down, "Abdallah went on radio and television to prevent false rumors from precipitating a bloodbath. He sat up all night with the Army chief of staff, phoning every one of the local commanders and ordering them to remain in barracks. Most observers credit Abdallah with saving Burundi from the genocidal frenzy that overtook Rwanda next door" (Ignatieff 1995, 39).

The Organization of African Unity (OAU) has recently overcome a reputation for ineffectiveness to become active in mediating conflicts related to democratic transitions (Amoo 1994). In mid-1993, the OAU Secretary-General obtained the agreement of factions in the Congo to accept mediation by Algerian diplomat Muhammad Sahnoun. In a two-week period of intense negotiations with Congolese and international actors, agreements were signed that prevented the escalation of violence (Sahnoun 1994, 30). The success of this traditional "jaw-boning" approach to diplomacy depends entirely on the skill of the mediator and the match between the mediator and the conflict. The appointment of Ambassador Richard Bogosian as the US Special Representative to Rwanda and Burundi is a welcome addition to the high-level diplomatic engagement with these countries.

One model of preventive diplomacy advocates constructing a regime that will be multi-lateral, layered and decentralized (Lund 1996). This decentralization applies also to the conduct of diplomacy within the US government, in which middle and lower levels of the State Department will conduct conflict resolution and prevention without raising the issue at higher levels of the government. In practice, this would mean that the State Department could jaw-bone and call together actors for meetings, but would have at its command few economic and coercive options. The power of socialization apart from the application of coercive and material incentives, however, is likely to be quite limited.

By the same token, the use of material resources and coercive incentives carries no guarantee of success in resolving internal conflicts. In a series of operations since 1990, the United Nations Security Council authorized deployment of military forces and political initiatives to carry out complex missions (Damrosch 1993). Each of the operations in northern Iraq, Somalia, Cambodia, Angola, and the Former Yugoslavia combined mandates for traditional peacekeeping with the consent of the parties; coercive diplomacy involving the threat or use of force; mediation to promote a negotiated political settlement; humanitarian assistance to deliver material aid; and humanitarian protection to prevent, punish, or simply protest abuses of human rights. These multi-mandate operations achieved a measure of success; but where they failed they were marked by a "doctrinal void—a failure to think through the strategic logic of new military operations that are neither neutral peacekeeping nor all-out warfighting" (Ruggie 1994, 180).

Multi-mandate missions in which the UN does everything can be successful in post-conflict situations where parties to a conflict make an agreement. However, such missions are less likely to work in ongoing violent conflicts, especially when the political will of major power countries is soft, and the local warring parties hold the tactical option to play against each other the components of the UN mandate. The UNPROFOR preventive deployment in Macedonia, including a contingent of US troops, was successful in preventing conflict escalation to that region, in combination with an array of other policy instruments (see Chapter 7). UNAMIR failed to prevent or stanch genocide in Rwanda, however, and military deployment is ruled out as an option by nearly all parties involved in Burundi. The perceived failure of international coercive incentives in the African context reflects a lack of political will on the part of major powers rather than the inherent disutility of coercive policy tools.

Economic sanctions, as they have been implemented in recent years, suffer serious moral and practical deficiencies as a tool to prevent conflict. First, the sanctions that are easiest to apply are indiscriminate in their effects and therefore exacerbate structural cleavages. When conflicts are driven by existing economic inequities that are politicized by mobilization of group cultural identities, economic sanctions amplify conflict by increasing the structural inequities and reinforcing the cultural identities of victimization. They may contribute to the long-term demise of a state elite, such as in South Africa, but this is a process of causing political change by promoting conflict, not by preventing it. Second, sanctions are unyielding to tactical manipulation when they are placed under multilateral legalistic jurisdiction. To have an effect on short-term political events their degree and scope must be carefully timed and targeted. This manipulation of threats and incentives is difficult when sanctions are imposed under a legal-moral regime of universal norms. Finally, sanctions allow third-party governments to affirm international norms without taking decisive action. Recent research on "smart sanctions" that can be effectively targeted at offending elites, and calibrated to provide carefully timed incentives for action, suggests that sanctions may become a more effective instrument for conflict prevention in the future (Cortright 1997).

In sum, third-party governments and intergovernmental organizations have a broad range of both non-coercive and coercive policy tools at their disposal, including diplomacy, economic sanctions and incentives, and threats and use of force. It should not be assumed that the rubric of preventive diplomacy applies exclusively to multilateral initiatives. When a major power government perceives the prevention of a particular conflict as a vital national interest, its leaders will consider the entire range of policy options—multilateral and unilateral, non-coercive and coercive, open and covert. It is a great irony that the extent to which major powers rely on multilateral, non-coercive and open policy tools in a particular case may indicate the low priority they place on conflict prevention, and the likelihood that they will fail to muster the political will to insure that such principled methods succeed.

In addition to governments and IOs, international non-governmental organizations can also contribute to early warning and conflict prevention. Indeed, NGOs are lauded as being on the front line of preventive action due to their ubiquitous presence in urban and rural areas of the Third World, their potential to act as both sources of information and agents of policy, and their relatively low cost of operation. The mandates of relevant NGOs embrace a panoply of issues: emergency relief, development assistance, human rights monitoring and advocacy, building civil society and democratic institutions, aid for refugees and displaced persons, and many combinations and variations of the above.

In the aggregate, NGOs channel complex international transactions of information, resources and socialization. NGOs collect information and channel it from South to North through both public and private conduits. Some, but by no means all, of this information can contribute to early warning. NGOs channel resources from North to South, mainly for relief and development. However, the information they collect may leverage other international aid resources. By publicizing a pocket of starvation an NGO can increase donor resource flows; or by triggering a negative aid conditionality with information on human rights abuses an NGO can reduce such flows. All NGOs, even those with the lowest political profiles, carry the seeds of political socialization in their discourse and practice. The principled mandate of each NGO embodies an ideal relationship between state and civil society found in the political culture of its home nation, and projects that ideal into "developing areas." The standard practices and policies of each NGO introduces these models in foreign societies, whether or not the NGO engages in public advocacy.

There is a rough division of labor in which four communities of NGOs each address different dimensions of conflict. The division of labor works roughly as follows: relief and development NGOs address structural cleavages, conflict resolution NGOs address cultural tensions, civil society NGOs address the institutional legitimacy of democratic transitions, and human rights NGOs address escalation dynamics.

Humanitarian relief and development NGOs have long considered it their mission to ameliorate the *structural cleavages* in societies. A relatively new concern, the focus of several recent conferences and research projects, asks how humanitarian assistance may prolong conflicts (Anderson 1994, 1995). NGOs are admonished to be aware of how their activities can prolong conflict and to minimize these effects. They are also attempting to carry out their primary missions "in ways that build bridges across the lines of communal conflict" (Menkhaus 1995, 12). A good example of such "indirect peace building" is the Catholic Relief Services project in Macedonia to bring together groups of parents of mixed ethnic identities to plan how to improve the schools for all their children. Indirect peace building is attractive to many NGOs because it can be perceived as apolitical by national authorities, yet it opens lines of communication between ethnic communities in a politically neutral and safe environment.

NGOs that confront the consequences of structural adjustment on a daily basis could do more than mitigate its impact on the poor. They could take on a prophetic role of protesting and working to adjust structural adjustment to reduce its poverty producing effects. Active engagement by relief and development NGOs with the World Bank and IMF would be required to convey the message and explore alternative policies. This is an underutilized niche for NGO humanitarian action.

Cultural differences in themselves do not necessarily contribute to conflict. Culture can become a resource for conflict when it is incorporated into a strategy of political mobilization. Culture as ideology defines citizenship rights in restrictive communal terms that exclude outsiders. A small number of established NGOs, such as Mennonite Central Committee and American Friends Service Committee, have long defined their mandates in terms of conflict resolution. These are joined by a relatively new generation of conflict resolution NGOs that have developed techniques to directly address the form of cultural tension that can be transformed into violent conflict. The Catholic Relief Services education project described above does this at one level. Search for Common Ground is an NGO innovator in catalyzing initiatives for non-violent conflict management. In Macedonia,

Search has brought together a team of journalists from Macedonian, Albanian and Turkish ethnic communities to conduct a joint investigative reporting project, the articles from which were published by each reporter's newspaper. It has also produced and broadcast a five-part "Path to Agreement" television series on controversial ethnic issues. In Burundi, Search has installed an audio recording and editing studio for production of a daily radio program for broadcast on Burundi National Radio. In collaboration with the UN Secretary-General's office and indigenous women's organizations, Search convened a national conference on "Women for Peace and Non-Violence" to lay the groundwork for a women's peace movement.

These innovative tactics target groups of societal leaders and give them an opportunity to practice their profession or pursue group goals outside of an ethnic definition of threats and rights. The approach plants the seeds of conflict resolution among groups with great potential influence on the shaping of cultural identities.

A few innovative NGOs are taking on the complex of tasks required to facilitate the transition from civil war to democratic governance. These NGOs are directly addressing the *institutional legitimacy* of new structures for democratic politics. This cluster of mandates is still undergoing rapid evolution and has received little academic analysis, but it includes a variety of tasks related to building civil society to support democratic institutions (Blair 1995), as well as demobilizing soldiers and helping them re-enter civilian life (Refugee Policy Group 1994).

During the Cold War, many human rights NGOs found themselves contending with American administrations concerning the facts of human rights situations, especially in countries where the abusive government was a client of the United States. During the 1980s, Human Rights Watch issued an annual report that critiqued the official State Department's reports of human rights violations by recipients of US aid. In recent years, by contrast, NGOs find that the US government agrees with their factual assessment of human rights conditions in the vast majority of countries. The NGO challenge of the 1990s is to obtain fresh and reliable information quickly enough to influence US government policy. To be effective in containing humanitarian crises, the speed of the information flow must match the pace of escalation dynamics in a particular conflict. Human Rights Watch is a leader in linking timely information with the policy process. During the Rwandan genocide, from April through July 1994, HRW reported the killing in real time from a network of sources in Rwanda, and conveyed the facts to the highest levels of the UN Security Council and the US government (Burkhalter 1995). Information alone was not sufficient to catalyze a strong response, however, until after the genocide was over and the situation could be redefined as a refugee crisis (African Rights 1994).

To "cover the bases" is only to meet the most general criterion for effective conflict prevention. It insures an international linkage for monitoring and influence to all important dimensions and levels of a society. However, the strategy for covering the bases in one country cannot be transferred in a mechanical way to another distinct context. Precisely who and what must be monitored is not the same for every emerging conflict. Moreover, the consequences of a particular policy tool on the course of conflict differ from case to case. These particularities can only be discovered through deeper engagement with the local political process.

Monitor Through Engagement

Hypothesis of Political Access

Information to warn the international community of an impending conflict is produced in a political process through which multiple actors negotiate with local political elites for access to sensitive areas and populations. There is no remote monitoring; there is only engaged monitoring.

Criterion of Engagement

Effective early warning presupposes that international actors have already gained access to the conflict through negotiated engagement with one or more of the conflict parties. International actors *monitor through engagement;* they do not monitor before engagement. This process is indispensable for understanding the unique causes of each conflict; but the information it generates on causes and potential solutions is usually late, selective and contestable.

To understand why most formal early warning schemes have fallen short of their designers' expectations, and why a few have succeeded, it is useful to analyze the fundamental political logic of early warning. Early warning projects that can succeed share several features. They respect the political processes of both the production and consumption of early warning information. They also accommodate the tactical flexibility of actors, especially concerning the choice of public or confidential channels of information.

Early warning information is produced in a political process. It is an artifact of the negotiations by particular international actors with local political elites for access to sensitive areas and populations. The essence of early warning is gathering information concerning an incipient or ongoing internal conflict and conveying that information to international actors. The early warning function is overlaid on existing channels of diplomatic and NGO information flows. Early warning information is also consumed in a political process. Conflict prevention is always an ad hoc process of forging a unique coalition of international actors (governmental, inter-governmental and non-governmental) who can define their shared interests in favor of effective action (see "*Build Coalitions*" at p. 206).

In a cross-current phenomenon, early warning information flows out from the conflict to the international arena, and prevention influence flows from the international arena into the conflict. Under certain conditions, particular prevention initiatives may be broken up by this cross-current. Actors who provide early warning information based on their access to local groups may lose that access when international policy targets the local power structure. Alternatively, international actors may protect their access so jealously that they refrain from communicating significant early warning information.

Understanding the political structure of early warning leads to the conclusion that remote early warning is an illusion. There is only engaged early warning, which requires personnel on the ground in the conflict area. Such engagement presupposes that the engaged actor has already negotiated its access (explicitly or implicitly) with local political elites. The information that each actor produces is necessarily selective and filtered by its ongoing negotiations for access. The opportunity for local elites to manipulate the process of international monitoring is built into the political structure of monitoring through engagement.

This fundamental political structure of early warning—monitoring through negotiated engagement—applies across all categories and types of internal conflicts. For example, it is possible to distinguish between ongoing conflicts with high levels of direct political violence, and conflicts in which the parties have made a formal, internationally brokered agreement to end the violence. Recent agreements in South Africa, Cambodia, El Salvador, and Mozambique have involved international action to demobilize soldiers, conduct or monitor elections, monitor human rights, repatriate refugees, and implement truth commissions to establish minimal accountability for past abuses. Where there is a brokered peace agreement, even when violence does not completely end, early warning and prevention policy can converge around monitoring the adherence of the conflict parties to the terms of their own agreement. However, this distinction loses some of its clarity in light of policy experience. The Rwandan case illustrates the extremes of uncertainty that can accompany peace agreements. The immediate trigger for the 1994 genocide was the dissatisfaction of groups within the political clique of the Rwandan President with the terms of the internationally brokered Arusha Accords between the government of Rwanda and the rebel Rwandan Patriotic Front. In response to an international agreement designed to resolve a civil war, dissatisfied groups launched a genocide. The international community was insufficiently engaged with Rwandan elites to anticipate and deter this tactical use of mass murder. Even the best of such peace agreements are "obsolescing bargains" that must be continually adjusted and renegotiated, and that require considerable international political creativity to sustain and implement (Doyle 1995). Neither a peace agreement nor elections can guarantee that the violence is in the past; therefore early warning and prevention remain relevant during the period of apparent reconciliation. Moreover, it is not only violations of the terms of the actual agreement by the official parties that must be monitored. Early warning must also be vigilant for violations using innovative tactics by splinter groups from the major coalitions.

In most early warning and prevention schemes, NGOs are relied upon as primary monitors and sources of information. This reliance builds a stubborn dilemma into the project of preventive diplomacy. The success of NGOs is based on their credible claim to serve the needs and rights of persons qua persons, regardless of their political utility. This claim to act "above politics" clashes with the political character of early warning in two ways. First, most NGO information is not useful for early warning, because it is selective, politically superficial, and can only be generated after the conflict is already underway. The "Dirty War" in Argentina illustrates the long time-frame necessary to generate accurate information—a consensus on the number of disappeared persons during the 1970s and early 1980s is still indeterminate after more than a decade of extraordinary efforts toward documentation (Brysk 1994). Most relief, development or human rights NGOs do not have as their primary mission either early warning or conflict prevention. The utility of this information in its raw form is mixed; it can be translated into a strategic assessment of the emerging conflict only through a process of political analysis that most NGOs resist.

Second, when humanitarian actors do generate early warning information that penetrates the methods and objectives of the conflict parties, the information acquires the power and sensitivity of strategic intelligence—it addresses the fundamental political economy of the conflict and the strategies of the warring parties. Such information will never be expressed in a broad consensus of NGO opinion because most NGOs will deny its validity in order to protect their humanitarian access agreements, and those that articulate such warnings will run risks of losing their humanitarian identities. The risks may include loss of personal security as well. Frederick Cuny, veteran humanitarian activist and editor of the journal *Disasters,* published a hard-hitting article criticizing the deplorable humanitarian consequences of Russian military strategy in Chechnya on April 6, 1995 (Cuny 1995). He disappeared in Chechnya three days later, and family members now accuse Russian intelligence of setting him up for assassination as retaliation for the article (Stanley 1995).

Within these limitations, NGOs are learning to accept limited responsibility and risk for early warning. NGO staff from the field level to the director are incorporating an early warning "peripheral vision" into normal analysis and decision making.

We have suggested that effective early warning techniques must respect the politically conditioned production and consumption of early warning information, and they must accommodate the tactical flexibility of actors, especially the choice of public or confidential channels of information. These criteria are useful for distinguishing between early warning schemes that can work and those that are unlikely to be effective. Bound to fail are systematic, universal criteria of conflict escalation, formal information matrices, and mechanical conflict or refugee flow models. All of these treat inherently political phenomena as if they were technical matters. Quantitative data sets on violent conflict or organized ethnic groups, whether they are assembled by academic analysts or policy analysts within government, tend to greatly overestimate the reliability and technical nature of data, and are incapable of reading or capturing the cultural dimensions of conflict. Such data sets, and analysis based upon them, may be useful in creating a global view of the scale and evolution of conflicts, or the diffusion of particular tactics. They may also serve a significant social construction function by bringing conflict actors into view in policy capitals of Washington, New York, Geneva, Paris, and London. Data sets on war during the Cold War were constructed in a way that excluded from view the micro-conflicts and micro-contestants that have become more significant in both politics and data sets since 1990.

Those schemes that can work allow the space for the political processes inherent in preventive diplomacy to play out, and respect the tactical flexibility and variability of actors. A good example is the pattern of NGO liaison with the Organization for Security and Cooperation in Europe (OSCE). Relations between NGOs and the OSCE preserve the tactical option to convey sensitive early warning information through either public or private information channels, and institutionalize opportunities for networking and coalition-building. Another secret of OSCE success is that its response to a particular situation is neither automatic nor consistent. From the jungle of often inconsistent standards and institutional mechanisms that exist on paper, officials can select those that fit the political context of each situation. Often the OSCE itself acts more like an NGO than an IO—it sends missions on its own initiative rather than at the request of a member government, it tailors normative principles to the situation at hand, and it can maintain a low political profile. Yet, at the same time, OSCE missions maintain the tactical option to mobilize the official, high profile, inter-governmental side of the organization to put pressure on a member government.

International actors monitor through engagement; they do not monitor before engagement. Hence, theoretical models that conceptualize early warning as disengaged from direct involvement with a society and its leaders are misleading. The process of engagement is indispensable for understanding the unique causes of each conflict; but the information it generates on causes and potential solutions is usually late, selective, and contestable. International actors who understand the partiality of their own information, and their need to learn from, and coordinate strategies with, other actors engaged in conflict prevention, seek to overcome these limitations by forming network relationships with other actors.

Cultivate Networks

Hypothesis of Synergy

Conflict prevention is policy artifice that sets in motion simultaneous peace processes in multiple levels and dimensions (cultural, institutional, and structural) of a society. The combination generates synergies across the levels and dimensions until peace develops a life of its own. Peace entrepreneurs not only invent processes for each dimension and subgroup of society, they also actively deter or neutralize the negative synergies created by conflict entrepreneurs or by the inadvertent effects of international intervention.

Criterion of Decentralized Coordination

Actors engaged in conflict prevention *cultivate networks* as a source of power. Policy networks are self-selected clusters of governmental, inter-governmental and non-governmental actors that share information through dense interactions, and in which each member modifies its own policies in light of that information. Policy networks for conflict prevention engage significant sectors of a society, correct negative synergies and enhance positive ones through decentralized coordination, and maximize the effectiveness of limited resources and political will. International actors—governments, IOs and NGOs—act as a loose and often uncoordinated network rather than a unitary "system" that single-mindedly maximizes its effectiveness. The members of the network are independent decision makers, many of which pursue other objectives in addition to conflict prevention. There is no guarantee that their independent tactics will not clash with one another. The challenge of inventive diplomacy is to maximize the positive synergy between the tactics of independent actors through consensual rather than authoritative coordination. Meeting this challenge is made more difficult by the context of uncertainty and imperfect information within which policy decisions must be made, and the relatively low and unreliable levels of resources and political will available to support policy initiatives.

To understand how conflict prevention policy can overcome these difficulties, it is useful to learn from the techniques of conflict escalation practiced in the developing world. Kenyan President Daniel Arap Moi is a master practitioner of both the prevention and escalation of conflict. To resist and then control the process of democratic transition in the 1990s, Moi argued that multi-party democracy in multi-ethnic Kenya would inevitably lead to violent conflict. He then used the coercive resources of the state to engineer ethnic violence and fulfill his own prophecy. In a Hobbesian sleight-of-hand, he generated just enough of a "war of all against all" to make the Leviathan of his own rule indispensable.

The structural and cultural background conditions of unequal land access and historical land disputes between ethnic groups had existed for decades in Kenya, but their conflict potential had been checked by an array of domestic conflict prevention measures, ironically including Moi's skillful brokering of land disputes (Amisi 1996). The legitimacy and effectiveness of these conflict prevention institutions did not simply break down; they were actively reversed. Moi deployed policies of escalation simultaneously and synergistically in the cultural, institutional, and structural dimensions of Kenyan politics. In the *cultural* dimension, politicians in Moi's political party ethnicised political discourse by threatening particular ethnic groups during regional political rallies. The *institutional* dimension came into play when Moi openly used political parties and political rallies (a central institution in Kenyan politics) to polarize ethnic groups. He also used the national military to transport ethnic "warriors" and selectively protect victims of violence. Using national political institutions as weapons in ethnic conflict weakened their civic legitimacy as representative of all Kenyan citizens regardless of ethnic identity. Finally, *structural* conditions were altered by large internal migrations driven by ethnic violence. Previously mixed areas became homogeneous, or influxes of particular ethnic groups exacerbated ethnic relations in the receiving regions.

The key to understanding Moi's strategy is to recognize the artificiality of linkages between these dimensions of conflict. The rhetorical conflict at political rallies (cultural dimension) was staged to appear to cause the physical violence (structural dimension), when actually the physical violence was launched by armed gangs orchestrated by Moi. Thus, the artifice of setting in motion several simultaneous conflict processes created synergies between cultural, institutional and structural dimensions that gave ethnic conflict a life of its own. Artifice became reality to the extent that Kenyans and international observers now wonder whether ethnic conflict will escalate beyond even Moi's capacity to regulate it.

In spite of the background conditions of cultural differences and material inequalities in Kenya, it was not easy for President Moi to generate ethnic conflict. He relied on synergistic interaction effects across cultural, structural and institutional dimensions of society, and across levels of society, to give momentum to conflict. The hypothesis of synergy suggests that an analogous process can be found in the development of conflict in other societies.

Conflict escalation can be inadvertent or purposeful. Its dynamics encompass the variety of factors that can trigger a significant increase in the scale, intensity or field of conflict. Escalation can be vertical, to higher stakes and means, or horizontal, to include more issues and social groups within a country or to spread into international conflict.

If synergy is a source of power for conflict entrepreneurs, it can also be used to create leverage for peace. The hypothesis of synergy suggests, and Table 8.1 depicts, that conflict prevention policy works in just this way. Effective conflict prevention uses policy artifice to set in motion simultaneous peace processes in the cultural, institutional, and structural dimensions of a society, and to generate synergies between the dimensions until peace develops a life of its own. This includes a positive mission to invent peace processes for each dimension and subgroup of society, and a negative mission to actively deter or neutralize the efforts of conflict entrepreneurs.

To the extent this hypothesis represents reality, it should encourage policymakers working with inadequate budgets against entrenched patterns of conflict. It suggests that the whole of conflict prevention may be greater than the sum of its parts; that successful peace initiatives in a limited realm can resonate with other efforts. The challenge for policymakers in governments, IOs, or NGOs is to activate peace synergies that respond to the particularities of each distinct society.

The propensity of actors engaged in conflict prevention to form complex policy networks can be understood in light of the hypothesis of synergy. Policy networks are self-selected clusters of governmental, inter-governmental and non-governmental actors that share information through dense interactions, and in which each member modifies its own policies in light of that information. In the field of conflict prevention, policy networks are sources of power in two respects. First, networks channel information to overcome the selectivity of each actor's monitoring of the conflict. Second, they provide a forum for decentralized coordination of each actor's policies with those of others. Hence, policy networks enhance the possibility of learning the causes of conflict in time to counter them, and the possibility of coordinating interventions to create mutually reinforcing synergies for peace.

Forming policy networks is often a spontaneous process, but recent examples illustrate an increasingly self-conscious effort to strengthen the inherent advantages of the organizational form (Ronfeldt and Thorup 1995). Several experimental initiatives are underway for networking between NGOs and US government officials. NGOs have long had extensive linkages with USAID, certain bureaus of the State Department, and even the National Security Council. In the past, these were affected by the adversarial atmosphere of the Cold War. By the mid-1990s, however, the character of government-NGO relationships has become more collaborative and non-hierarchical.

The Burundi Policy Forum is a good example of current innovations. Sponsored by four unconventional NGOs, the Forum has met in Washington almost monthly since January 1995.[1] Approximately seventy-five to one hundred people, from a variety of NGO, United Nations, and US government agencies and sometimes including Burundi nationals and government representatives, meet for two hours in a neutral location, often a university or foundation meeting room. Invitations are broadcast widely through a fax network. Academics and reporters are welcome, and everyone present states their name and affiliation at the start of each meeting; however, the ground rules forbid quotation with attribution. Hence, the meeting is designed to maximize openness of attendance and exchange of information.

The Burundi Policy Forum is new in two respects. First, it represents perhaps an unprecedented degree of cooperation between NGO and government sectors toward common goals. The meeting attracts officials from several bureaus of the State Department, USAID, the Pentagon, and the intelligence community; as well as representatives of NGOs specializing in human rights, relief assistance, refugee advocacy, democratization, and conflict resolution. The working assumption is that preventing a humanitarian crisis in Burundi is a shared goal of all participants. Second, for the government officials, the purpose of the Burundi Policy Forum is not the traditional foreign policy objective of relative gain over an adversary or competitor country, but rather mutual gain to prevent an outcome that would hurt all actors.

That said, it should also be recognized that the innovation of the Forum is more procedural than substantive. In fact, the poverty of substantive policy tools to reliably prevent conflict escalation in Burundi is precisely what drives the procedural innovation of the Forum. Its strength is that it can provide the *opportunity but not the guarantee* for creating informal networks of information and ad hoc coalitions for preventive action. According to participants, the Forum has faced certain practical limitations. Some ethnic Hutu and Tutsi have attended the Forum and promptly reported back to Bujumbura their impressions of whose side the Forum was on, thereby using conflict resolution to fuel conflict. In addition, the broad Forum has proven more useful for exchanging information on initiatives already underway than for designing new policy options. A parallel Burundi Security Forum has developed for collaborative problem solving among NGO and government representatives. This group of ten to fifteen persons has a restricted attendance, meets every two weeks, and deals with more sensitive topics such as how to monitor and stanch arms flows to Rwandan refugees in Zaire, and how to focus sanctions on extremist leaders in Burundi.

The Burundi Policy Forum may represent a growing pattern of government/NGO collaboration. In the future, according to one Forum leader, task forces or working groups within the US government will either have NGOs actively participating, or there will be parallel groups that include NGOs. If this comes to pass, such fluid, tactically innovative networks will redefine the meaning of humanitarian neutrality. The process of government/NGO collaboration is driven by the organizational imperative to search for new humanitarian and political missions after the Cold War, by budget cuts that require privatizing elements of US foreign policy, and by new humanitarian crises fueled by ethnic conflict and collapsed states. This trend carries risk as well as promise. On the one hand, closer government/NGO collaboration promises to stem conflicts before they generate expensive and destabilizing humanitarian disasters. On the other hand, the merging of the humanitarian and political realms could sap the neutrality that humanitarian organizations require to gain acceptance in conflict situations, and could deprive the government of independent sources of normative critique and legitimacy.

A corollary of the hypothesis of synergy is that international interventions can create unintended side-effects as well as positive synergies for peace. International actors—including governments, global and regional IOs, and NGOs are responsible for the effects of their policies on the escalation of violence or the prevention of conflict. Each international actor is responsible not only to monitor and promote the intended consequences of its policies, but also to monitor and manage the critical side-effects of its policies on the prospects for peace. This demands that policymakers cultivate a kind of peripheral vision, alert to inadvertent consequences in the broader political context. Hearing the views and observations of a wide range of policy actors by participating in a network such as the Burundi Policy Forum is an effective means to develop peripheral vision.

Toolbox approaches to early warning and conflict prevention do not make clear that the same policy tools can have different effects and uses, in different combinations, in each distinct conflict. These must be discovered in order to avoid exacerbating negative synergies. The themes of early warning and conflict prevention are gaining influence and reshaping the mandates of refugee assistance and protection, human rights advocacy, and relief and development aid. A consensus is developing that humanitarian action in a conflict situation *always* influences the course of the war, and that responsible humanitarian professionals should minimize the conflict prolongation effects and maximize the conflict resolution effects of their operations. In this way, the imperative of conflict prevention is subtly reshaping the very concept of humanitarian neutrality. It is important to realize that this consensus departs fundamentally from the traditional concept of humanitarian neutrality in International Humanitarian Law and in the operational mandate of the International Committee of the Red Cross. In the Red Cross tradition, neutrality means to conduct humanitarian action in a manner that has no significant effects on the strategic interests of the warring parties or the course of the conflict. To resolve a conflict is to influence its course. Realizing this plurality of meanings for "neutrality" is essential, if only because the ICRC continues to guide its operations with a traditional concept of neutrality, and the ICRC works side by side with a plethora of NGOs and IOs in most humanitarian crises. The clash between contending neutralities is one of the unexamined sources of inadvertent consequences from international responses to intrastate conflict.

Some of the concepts that scholars use to understand conflict processes may actually obscure a clear vision of unintended policy side-effects. In an effort to gain some analytical leverage on the bewilderingly complex causality of internal conflicts, much energy is spent attempting to construct categories into which conflicts can be sorted, or to identify the phases through which all conflicts must pass. This emphasis in the academic literature bears little connection to policy experience.

In both the theoretical and empirical components of this study we have followed an expansive conception of preventive diplomacy to include pre-, intra- and post-conflict prevention. Theories of the stages of conflict play little role in our framework (see Chapter 2). The theoretical dichotomy between prevention located exclusively in the early stage of incipient conflict, and conflict resolution in the final stage leading to reconciliation, does not reflect political reality. Emerging practice treats "early warning and prevention" as a broad rhetorical theme uniting diverse policies. In a protracted conflict such as Burundi, each initiative to *prevent* the next episode of mass murder, forced migration, or armed conflict is also part of an attempt to *resolve* the historic conflict between Hutu and Tutsi. Macedonia can also be viewed as a protracted political conflict extended over decades, so interventions to address the conflict necessarily have a *rehabilitative* dimension oriented to the past, a *resolutive* dimension oriented to the present and a *preventive* dimension oriented to the future.

We can never know with certainty the stage of a conflict. Defining the stage is actually part of the political struggle. Those who want a conflict to end attempt to create a consensus that it is moving toward resolution. In Rwanda during 1994, the international community concentrated on resolving a civil war when it should have paid more attention to preventing a genocide. The Arusha Accords, to which the international community pressured the warring parties to agree, inadvertently triggered the defection of government extremists who launched the genocide. The illusion that the Rwandan conflict was advancing toward resolution helped to confuse and paralyze the international community long enough for the genocide to succeed. The policy implication is that international actors in conflict-prone settings must carry out simultaneously the missions of post-conflict reconstruction, resolution of ongoing conflict, and early warning of future conflict escalation. While one member of the policy triad of prevention, resolution, or rehabilitation may be primary at a particular moment, the other two orientations must be built into policy practice.

Some attempts to build formal NGO networks of information are based on misunderstandings of the dynamics of both NGOs and networks. Attempts to encourage the construction of systematic networks of indigenous NGOs for early warning ignore the nature of NGO relationships. NGO personnel, from the field level to the highest executive levels, conduct routine business through personal relationships based on trust and experience. This is also the tenor of relations between northern NGOs and their southern partner organizations. Sensitive information concerning early warning of impending conflict will only flow through personal relationships that have been cultivated over time.

NGOs treat transparency as a tactical choice. For all NGOs, some information is conveyed through public channels and some confidentially. The mix varies widely. Indigenous and international NGOs work primarily through informal networks of personal contact through which early warning signals may flow. NGOs tend to resist participating in formal, public networks that threaten to tie their hands tactically concerning choices of how to deal with information that comes their way. What can be done is to create opportunities for informal networking. Conferences and trips that bring together members of indigenous NGOs and international NGOs as well as influential policymakers and individuals create the opportunity for creating informal networks. But these networks are created more during the breaks than during the formal sessions. We recommend, not entirely facetiously, that such conferences have regular and generous breaks. Communication technologies can make a difference, but not in predictable ways. The availability of phone, fax, computer internet, and video technologies to indigenous NGOs gives them increased tactical flexibility for channeling information to international audiences. But these technologies will be utilized in unpredictable ways, just as actors who seek to thwart early warning will attempt to use the same technologies to distort or counter the clarity of the messages.

The existing literature offers two distinct, and mutually incompatible, metaphors for the global project of early warning and conflict prevention. The first is a "system" that would require the development of a predictive social science applied to intrastate conflict. Such a social science would specify key criteria for early warning, and predict the timing, mode, and consequences of social and political explosions. The second metaphor is a "network" of decentralized actors gathering information and exercising independent but informed political judgments about whether and how to take action. The second metaphor is how early warning really works, both when it succeeds and when it fails. The first metaphor of a tight system is how some theorists and practitioners talk about early warning to promote it before various constituencies. The second metaphor ought to be the basis for realistic planning and cumulative improvement of policy practice.

The notions of networks as a source of power, and interactive synergies that mesh and amplify the effects of isolated peace initiatives, should not be regarded as panaceas or substitutes for providing adequate funding and political support for conflict prevention policies. In fact, one of the most important functions of policy networks is precisely to build political coalitions to support conflict prevention.

Build Coalitions

Hypothesis of Political Interest

The political will and material resources available for conflict prevention, and even the threshold of violence that defines the early warning task, differ from case to case and reflect the perception of interests by major powers and leading regional states. These interests are not fixed or given, particularly after the Cold War, but emerge from fluid coalitions of political leaders, bureaucrats, public opinion, mass movements, NGOs and other actors.

Criterion of Coalition Building

Actors committed to effective conflict prevention continuously *build supportive coalitions* by mobilizing constituencies, shaping perceptions, and generating policy options.

Scholars concerned with early warning and preventive diplomacy tend to assume that after the Cold War the national interests of major power countries are virtually identical with the humanitarian interest to resolve and prevent conflicts in the Third World and former socialist bloc. This is a false and misleading assumption. In reality, the general enthusiasm for the project of early warning and conflict prevention is a post-Somalia, post-Bosnia phenomenon of American foreign policy. It reflects a chastened, timid internationalism that is a compromise between isolationism and the muscular interventionism of Operation Provide Comfort in northern Iraq or Operation Restore Hope in Somalia. The argument used in Washington to defend the State Department and USAID from drastic budget cuts advocated by isolationists in Congress acknowledges that major powers are generally unwilling to spend the blood and treasure required to repair the largest war-linked humanitarian catastrophes, and proposes, instead, to allocate much lower levels of resources to anticipate and prevent such conflicts from escalating.

The political appeal of early warning is precisely as a cheap and low-risk option for policymakers. Intrinsic to conflict prevention, therefore, is reliance on relatively low and unreliable levels of resources and political will from major power sponsors. This political context of early warning generates both opportunities and hazards for the actors involved. Before analyzing these, however, it is important to recognize that the relatively soft and unprincipled multilateralism that has characterized American and major power foreign policy since Somalia was not an inevitable development.

One great sin of omission in world politics at the turn of the millennium is the failure to base a limited internationalism on a firm opposition to massive genocide. In both Bosnia and Rwanda since 1992, major powers permitted genocide when they had timely intelligence and the capacity to stop the violence at an acceptable cost. The United States in particular using the scale of diplomatic, economic and military resources it devoted to influencing any one of fifty countries during the Cold War could have cajoled, bribed, threatened, coerced or removed the elites that perpetrated the violence in Bosnia and Rwanda. That it did not do so, nor did Britain or France, is not properly explained by the lack of ready-made grassroots political support. The coalition of domestic and international support necessary to sustain such a policy was not mobilized by leaders in a position to do so. By celebrating the events that marked the fiftieth anniversary of the defeat of the genocidal Nazi regime, while ignoring, or neglecting to act against, ongoing genocide in Bosnia and Rwanda, Bill Clinton, François Mitterrand, and John Major failed to incorporate a clear "No To Genocide" into the reconstructed strategic interests of the West.

Responsibility is shared, of course, by the United Nations, the tangle of European multilateral organizations, and the moribund peace and human rights movements of Europe and North America. But ultimately it was a failure of leaders. The clear and credible message to ambitious men that they are not permitted to build states on genocide would have won sufficient popular support at home, discouraged countless mimic ethnic state-builders, and applied to Bosnia forged a powerful alliance for basic human rights between Western and Muslim worlds. This was a missed opportunity of historic proportions to define the relationship between the national interest and the human interest. Alternate historical trajectories notwithstanding, there are clear limits to the costs major powers will incur to prevent or resolve conflicts. As a matter of practical action if not conviction, many policymakers in Europe and North America view the confinement of war to internal conflict, and the containment of humanitarian disasters to peripheral regions of the Third World, as the solution, not the problem. Only when war and its consequences spill beyond these containers do they attract serious attention in world capitals.

Macedonia and Burundi, the countries selected as case studies for this volume, illustrate the international community's variable threshold of attention to early warning. Each is perceived as the twin of an adjacent country in which conflict was allowed to spiral out of control, imposing substantial costs on major powers. In each country, peace is pursued in the shadow of a genocide. However, a few political killings are considered serious violence in Macedonia, where the prospect of an expanded war drawing in Greece and Turkey on opposing sides would threaten the stability of NATO. The only American soldiers serving in UNPROFOR were five hundred troops deployed to Macedonia as a clear, though never publicly acknowledged, signal to the Serbs that *this* is where we draw the line. In Burundi, by contrast, a death toll of several *hundred* political killings per week has not attracted a firm response from the international community, whose threshold of tolerance in Africa can accommodate anything short of "another Rwanda."

If the band of overlap between the human interests of victims of conflict and the political interests of major powers is somewhat wider in Macedonia than in Burundi, it is relatively narrow in all cases. The basic challenge, which must be faced afresh in each distinct conflict, is to discover or fashion a coalition for peace that includes all significant international and national actors. The mid-level State Department and embassy staffs, UN officials, and NGO personnel who are responsible for warning and prevention face three broad options for doing this in a context of soft political support for the enterprise in higher policy circles. The first option is to recognize and take advantage of those rare cases in which a favorable structure of incentives is given by circumstances. The Organization for Security and Cooperation in Europe (OSCE) is effective in certain Central European and Baltic countries where conflict has not escalated to large-scale violence. The government of Estonia, for example, permits a strong OSCE presence to monitor and shape its treatment of the Russian minority in Estonia. The regional political context underpins the OSCE role with both a carrot and a stick. The government of Estonia seeks to strengthen its ties with Europe in the hope of gaining membership in the European Union (the carrot), and it uses OSCE monitoring of human rights conditions to satisfy the concerns of Moscow and to prevent a feared Russian intervention on behalf of ethnic Russians in Estonia (the stick). Even where the regional context provides a favorable structure of incentives for peace, these incentives must be translated through skillful diplomacy by governmental, intergovernmental, and non-governmental actors. International actors can focus the incentives for national elites, shape their perceptions, and provide attractive policy options.

The relative success of the OSCE in conflict prevention cannot easily be duplicated outside of Europe. The ambiguous promise of membership in the European Union and NATO provides the political impetus for OSCE effectiveness. In Africa, for example, there is no thriving intergovernmental economic organization to which all regional states wish to belong. The African political context offers few "carrots," or positive incentives for responsible leadership, although the economic and political success of democratic South Africa may cultivate some in the future.

The second option for conflict prevention is to create new political will by mobilizing public opinion. Several NGOs attempted, with mixed success, to do this around the genocide in Rwanda. The killing of more than 500,000 ethnic Tutsi was reported *as it occurred* from April through July 1994 by a representative of Africa Watch, who personally briefed representatives of the permanent members of the UN Security Council, and staff of the US National Security Council. The officials acknowledged the accuracy of her account, but took no significant action to stop the genocide. In this case, Africa Watch successfully shaped the perceptions of policymakers, but failed to mobilize a constituency or create attractive policy options. When the rebel Tutsi army captured the capital in July, the former government that had orchestrated the genocide fled to Zaire with a million refugees. Refugees International (RI), a Washington-based advocacy NGO, sent a staff person to Zaire to report on the first flows of refugees and the unpreparedness of the UN relief effort. RI faxed these reports to hundreds of NGO and government offices, including the US National Security Council. Then the president of RI conducted a media blitz to lobby—successfully—for the US Air Force to deliver humanitarian relief to the refugees streaming into Zaire. In this case, an NGO not only shaped the perceptions of policymakers, but also mobilized a constituency for a particular policy option. In these initiatives, NGOs acted as both direct agents of early warning and pressure groups for preventive action by governments and the UN.

The third option for doing conflict prevention in a context of low political will is to muddle through, simply to do what can be done with the resources at hand. The option of muddling through characterizes much of the work of conflict prevention in Burundi. In mid-1996, there was a general consensus that the appropriate response to the ongoing massacres of Hutu by the Burundi army was a multilateral military threat or strike to stop the violence. Yet no major power was willing to provide the troops, so the action was left undone and an effort to extend the War Crimes Tribunal to cover violations in Burundi was the fallback position.

Hence, three opportunities present themselves to meet the policy challenge of conflict prevention under current conditions: take advantage of contingent circumstances that establish incentives for peace; create political will by mobilizing public opinion; or simply muddle through with low levels of major power commitment.

The opportunities and hazards of conflict prevention can be construed another way—as affecting the organizational and personal interests of the actors that must cooperate to sustain peace. As the Cold War drew to a close—those years when the phrases "New World Order" and "End of History" could be used with more assurance than irony—the focus was on opportunities. National elites in Eastern Europe and the Third World could build political futures on the plausible prospect of electoral democracy and economic development. UN entities and NGOs had an array of new mandates and responsibilities thrust upon them, from demobilizing soldiers to monitoring elections to accompanying enforcement operations into civil war zones, to test their capacities and expand their operations. Military organizations in the United States, as well as middle and minor powers, could look to multilateral operations, from enforcement to peacekeeping and everything in between, as a source of new missions. From this euphoria for new mandates and missions a few years ago, the mood has shifted to one of chastened optimism as the hazards of democratic transition and conflict prevention have become more clear.

In the light of experience, it is now possible to confront more realistically the political and organizational hazards that face three partners in the coalition of conflict prevention: national elites, the US military, and NGOs.

National elites are the crucial stakeholders who make the choices to pursue power through peaceful or violent means. While they face divergent realities of national politics, the strategies and resources available in the international arena also influence their choices. Many of the states that are the focus of current conflict prevention efforts gained independence during the Cold War or its aftermath. Their leaders were formed in the cauldron of Cold War militarism and superpower clientelism. They had to be carefully taught to build elaborate security apparatuses and military establishments to protect themselves from their own people (Wendt and Barnett 1993).

International economic resources also buoyed Third World elites until recently. Repressive authoritarian leaders could invoke the plausible promise of economic development to legitimate their rule. A relatively benign international environment for economic growth from 1945 through the 1970s, and the availability of foreign military and economic aid through the Cold War, allowed Third World states to draw on international resources to fund investment, maintain social peace by subsidizing the cost of basic goods and services for the urban poor, and employ the middle class in the state bureaucracy.

Since 1990, however, the Third World state draws fewer resources from international sources. The drastic reduction in the scale of international resources available to the elites of peripheral states changes the options available for the politically ambitious to pursue power. The authoritarian welfare state of the Cold War era is no longer an option except for a few oil-rich regimes and special client states. For many countries that fail to secure a niche in the competitive global export economy, few options remain. On economic policy, privatization and structural adjustment are virtually universal. On the political side, the most popular alternatives are electoral democracy or ethnic warfare. The greatest benefit of electoral democracy is to reduce political violence for all citizens. In current practice, however, democracy often reinforces the exclusion of the poor from immediate economic benefits on the basis of a receding promise of eventual economic development. Ethnic war wields political violence to capture the reduced economic resources available to the state for an exclusive portion of the national population. It is a defensive, if usually self-defeating, response to the prospect of downward political and economic mobility.

Hence, the fundamental task of preventive diplomacy, in all its forms, is to steer national elites toward democracy and away from ethnic war. Given the constraints of the current international context, this task demands an extraordinarily high quality of political leadership. Figures such as Nelson Mandela in South Africa, Fernando Henrique Cardoso in Brazil, and Jean Bertrande Aristide in Haiti—all former socialists leading their countries into the global free market as popularly elected presidents—illustrate both the heroic and the ironic dimensions of the leadership challenge.

In countries where democratic leaders and processes are vulnerable to violent opposition, the response of the international community can be a crucial variable. However, the clearest evidence of the lack of major power commitment to conflict prevention is the difficulty in mustering coercive military actions against ethnic aggressors in internal conflicts. Bosnia, for example is perhaps the highest global priority for conflict resolution and prevention. NATO bombing of Bosnian Serb targets formed part of a configuration of carrots and sticks used to bring the parties to a peace agreement. Nevertheless, the implementation of the Dayton Peace Accords appears to leave IFOR troops from the United States, Britain, and France impotent to apprehend indicted war criminals Karadic and Mladic. The bootlessness of coercive multilateral incentives is rooted partly in reparable deficiencies of leadership, and partly in the nature of military humanitarianism.

In the theory of coercive diplomacy, the credible threat of force, if properly tailored to the political realities of each context, should effectively contain escalation dynamics and buy time for diplomacy to work. After Somalia, however, how can such threats be made credibly? Effective coercive diplomacy relies less on the actual use of force than on the ability to project a credible commitment to use more force in the future. No multilateral committee or coalition can convey such a threat effectively, because it is too easy for the target of the threat to split the coalition through political maneuvering. A unilateral, even personal, component is essential to anchor credibility. The United Nations or a regional organization can provide the normative warrant for action, but the threat must be made by a major power president or prime minister who is personally prepared to cultivate domestic political support for action, and to act with or without coalition partners. Coercive humanitarian diplomacy, therefore, requires the engagement of major power governments at the highest level.

In theory, any major power will do. However, in practice—based on history, custom and sheer capability—this leadership role is reserved for the President and military organization of the United States. Such an operation—a US threat of force for humanitarian objectives has been carried out successfully only two or three times. In Operation Provide Comfort, the Gulf War coalition led by the United States effectively prevented the Iraqi military from operating in Northern Iraq to allow Kurdish refugees to return from the border with Turkey. The strategic logic of the operation was a combination of *denial*—enforcing a no-fly zone by shooting down any Iraqi aircraft that violated it, and *deterrence*—warding off ground troops by deploying UN "guards" in the area as a trip wire for a strike force stationed in Turkey. President Bush was able to bring this off because the American military was already deployed to the region in force, his public support was high, fresh from victory in the Gulf War, and Turkey—an important coalition partner and NATO member—was imperiled by the refugee flow. In the second case, coercive diplomacy was implemented almost inadvertently. President Clinton, backed into a political corner by the continued flow of Haitian refugees to Florida, ordered an American invasion force into the air to oust the military government and restore President Aristide. The strike force, salted with a few hundred Caribbean troops and underwritten by UN and OAS resolutions, was successful as a *threat* rather than a shooting war only because the almost-freelance negotiating team of Jimmy Carter, Colin Powell, and Sam Nunn was in Port au Prince to spell out the alternatives to General Cedras and secure an agreement before the force landed. The possible third case is the five hundred US troops deployed to UNPROFOR in Macedonia. Were they a trip-wire for US military action in the event the war widened to Macedonia? Was a direct threat conveyed to the Serbs?

In practical terms, successful coercive humanitarian diplomacy requires that the President of the United States be willing to do three things. First, to order a use of force previously threatened. Second, to make the television speeches mobilizing public and Congressional support for the initial action and its aftermath. And third, to make the funeral speeches that hallow the blood of the American soldiers who die in the operation. Only if he is committed to following through on all three fronts will the President make a military threat. Only if he *appears* to be committed to take all these political risks will the threat be believed.

After Somalia, leaders of the US military apparently concluded, with considerable justification at the time, that Presidents were more likely to resort to multilateral UN peace enforcement operations as a means to avoid political risk and commitment rather than to embrace them. In any case, the military negotiated with the Clinton administration Presidential Decision Directive 25 that severely restricted the range of multilateral operations in which the US military could be deployed. One important consequence of PDD-25 was to protect the American military from being sent on a mission that the President was unwilling to back politically through to its completion. Unfortunately, this initiative to block the politically irresponsible use of the US military has the added consequence of thwarting effective coercive humanitarian action on those occasions when it is politically possible.

Canadian General Romeo Dallaire, the commander of UNAMIR peace-keeping troops in Rwanda during the genocide in 1994, has since stated that with 1,800 soldiers, the right equipment and permission to act he could have stopped the killing of 500,000 people. The US military, so determined to avoid another Somalia that it opposed any assertive multilateral operation for fear that American troops would be called in to rescue it, was a key actor in blocking UN authorization of General Dallaire's request (Burkhalter 1995).

If the quality of political leadership is a reparable weakness of coercive humanitarian diplomacy, the enterprise also suffers several inherent strategic problems. To intervene in an ongoing civil war with threats of force aimed at reducing the violence is to attempt *compulsion*—forcing the target to stop doing something it is already doing. According to both theory and practice, compulsion is considerably more difficult to bring off successfully than its cousin deterrence. In addition, the threat of force hands to the target the tactical initiative to escalate the violence, leaving the threatener with the choice either to withdraw or to fight what resembles a protracted counterinsurgency war. The international peace enforcer, perhaps in partnership with a national government constituted by former warring parties, takes the role of the counterinsurgent against the recalcitrant warring parties in the role of the insurgent.

In Somalia, General Aideed successfully used this tactic, which hamstrings peace enforcement in two ways. First, the international force will sustain casualties, which sponsoring countries may be unwilling to tolerate. Even if the international force survives this first political test, the second is more demanding. A classic strategy of insurgency is to make the war longer, more expensive and more violent than the counterinsurgent can endure politically. When the insurgents take shelter among the civilian population, as General Aideed did in crowded neighborhoods of Mogadishu, counterinsurgency pursuit requires a willingness, not only to suffer military casualties, but also to inflict civilian casualties on a potentially large scale. It is axiomatic that such a war cannot be waged for a purely humanitarian mission to promote the human rights and welfare of the local population. The paradoxical policy conclusion is that credible and effective coercive diplomacy for conflict prevention requires that the core mission be defined in non-humanitarian terms. More generally, coercive humanitarian diplomacy will be rarely attempted, and rarely successful. It can work when either contingent circumstances or creative policies render the operation politically sustainable for the United States, and also counter its inherent strategic paradoxes.

For every conflict in which multilateral military action is authorized, or even considered, several conflicts receive the standard treatment of governmental and non-governmental diplomacy. Indeed, early warning and conflict prevention reserves a particularly prominent role for NGOs. "We're really at the table now!" commented an NGO representative at a 1994 Washington conference on conflict prevention and management. It is becoming increasingly clear, however, that NGO prominence in civil wars can bring hazards and vulnerabilities as well.

In many protracted humanitarian crises, particularly in Africa, humanitarian NGOs find themselves operating amidst gradations of state collapse (Zartman 1995). This new environment poses operational challenges that have only begun to be conceptualized. For relief and development organizations, state collapse creates an immediate operational challenge. There may be no central authority, whether government or rebel force, with whom the agency can negotiate a reliable agreement to provide operational security. The NGO may then be forced either to withdraw, or to construct a local governmental structure under which humanitarian relief can be delivered to the population. It is well-known that NGOs hired their own armed guards to protect humanitarian relief in Somalia. In addition, humanitarian agencies have organized elections among relief recipients for committees to control food distribution in Sudan, negotiated distribution policies with traditional village elders in rural Somalia, and hired young refugee men to supervise relief activities in Zaire.

Such actions are often justified under a conflict prevention mandate as "enhancing local capacity," "empowering moderate social forces," and "building structures of participatory decision making." These upbeat phrases obscure the political reality that to create a local government structure in a context of civil war or state collapse is to institutionalize a power base that will inevitably clash with, or be absorbed by, competing power centers. The more general problem, in collapsed states, is that humanitarian NGOs are increasingly asked to undertake the political as well as the humanitarian tasks necessary for facilitating humanitarian action. Under what circumstances is this possible? What division of labor between humanitarian organizations and third-party governments is optimal in collapsed state situations? These questions urgently require more research and reflection.

As NGOs are drawn into a diplomatic context that makes conflict prevention the highest political and humanitarian priority, they should be aware of dangers endemic to such a project. The greatest danger is that conflict prevention tactics can be used to promote a veiled neglect of humanitarian protection. In theory, conflict resolution and prevention add a new dimension that can only enhance the overall effectiveness of humanitarian action. The promise is that humanitarian action will not only mitigate the violence and deprivation that are the human consequences of conflict, it will also address the roots of humanitarian crisis by resolving and preventing conflict. In practice, however, a pattern is developing in which international political support is reliable for only a truncated conflict prevention.

Prevention has been effective in containing internal conflicts from spreading horizontally into international conflicts and refugee flows. However, the solution often involves a denial of protection from immediate abuse. Humanitarian NGOs are drawn into such operations to provide material assistance to the victims, but the victims are denied protection in the form of refugee asylum, safe havens for internally displaced persons, or decisive political and military actions to deter and punish the perpetrators of the abuse. This is *less* protection than was provided during the Cold War when refugee asylum was more generous. War Crimes Tribunals are significant advances in their own terms, but in a broader perspective they may serve as a veil for the withdrawal of humanitarian protection.

The implication is that, after the Cold War, NGOs ought to have a looser, rather than tighter, relationship with their home governments. They ought to be more ready to publicly critique their government's policies in particular cases. NGOs ought to think in terms of tactical alliances with their own government where and when goals sufficiently overlap, and be willing to break the alliance when government policies generate significant anti-humanitarian consequences. This may be going too far for many NGOs. At a minimum, nevertheless, they can sensitize their political antennae and develop their internal policy dialogue and contingency planning for new political realities.

Discovering or creating the political will for preventive action is a task done one conflict at a time. Each coalition is built individually, and its members will not necessarily cooperate on the next conflict or country. When it works, conflict prevention is always ad hoc, relying on a unique conjuncture of factors and constellation of interests. There will be no global system for early warning and prevention. The information needed for warning, and the leverage required for prevention, are particular to the political economy of each conflict. Policymakers and journalists know this, if academics do not. The energy scholars invest in mining each case for policy precedents on which to build a global system would be more fruitfully applied to identifying the brilliant one-off performances of tactical innovation and creative coalition-building. Just as generals often prepare to fight the last war, so too peacemakers risk working to prevent the last conflict. There is no substitute for cultivating excellence in working with the particular resources and interests at hand.

Conclusion: The Indispensability of Political Judgment

Our conclusions offer no shortcuts to effective conflict prevention. They yield neither a formula for designing effective policy in disparate cases, nor an exhortation to adhere to universal principles that apply to all situations. No "system" of early warning and conflict prevention—in the sense of a global, unitary, rule-governed bureaucracy or regime—is likely to emerge to regulate societies that choose their rulers through civil war. "Who rules?" is the perennial political question; its answer inevitably sets in motion a political process of struggle, uncertainty and innovation. Nevertheless, much can be done to guide societies away from the shoals of violence, civil war and genocide and through the narrow channel of peaceful development.

The international community responds to each new challenge of conflict prevention in a necessarily ad hoc manner. Experience helps. But experienced actors understand that they must start over in each new case to:

- cover the bases by engaging key societal actors
- monitor through engagement to discover the causes of conflict
- cultivate networks as a source of power through synergy and self-coordination
- build coalitions of political support for peace

The performance of each of these tasks is a necessary but not sufficient condition for successful conflict prevention. The sufficient condition is that international and domestic actors somehow find a way to make peace by matching the reality of the particular society with the available policy tools and coalition partners. In short, conflict prevention requires a concurrent exercise of excellent political judgment by an array of international and domestic actors. Political judgment is indispensable for the inventive diplomacy of conflict prevention. We can best learn from previous cases by identifying examples of excellence in such inventive diplomacy.

Notes

1. In 1997, the Burundi Policy Forum was joined by International Watch on Zaire/Congo, to become the Great Lakes Policy Forum and Security Working Group sponsored by the Center for Preventive Action of the Council on Foreign Relations, Search for Common Ground, Refugees International, and the African Studies and Conflict Management Program of The Nitze School of Advanced International Studies of Johns Hopkins University.

REFERENCES

Abdallah, Ahmedou Ould. 1996. *La Diplomatie Pyromane: Burundi, Rwanda, Somalie, Bosnie...Entretiens avec Stephen Smith*. Paris: Calmann-Lévy.

Abrams, Jason S. 1995. Burundi: Anatomy of an Ethnic Conflict. *Survival* 37(1): 144–64. 1998. Burundi: Secrets and Splits. *Africa Confidential* 39(8) April 17.

African Rights. 1994. Humanitarianism Unbound? Current Dilemmas Facing Multi-mandate Relief Operations in Political Emergencies. Discussion Paper No. 5. (November). London: African Rights. Stockholm: Norstedts.

Agnew, John. 1989. Beyond Reason: Spatial and Temporal Sources of Ethnic Conflicts. In *Intractable Conflicts and their Transformation*, ed. Louis Kriesberg, Terrell Northrup and Stuart Thorson, 41–52. Syracuse, NY: Syracuse University Press.

Albert, Ethel, M. 1960. Socio-Political Organization and Receptivity to Change: Some Differences Between Ruanda and Urundi. *Southwestern Journal of Anthropology* 16: 46–74.

Alden, Chris. 1995. The UN and the Resolution of Conflict in Mozam-bique. *Journal of Modern African Studies* 33(1): 103–28.

Alker, Hayward R. 1994. Early Warning Models and/or Preventative Information Systems? *Journal of Ethno Development* 4(1): 117–23.

Amisi, Bertha. 1996. Conflict in the Rift Valley and Western Part of Kenya. Photocopy. Kroc Institute for International Peace Studies: University of Notre Dame.

Amnesty International. 1996. Burundi: More Than 6,000 People Have Been Killed Since the Coup d'Etat. London. August 22. *http://www.amnesty.org.uk/press/burundi_aug22.html* (accessed May 24, 1998).

Amoo, Sam G. 1994. Role of the OAU Past, Present, and Future. In *Making War and Waging Peace: Foreign Intervention in Africa*, ed. David R. Smock. Washington, DC: United States Institute of Peace.

Anderson, Mary B. 1995. *The Experience of NGOs in Conflict Intervention: Problems and Prospects*. Cambridge, MA: Collaborative for Development Action, Inc.

———. 1994. *Promoting Peace or Promoting War? The Complex Relationship Between International Assistance and Conflict*. Cambridge, MA: Collaborative for Development Action, Inc.

Anderson, Scott. 1996. Lost in Chechnya. *The New York Times Magazine,* February 25: 44–53, 68, 80–86.

Andreev, Velko, et. al. 1995. *The Republic of Macedonia*. Skopje, Macedonia: Goce Delcev.

Archer, Clive. 1994. Conflict Prevention in Europe: The Case of the Nordic States in Macedonia. *Cooperation and Conflict* 29(4): 367–386.

Arend, Anthony Clark and Robert J. Beck. 1993. *International Law and the Use of Force.* London: Routledge.

Atanasov, Peter. 1994. Peace to Keep. *Balkan War Report,* September: 22–23.

Auvinen, Juha. 1993. *Economic Performance, Adjustment and Political Instability.* Unpublished licentiate thesis. Department of Political Science, University of Helsinki.

Ayissi, Anatole N. 1994. *Le défi de la sécurité régionale en Afrique après la guerre froide: vers la diplomatie préventive et la sécurité collective.* Institut des Nations Unies pour la recherche sur le désarmement. Travaux de recherche, No. 27. Geneva.

Azar, Edward. 1990. *The Management of Protracted Social Conflict.* Brookfield, VT: Gower.

Baldwin, David. 1985. *Economic Statecraft.* Princeton, NJ: Princeton University Press.

Ball, Nicole and Tammy Halevy. 1996. Making Peace Work: The Role of the International Development Community. Overseas Development Council: Washington, DC.

Barnabé, Jean-François. 1994. À Burundi aussi, les médias de la haine . . . *La Lettre de Reporter Sans Frontiers* 63 (November).

Beinart, Peter. 1996. An American Stepchild's Plight: Born in the USA. *The New Republic,* May 13: 16–19.

Bennett, Jon, et al. 1995. *Meeting Needs: NGO Coordination in Practice.* London: Earthscan Publications.

Bercovich, Jacob and Jeffrey Langley. 1993. The Nature of Disputes and the Effectiveness of International Mediation. *Journal of Conflict Resolution* 37(4): 670–91.

Berdal, Mats. 1994. The Political Economy of Demobilization. Background Paper to the IISS 36th Annual Conference, Vancouver, BC, September 8–11.

Berkeley, Bill. 1996. An Encore for Chaos? *The Atlantic Monthly,* February: 30–36.

Beyer, Gregg A. 1992. Human Rights Monitoring: Lessons Learnt from the Case of Issaks in Somalia. In *Early Warning and Conflict Resolution,* ed. Kumar Rupesinghe and Michiko Kuroda, 15–39. New York: St. Martin's Press.

Birkenbach, Hanne-Margret. 1994. Fact-Finding as Part of Preventative Diplomacy Experience of the Citizenship Conflicts in Estonia and Latvia. Paper presented to General Conference of the International Peace Research Association, Malta, October 30 – November 4.

Black, Cyril E., Richard A. Falk, Klaus Knorr and Oran R. Young. 1968. *Neutralization and World Politics.* Princeton, NJ: Princeton University Press.

Blair, Harry. 1995. Civil Society and Building Democracy: Lessons from International Donor Experience. Paper presented at the Annual Meeting of the American Political Science Association, Chicago, IL, August 31–September 3, 1995.

Block, Robert. 1994. City of the Future. *New York Review of Books* 41(11): 50–51.

Bloed, Arie. 1993. Monitoring the CSCE Human Dimension: In Search of Its Effectiveness. In *Monitoring Human Rights in Europe*, ed. Arie Bloed, 45–92. Dordrecht: Martinus Nijhoff.

Boban, Ljubo. 1992. Jasenovac and the Manipulation of History. *East European Politics and Societies* 4(4): 550–92.

Boidevaix, Francine. 1997. *Une diplomatie informelle pour L'Europe. Le Groupe de Contact Bosnie.* Paris: Fondation pour les Etudes de Defense.

Bond, Doug and Brad Bennett. 1994. The Practice of Democracy: Global Patterns and Processes in 1990. Paper originally prepared for presentation at the XVI World Congress of the International Political Science Association in Berlin, August 25. Last revised November 4.

Bond, Doug and William B. Vogele. 1995. *Profiles of International "Hotspots."* Cambridge, MA: Program on Nonviolent Sanctions and Cultural Survival, Harvard University.

Bonner, Raymond. 1995. Economic and Ethnic Woes Endanger Macedonia as Serbia Looms Large. *International Herald Tribune*, April 10.

Botes, Johannes and Christopher Mitchell. 1995. Constraints on Third Party Flexibility. *The Annals of the American Academy of Political and Social Science*, 542: 168–84.

Boutros-Ghali, Boutros. 1992. *An Agenda for Peace: Preventive Diplomacy, Peacemaking and Peacekeeping.* New York: The United Nations.

———. 1993. An Agenda for Peace: One Year Later. *Orbis* 37(3): 323–32.

———. 1995. Supplement to an Agenda for Peace. The United Nations, General Assembly, Fiftieth Session. A/50/60. January 3.

Braeckman, Colette. 1995. L'Interminable descente aux enfers du Burundi. *Le Monde Diplomatique* (July): 13–14.

———. 1996a. Hantise du genocide au Burundi. *Le Monde Diplomatique* (March): 16.

———. 1996b. *Terreur Africaine Burundi, Rwanda, Zaïre: Les Racines de la Violence.* Paris: Feyard.

Brecher, Michael. 1996. Crisis Escalation: Model and Findings. *International Political Science Review* 17(2): 215–30.

Brown, Kenneth. 1995. By the Time of the Cease Fire. *Mediterraneans* 7: 12–24.

Brown, Lester. 1995. *Who Will Feed China? Wake-Up Call for a Small Planet.* New York: W.W. Norton.

———, Nicholas Lenssen and Hal Kane. *Vital Signs 1995. Trends That Are Shaping Our Future.* Washington, DC: Worldwatch Institute.

Brown, Seyom. 1994. *The Causes and Prevention of War.* 2nd ed. New York: St. Martin's Press.

Brysk, Alison. 1994. The Politics of Measurement: The Contested Count of the Disappeared in Argentina. *Human Rights Quarterly* 16(4): 676–92.

Buckley, Stephen. 1996a. Putting Aid Workers in the Crosshairs. *The Washington Post National Weekly Edition*, January 29–February 4: 18.

———. 1996b. Burundi Leader Flees to Home of U.S. Envoy. *The Washington Post*, July 25: A1.

Burkhalter, Holly J. 1995. The Question of Genocide: The Clinton Administration and Rwanda. *World Policy Journal* 11(4): 44–54.

Buzan, Barry. 1995. The Level of Analysis Problem in International Relations Reconsidered. In *International Relations Theory Today*, ed. Ken Booth and Steve Smith, 198–216. London: Polity Press.

Carnegie Commission on Preventing Deadly Conflict. 1997. *Preventing Deadly Conflict. Final Report.* Washington, DC: Carnegie Corporation of New York.

Carter Center. 1995. Cairo Declaration on the Great Lakes Region. November 29. *http://www.emory.edu/CARTER_CENTER/RLS95/cairodec.htm* (accessed June 29, 1998).

Cervenka, Zdenek and Legum, Colin. 1994. *Can National Dialogue Break the Power of Terror in Burundi?* Uppsala: Nordiska Afrikainstitutet.

Chigas, Diana et al. 1996. Preventive Diplomacy and the Organization for Security and Cooperation in Europe: Creating Incentives for Dialogue and Cooperation. In *Preventing Conflict in the Post-Communist World. Mobilizing International and Regional Organizations*, ed. Abram Chayes and Antonia Handler Chayes, 25–97. Washington, DC: Brookings Institution.

Chrétien, Jean Pierre. 1994. Burundi Pogromes sur les Collines. *Esprit* (July): 16–30.

Claude, Jr., Inis L. 1964. *Swords into Plowshares: The Problems and Progress of International Organization.* 3rd ed. New York: Random House.

Cohen, Lenard J. 1995. *Broken Bonds: Yugoslavia's Disintegration and Balkan Politics in Transition.* Boulder, CO: Westview Press.

Cohen, Roberta and Francis M. Deng. 1998. *Masses in Flight: The Global Internal Displacement.* Washington, DC: Brookings Institution Press.

Commission on Global Governance. 1995. *Our Global Neighborhood.* Report by the Commission on Global Governance. Oxford: Oxford University Press.

Conference on Security and Cooperation in Europe (CSCE) 1992a. Report of the CSCE Conflict Prevention Center Fact-Finding Mission to Kosovo, Vienna, 5 June.

Conference on Security and Cooperation in Europe (CSCE) 1992b. CSCE Spillover Monitor Mission to Skopje. CSCE Communication No. 282. Secretariat of the CSCE, Prague, 16 September.

Conference on Security and Cooperation in Europe (CSCE). 1993. Report of the CSCE Rapporteur Mission to the Former Yugoslav Republic of Macedonia. CSCE Communication No. 183. Secretariat of the CSCE. Prague, June 24.

Conference on Security and Cooperation in Europe (CSCE) 1994a. The CSCE Mission to Skopje, *CSCE Facts*, CSCE Secretariat, Department for Chairman-in-Office Support, Vienna, Austria, October 7, 1994: 37.

Conference on Security and Cooperation in Europe (CSCE) 1994b. CSCE Monitor Mission. Skopje. Special Report (No. 59). 1994 Overview. December 23.

Conference on Security and Cooperation in Europe (CSCE) 1995. OSCE Spillover Monitor Mission to Skopje *Biweekly* 64. February 28–March 15.

Conflict Managment Group. 1994. *Methods and Strategies in Conflict Prevention*. Report of an Expert Consultation on the Activities of the CSCE High Commissioner on National Minorities, Cambridge, MA.

Cortright, David. 1997. Incentives and Cooperation in International Affairs. In *The Price of Peace: Incentives and International Conflict Prevention*, ed. David Cortright, 3–20. Lanham, MD: Rowman and Littlefield.

Cortright, David and George A. Lopez, eds. 1995. *Economic Sanctions: Panacea or Peacebuilding in a Post–Cold War World?* Boulder, CO: Westview.

Coser, Lewis. 1956. *The Functions of Social Conflict*. Glencoe, IL: The Free Press.

Crépeau, Pierre. 1981. The Invading Guest: Some Aspects of Oral Tradition. In *The Wisdom of Many: Essays on Proverbs*, ed. Wolfgang Mieder and Alan Dundes, 86–110. New York: Garland Publishing Co.

Crocker, Chester A. 1992. Conflict Resolution in the Third World: The Role of Superpowers. In *Resolving Third World Conflict: Challenges for a New Era*, ed. Sheryl J. Brown and Kimber M. Schraub, 193–210. Washington, DC: United States Institute of Peace Press.

Crumm, Eileen M. 1995. The Value of Economic Incentives in International Politics. *Journal of Peace Research* 32(3): 313–30.

Cuny, Frederick C. 1995. Killing Chechnya. *The New York Review of Books,* April 6: 15–17.

Cviic, Christopher. 1994. An Awful Warning: The War in ex-Yugoslavia. *Balkan Forum* 2: 29–76.

Daalder, Ivo H. 1996. The United States and Military Intervention in Internal Conflict. In *The International Dimensions of Internal Conflict*, ed. Michael E. Brown, 461–88. Cambridge, MA: The MIT Press.

Damrosch, Lori Fisler. 1994. The Collective Enforcement of International Norms through Economic Sanctions. *Ethics and International Affairs* 8: 59–75.

————, ed. 1993. *Enforcing Restraint: Collective Intervention in Internal Conflicts*. New York: Council on Foreign Relations Press.

Darilek, Richard E. 1995. Conflict Prevention Measures: A Distinctive Approach to Arms Control? Center for International and Security Studies. PRAC Paper No. 14. University of Maryland at College Park.

Dedring, Jürgen. 1995. Conflict Prevention and Conflict Resolution: Avoiding and Abating Violent Conflict. In *Peacemaking and Preventive Diplomacy in the New World (Dis)order*, ed. David R. Black and Susan J. Rolston, 19–33. Halifax,

NS: Center for Foreign Policy Studies, Dalhousie University.

————. 1994. Early Warning and the United Nations. *Journal of Ethno Development* 4(1): 98–104.

de Gaay Fortman, Bas and Chris Kortekaas. 1994. *Conflict Susceptibility in a Socio-Economic Context. An Entitlement System Approach.* Paper prepared for the Seventh Annual Meeting of the Academic Council on the United Nations System. The Hague, June 22–25.

De Heusch, Luc. 1966. *Le Rwanda et la Civilisation Interlacustre.* Brussels: Institut de Sociologie de l'Université Libre de Bruxelles.

DeMars, William. 1994. *Early Warning and Humanitarian Action After the Cold War.* Joan B. Kroc Institute for International Peace Studies, University of Notre Dame (unpublished paper).

Deng, Francis M. 1993. *Protecting the Dispossessed. A Challenge for the International Community.* Washington, DC: Brookings Institution.

Des Forges, Alison. 1994. Burundi: Failed Coup or Creeping Coup? *Current History* 93 (May): 203–207.

De Soto, Alvaro and Graciana del Castillo. 1994. Obstacles to Peacebuilding. *Foreign Policy* 94:69–83.

Dessler, David. 1991. Beyond Correlations: Toward a Causal Theory of War. *International Studies Quarterly* 35(3): 337–55.

Deutsch, Morton. 1991. Subjective Features of Conflict Resolution: Psychological, Social and Cultural Influences. In *New Directions in Conflict Theory*, ed. Raimo Väyrynen, 26–56. London: Sage Publications.

de Waal, Alex. 1990. A Re-assessment of Entitlement Theory in the Light of Recent Famines in Africa. *Development and Change* 21(4): 469–90.

————. 1997. *Famine Crimes. Politics and Disaster Relief Industry in Africa.* James Currey: Oxford.

Diehl, Paul. 1992. What Are They Fighting For? The Importance of Issues in International Conflict Research. *Journal of Peace Research* 3(29): 333–44.

Dimitrijevic, Vojin. 1993. The Monitoring of Human Rights and the Prevention of Human Rights Violations Through Reporting Procedures. In *Monitoring Human Rights in Europe*, ed. Arie Bloed et al., 1–24. Dordrecht: Martinus Nijhoff.

Doom, Ruddy. 1995. Early Warning and Conflict Prevention. Minerva's Wisdom? Brussels: Vlaamse Interuniversitaire Raad.

Dowty, Alan. 1994. Sanctioning Iraq: The Limits of the New Wold Order. *The Washington Quarterly* 17(3): 179–98.

Doyle, Michael W. 1995. Managing Global Security, The United Nations: Not a War-Maker, a Peace Maker. Paper presented at the American Political Science Association Convention, Chicago, IL, September 1, 1995.

Drèze, Jean. 1990. Famine Prevention in Africa: Some Experiences and Lessons. In *The Political Economy of Hunger, Vol. 2: Famine Prevention*, ed. Jean Drèze and Amartya Sen. Oxford: Clarendon Press.

———— and Amartya Sen. 1989. *Hunger and Public Action.* Oxford: Clarendon Press.

Druckman, Daniel. 1994. Nationalism, Patriotism and Group Loyalty: A Social Psychological Perspective. *Mershon International Studies Review* Supplement 1(38): 43–68.

————. 1993. An Analytical Research Agenda for Conflict and Conflict Resolution. In *Conflict Resolution and Practice. Integration and Application,* ed. Dennis J.D. Sandole and Hugo van der Merwe, 25–42. New York: Manchester University Press.

Dudwick, Nora. 1993. Armenia: The Nation Awakens. In *Nations and Politics in the Soviet Successor States,* ed. Ian Bremmen and Ray Taras, 261–87. New York: Cambridge University Press.

Eggers, Ellen K. 1997. *Historical Dictionary of Burundi.* Lanham, MD: Scarecrow Press.

Ehrenreich, Frederick. 1996. Burundi: The Current Political Dynamic. United States Institute of Peace. Conference on Burundi. September 12. *http://www.usip.org/grants/burundi/burehren.htm* (accessed November 9, 1997).

Eland, Ivan. 1995. Economic Sanctions as a Tool of Foreign Policy. In *Economic Sanctions. Panacea or Peacebuilding in a Post–Cold War World,* ed. David Cortright and George A. Lopez, 29–42. Boulder, CO: Westview.

Elias, Michel. 1995. Burundi: Une Nation Pétrifiée Dans Ses Peurs. *Les Temps Modernes* (583) Juillet-Août: 34–62.

Eliassen, Jan. 1995. Responding to Crises. *Security Dialogue* 26(4): 405–12.

Englebert, Pierre and Hoffman, Richard. 1994. Burundi: Learning the Lessons. In *Adjustment in Africa,* ed. Ishrat Husain and Rashid Faruqee, 11–71. Washington DC: The World Bank.

Enzensberger, Hans Magnus. 1994. *Civil Wars from L.A. to Bosnia.* New York: The New Press.

Esman, Milton J. 1994. *Ethnic Politics.* Ithaca, NY: Cornell University Press.

————. 1997. Can Foreign Aid Moderate Ethnic Conflict? Peaceworks No. 13. Washington, DC: The United States Institute of Peace.

Evans, Gareth. 1993. *Cooperating for Peace. The Global Agenda for the 1990s and Beyond.* Boston: Allen and Unwin.

————. 1994. Cooperative Security and Intrastate Conflict. *Foreign Policy* 96: 3–20.

Evans, Glynne. 1997. Responding to Crises in the African Great Lakes. Adelphi Paper no. 311. London: International Institute for Strategic Studies.

Ezell, Walter K. 1992. Newspaper Responses to Reports of Atrocities: Burundi, Mozambique, Iraq. In *Genocide Watch,* ed. Helen Fein, 87–112. New Haven, CT: Yale University Press.

Fearon, James D. 1991. Counterfactuals and Hypothesis Testing in Political Science. *World Politics* 43(2): 169–95.

Fialka, John J. 1991. *Hotel Warriors: Covering the Gulf War.* Washington, DC: The Woodrow Wilson Center Press.

Fondation Hirondelle. 1998. Tanzanie-Burundi—Six États Africains Represents Aux Pourparler De Paix D'Arusha. June 12. *http://www.hirondelle.org* (accessed June 12, 1998).

Forsythe, David P. 1994. Politics and the International Tribunal for the Former Yugoslavia. *Criminal Law Forum* 5(2–3): 401–422.

Foundation on Inter-Ethnic Relations. 1997. *The Role of the High Commissioner on National Minorities in OSCE Conflict Prevention. An Introduction.* June. The Hague, The Netherlands.

Friedman, Thomas. 1996. The Next Rwanda. *New York Times,* January 24: A15.

Friends World Committee for Consultation. 1994. Quaker United Nations Office—Geneva: Report on the 1994 UN Commission on Human Rights. 31 January to 11 March 1994. Geneva, Switzerland: Quaker House.

Gahama, Joseph. 1995. Limites de contradictions au processus de démocratisation au Burundi. In *Les Crises Politiques au Burundi et au Rwanda (1993–1994),* ed. André Guichaoua, 77–88 . Paris: Karthala.

George, Alexander L. 1983. Crisis Prevention Rexamined. In *Managing U.S.-Soviet Rivalry. Problems of Crisis Prevention,* ed. Alexander L. George, 365–98. Boulder, CO: Westview.

———. 1991. *Forceful Persuasion. Coercive Diplomacy as an Alternative to War.* Washington, DC: United States Institute of Peace Press.

———, David K. Hall and William E. Simons. 1971. *The Limits of Coercive Diplomacy: Laos, Cuba, Vietnam.* Boston: Little, Brown and Co.

Glenny, Misha. 1995. Heading Off War in the Southern Balkans. *Foreign Affairs* 74(3): 98–108.

Gordenker, Leon. 1992. Early Warning: Conceptual and Practical Issues. In *Early Warning and Conflict Resolution,* ed. Kumar Rupesinghe and Michiko Kuroda, 1–14. New York: St. Martin's Press.

Gordon, Ruth. 1994. Article 2(7) Revisted: The Post Cold-War Security Council. Reports and Papers, No. 5. In *Article 2(7) Revisited,* ed. Abiodun Williams et al., 21–36. Providence, RI: The Academic Council of the United Nations Systems.

Gourevitch, Philip. 1996. Is Burundi Next? *The New Yorker.* February 19: 7–8.

Greco, Ettore. 1995. The OSCE After Budapest Summit: The Need for Specialization. *The International Spectator* 2(30): 3–19.

Gurr, Ted Robert. 1993. *Minorities at Risk: A Global View of Ethnopolitical Conflicts.* Washington, DC: The United States Institute of Peace Press.

———. 1994a. Testing and Using a Model of Communal Conflict for Early Warning. *Journal of Ethno Development* 4(1): 20–30.

———. 1994b. Peoples Against States: Ethnopolitical Conflict and the Changing World System. *International Studies Quarterly* 38(3): 347–77.

Gurr, Ted Robert and Barbara Harff. 1994. Conceptual, Research, and Policy Issues in Early Warning Research: An Overview. *Journal of Ethno Development* 4(1): 3–14.

———. 1996. *Early Warning of Communal Conflicts and Genocide: Linking Empirical Research to International Responses.* Tokyo: The United Nations University Press.

Gurr, Ted Robert and Mark Irving Lichbach. 1979. Forecasting Domestic Political Conflicts. In *To Augur Well: Early Warning Indicators in World Politics*, ed. J. David Singer and Michael D. Wallace, 153–93. Beverly Hills, CA: Sage.

Haass, Richard N. 1994. Military Force: A User's Guide. *Foreign Policy* 96: 21–37.

Hammarström, Mats. 1994. The Diffusion of Military Conflicts. *Journal of Peace Research* 31(3): 263–80.

Hansen, Peter. 1996. Old Concepts and New Approaches: Three States of Positive Prevention. In *Preventive Diplomacy: Stopping Wars Before They Start*, ed. Kevin M. Cahill, 285–302. New York: Basic Books.

't Hart, Paul. 1992. Symbols, Rituals and Power: The Lost Dimensions of Crisis Management. Paper presented at the ECPR Joint Sessions of Workshops, University of Leiden, April.

Hauge, Wenche and Tanja Ellingsen. 1998. Beyond Environmental Scarcity: Causal Pathways to Conflict. *Journal of Peace Research* 35(3): 299–317.

Heraclides, Alexis. 1990. Secessionist Minorities and External Involvement. *International Organization* 44(3): 341–78.

Hermann, Richard K. 1992. Soviet Behavior in Regional Conflicts: Old Questions, New Strategies, and Important Lessons. *World Politics* 44(3): 432–465.

Hilsum, Lindsey. 1995. Where is Kigali? *Granta* 51: 145–79.

Hirsch, Herbert. 1995. *Genocide and the Politics of Memory: Studying Death to Preserve Life.* Chapel Hill and London: University of North Carolina Press.

Holdsworth, David Geoffrey. 1989. Risk Assessment and National Standards: Philosophical Problems Arising from the Normalization of Risk, 563–71. In *Risk Assessment in Setting National Priorities*, ed. James J. Bonin and Donald E. Stevenson. New York: Plenum Press.

Holsti, Kalevi J. 1991. *Peace and War: Armed Conflicts and International Order 1648–1989.* Cambridge: Cambridge University Press.

———. 1996. *The State, War, and the State of War.* Cambridge: Cambridge University Press.

Homer-Dixon, Thomas F. 1994. Environmental Scarcities and Violent Conflict. Evidence from Cases. *International Security* 19(1): 5–40.

———. 1991. On the Threshold. Environmental Changes as Causes of Acute Conflict. *International Security* 16(2): 76–116.

Honig, Jan Willem and Both, Norbert. 1997. *Srebrenica: Record of a War Crime.* New York: Penguin Books.

Hoskins, Eric and Samantha Nutt. 1997. *The Humanitarian Impacts of Economic Sanctions on Burundi.* Occasional Paper #29. Providence: Thomas J. Watson Jr. Institute for International Studies.

Howell, Llewelyn D. and Brad Chaddick. 1994. *The Political Sociology of Foreign Investment and Trade: Testing Risk Models and Adequacy of Projection.* Occasional Papers. Glendale, AZ: American Graduate School of International Management. Department of International Studies.

Human Rights Watch. 1995. *Playing the Communal Card: Communal Violence and Human Rights.* New York: Human Rights Watch.

Human Rights Watch/Helsinki. 1994. *The Macedonians of Greece: Denying Ethnic Identity.* New York: Human Rights Watch.

Ignatieff, Michael. 1994. *Blood and Belonging. Journeys into the New Nationalism.* Toronto: Penguin Books.

———. 1995. Alone with the Secretary-General. *The New Yorker*, August 14: 33–39.

International Crisis Group. 1998. Burundi: Lever Les Sanctions, Relancer La Transition. London: International Crisis Group. April 28. *http://www.intl-crisis-group.org/projects/cafrica/reports/bu05f_1.htm* (accessed May 24, 1998).

International Helsinki Federation for Human Rights. 1994. Recommendations to the CSCE Budapest Review Conference (October 10–December 2, 1994). Vienna, Austria. August 1994.

Jackman, Robert W. 1993. *Power Without Force: The Political Capacity of Nation-States.* Ann Arbor, MI: University of Michigan Press.

Jackson, Robert H. 1991. *Quasi-States: Sovereignty, International Relations and the Third World.* Cambridge: Cambridge University Press.

Janis, Irving L. 1990. Reducing Avoidable Errors. A New Framework for Policy-Making and Crisis Management. In *Organizations and Nation-States: New Perspectives on Conflict and Cooperation,* ed. Robert L. Kahn and Mayer N. Zald, 249–308. San Francisco, CA: Jossey-Bass Publishers.

Janjic, Dusan. 1995. National Identities: Movements and Nationalism of Serbs and Albanians. *Balkan Forum* 3(1): 19–86.

Jentleson, Bruce W. 1996. Preventive Diplomacy and Ethnic Conflict: Possible, Difficult, Necessary. University of California, Davis. Institute of Global Conflict and Cooperation. Policy Paper # 27.

Jervis, Robert. 1993. Systems and Interaction Effects. In *Coping with Complexity in the International System,* ed. Jack Snyder and Robert Jervis. Boulder, CO: Westview.

Jones, Bruce D. 1995. 'Intervention without Borders': Humanitarian Intervention in Rwanda, 1990–94. *Millennium* 24(2): 225–50.

Jongman, Albert. 1994. The PIOOM Program on Monitoring and Early Warning of Humanitarian Crises. *Journal of Ethno Development* (4)1: 65–71.

Judah, Tim. 1997. *The Serbs: History, Myth and the Destruction of Yugoslavia.* New Haven and London: Yale University Press.

Juergensmeyer, Mark. 1993. *The New Cold War?* Berkeley, CA: University of California Press.

Kadende-Kaiser, Rose M. and Paul Kaiser. 1997. Modern Folklore, Identity, and Political Change in Burundi. *African Studies Review* (40)3: 29–54.

Kahler, Miles. 1993. Multilateralism with Small and Large Numbers. In *Multilateralism Matters: The Theory and Practice of an Institutional Form,* ed. John Gerard Ruggie, 295–326. New York: Columbia University Press.

Kay, Reginald. 1987. *Burundi Since the Genocide.* London: Minority Rights Group.

Keck, Margaret and Kathryn Sikkink. 1995. Transnational Issue Networks in International Politics. Paper presented at the 91st Annual Meeting of the American Political Science Association, Chicago, August 31–September 3.

Kennedy, Charles, Jr. 1987. *Political Risk Management: International Lending and Investing Under Environmental Uncertainty.* New York: Quorum Books.

Klotz, Audie. 1995. Norms Reconstituting Interests: Global Racial Equality and U.S. Sanctions Against South Africa. *International Organization* 49(3): 451–78.

Kriesberg, Louis. 1992. *International Conflict Resolution: The U.S.-USSR and Middle East Cases.* New Haven, CT: Yale University Press.

Kupchan, Charles. 1994. The Case for Collective Security. In *Collective Security Beyond the Cold War,* ed. George W. Downs, 41–67. Ann Arbor, MI: University of Michigan Press.

Kuper, Leo. 1982. *Genocide: Its Political Use in the Twentieth Century.* New Haven, CT: Yale University Press.

Laely, Thomas. 1992. Le destin du Bushingantahe: Transformation d'une structure locale d'autorité au Burundi. *Genève-Afrique* 30(2): 75–98.

———. 1995. *Authorität und Staat in Burundi.* Berlin: Dietrich Reimer Verlag.

Laurent, Martial. 1995. Panorama Succinct des Économies de la Régions des Grands Lacs Africains. In *Les crises politiques au Burundi et au Rwanda (1993–1994),* ed. A. Guichaoua, 403–433. Paris: Karatha.

Lazarov, Risto. 1995. The Albanians in Macedonia: Co-Citizenship or . . .? *Balkan Forum* 3(2): 19–48.

Leatherman, Janie. 1999. Catholic Relief Serrvices' Peacebuilding Role in the Republic of Macedonia. In *Theory and Practice in Ethic Conflict Management: Conceptualizing Success and Failure,* ed. Marc Howard Ross and Jay Rothman. New York: MacMillan.

Lederach, John Paul. 1994. Un marco englobador de la transformación de conflictos sociales crónicos. Centro de Investigación por la Paz Gernika Gogoratuz, San Sebastian, Spain. Documento no. 2.

———. 1997. *Building Peace: Sustainable Reconciliation in Divided Societies.* Washington, DC: United States Institute of Peace.

Lemarchand, René. 1970. *Rwanda and Burundi.* London: Pall Mall Press.

———. 1973. *Selective Genocide in Burundi.* London: Minority Rights Group.

———. 1977. Burundi. In *African Kingships in Perspective: Political Change and Modernization in Monarchical Settings,* ed. René Lemarchand, 93–126. London: Frank Cass.

———. 1992. Burundi: The Politics of Amnesia. In *Genocide Watch,* 70–86. New Haven, CT: Yale University Press.

———. 1993. Burundi in Comparative Perspective: Dimensions of Ethnic Strife. In *The Politics of Ethnic Conflict Regulation: Case Studies of Protracted Conflicts,* ed. John McGarry and Brendan O'Leary, 151–71. London: Routledge.

———. 1994a. *Burundi: Ethnocide as Discourse and Practice.* New York: Cambridge University Press.

———. 1994b. Managing Transition Anarchies: Rwanda, Burundi, and South Africa in Comparative Perspective. *Journal of Modern African Studies* 32(4): 581–604.

———. 1997. Patterns of State Collapse and Reconstruction in Central Africa: Reflections on the Crisis in the Great Lakes. *African Studies Quarterly* (1)2/3. 1–13. *http://www.clas.ufl.edu/africa/asq/v1/3/2.htm* (accessed November 25, 1997).

Levine, Alicia. 1996. Political Accommodation and the Prevention of Secessionist Violence. In *The International Dimensions of Internal Conflict,* ed. Michael E. Brown, 311–40 . Cambridge, MA: The MIT Press.

Lund, Michael S. 1996. *Preventing Violent Conflict: A Strategy for Preventive Diplomacy.* Washington, DC: United States Institute of Peace Press.

Luttwak, Edward, N. 1994. Where are the Great Powers? At Home with the Kids. *Foreign Affairs* 73(4): 23–28.

Macedonian Information and Liaison Service (MILS). 1993. *Certain Aspects on the Status of the Albanian Minority in the Republic of Macedonia.* May. Skopje, Macedonia.

Macedonian Information Center (MIC). 1994. *Independent Survey.* Skopje, Macedonia.

Mack, John, E. M.D. 1990. Leadership for the Politics of Transcendence. *Center Review* 4:1, 12–14. Center for Psychological Studies in the Nuclear Age, Harvard University.

Malkki, Liisa H. 1995. *Purity and Exile: Violence, Memory, and National Cosmology Among Hutu Refugees in Tanzania.* Chicago: University of Chicago Press.

Malnes, Raino. 1995. 'Leader' and 'Entrepreneur' in International Negotiations. *European Journal of International Relations* 1(1): 87–112.

Manirakiza, Marc. 1992. *Burundi: De la révolution au régionalisme, 1962–1966.* Bruxelles: Le Mât de Misaine.

Mansfield, Edward D. and Jack Snyder. 1995. Democratization and the Danger of War. *International Security* 20(1): 5–38.

Maresca, John J. 1995. Resolving Conflicts Without Enforced Solutions. In *Managing Ethnic Tension in the Post-Soviet Space*, ed. Maria Drohobycky, 59–64. Washington, DC: American Association for the Advancement of Science.

Martin, Lisa L. 1993. Credibility, Costs and Institutions. Cooperation on Economic Sanctions. *World Politics* 45(3): 406–32.

Maull, Hanns W. 1995–96. Germany in the Yugoslav Crisis. *Survival* 37(4): 99–130.

Mazrui, Ali A. 1995. The Blood of Experience: The Failed State and Political Collapse in Africa. *World Policy Journal* 12(1): 28–34.

McKinley Jr., James C. 1996. Chaos in Burundi Could Sow Misery Next Door. *The New York Times*, July 12: A3.

McMahon, Edward R. 1996. Discussion Memo: Institutional Reform in Burundi. United States Institute of Peace. Conference on Burundi. September 12. *http://www.usip.org/grants/burundi/burmcmahon.htm* (accessed November 9, 1997).

Melvern, Linda. 1997. Genocide Behind the Thin Blue Line. *Security Dialogue* 28(3): 333–46.

Menkhaus, Ken. 1995. Conflict, Peacebuilding and International Aid: The State of the Debate. *Life and Peace Review* 9(2): 10–13.

Miall, Hugh. 1992. *The Peacemakers*. New York: St. Martin's Press.

Midlarsky, Manus I. 1988. Rulers and the Ruled: Patterned Inequality and the Onset of Mass Political Violence. *American Political Science Review* 82(2): 491–509.

Miller, Benjamin. 1995. International Systems and Regional Security: From Competition to Cooperation, Dominance or Disengagement? *Journal of Strategic Studies* 18 (2): 52–100.

Mitchell, Christopher. 1991. Classifying Conflicts: Asymmetries and Resolution. *Annals AAPSS* 518 (November): 23–38.

Mojzes, Paul. 1994. *Yugoslavian Inferno. Ethnoreligious Warfare in the Balkans*. New York: Continuum.

Nairn, Allan. 1994. Occupation Haiti: The Eagle is Landing. *The Nation*, October 3: 344–48.

Ndarshikanya, Barnabé. 1995. Les intellectuels Burundais et la crise. In *Les crises politiques au Burundi et au Rwanda (1993–1994)*, ed. A. Guichaoua, 155–66. Paris: Kathala.

Netherlands Helsinki Committee. 1994. A Focus on the Future: Using an Enhanced Conference on Security and Co-operation in Europe. A Contribution to the Budapest Review Conference. A Report by the Netherlands Helsinki Committee. Utrecht. 15 August 1994.

Neuneck, Götz and Jörg Wallner. 1996. Präventive Rüstungskontrolle: Chance oder Utopie? In *Friedensgutachten 1996*, ed. Bruno Schoch, Friedhelm Solms and Reinhard Mutz, 322–32. Münster: LIT Verlag.

Newman, James L. 1995. *The People of Africa: A Geographic Interpretation*. New

Haven, CT: Yale University Press.

Nicolaïdis, Calypso. 1996. International Preventive Action: Developing a Strategic Framework. In *Vigilance and Vengeance. NGOs Preventing Ethnic Conflict in Divided Societies*, ed. Robert I. Rotberg, 23–69. Washington, DC: The Brookings Institution.

Nindorera, Eugéne. 1995. L'enjeu des droits de l'homme á la lumiére des derniers événements burundiais. In *Les Crises Politiques au Burundi et au Rwanda (1993–1994)*, ed. André Guichaoua, 89–98. Paris: Karthala.

Northrup, Terrell. 1989. The Dynamics of Identity in Personal and Social Conflict. In *Intractable Conflicts and their Transformation*, ed. Louis Kriesberg, Terrell Northrup and Stuart Thorson, 55–82. Syracuse, NY: Syracuse University Press.

Nossal, Kim Richard. 1994. *Rain Dancing. Sanctions in Canadian and Australian Foreign Policy*. Toronto: University of Toronto Press.

Our Global Neighborhood. 1995. *The Report of the Commission on Global Governance 1995*. London: Oxford University Press.

Overholt, William H. 1982. *Political Risk*. London: Euromoney Publications.

Panov, L. 1995. Making Sense of a Confusing Situation: MPO Urges Support of Loyalty. *Macedonian Tribune*, March 9: 1ff.

Pape, Robert A. 1997. Why Economic Sanctions Do Not Work. *International Security* 22(2): 90–136.

Paye, Olivier and Eric Remacle. 1994. The United Nations and the CSCE: Facing Conflicts in Abkhazia and Nagorno-Karabakh. *Peace and the Sciences* 3(25): 1–18.

Peck, Connie. 1998. *Sustainable Peace: The Role of the UN and Regional Organizations in Preventing Conflict*. Lanham, MD: Rowman and Littlefield.

Perry, Duncan. 1988. *The Politics of Terror*. Durham, NC: Duke University Press.

———. 1995. The Republic of Macedonia: Foreign Relations, Issues and Dilemmas. *Analysis of Current Events*. Association for the Study of Nationalities. May 2.

Perry, William J. 1996. Managing Conflict in the Post–Cold War Era. In *Managing Conflict in the Post–Cold War World: The Role of Intervention*, 55–61 Washington, DC: The Aspen Institute.

Pinheiro, Paulo Sérgio. 1995. Initial report on the human rights situation in Burundi submitted by Special Rapporteur, Mr. Paulo Sérgio Pinheiro, in accordance with Commission resolution 1995/90. New York: United Nations Commission on Human Rights, November 14, 1995.

———. 1996a. Initial report on the human rights situation in Burundi submitted by Special Rapporteur, Mr. Paulo Sérgio Pinheiro, in accordance with Commission resolution 1995/90, *Addendum*. New York: United Nations Commission on Human Rights, February 27, 1996.

———. 1996b. Interim report on the human rights situation in Burundi submitted by the Special Rapporteur of the Commission on Human Rights, pursuant to Commission on Human Rights resolution 1996/1 and Economic and Social Council decision 1996/254. October 7. New York: United Nations.

Poulton, Hugh. 1991. *The Balkans: Minorities and States in Conflict.* Great Britain: Minority Rights Group.

———. 1995. *Who Are the Macedonians?* Bloomington, IN: Indiana University Press.

Prendergast, John. 1996. *Frontline Diplomacy.* Washington, DC: The United States Institute of Peace Press.

Press, Robert M. 1995. Nomads and Farmers in Kenya War Over Increasingly Scarce Land. *Christian Science Monitor,* January 13.

Princen, Thomas. 1994. *Environmental NGOs in World Politics: Linking the Local and the Global.* New York: Routledge.

———. 1992. *Intermediaries in International Conflict.* Princeton, NJ: Princeton University Press.

Prunier, Gérard. 1996. Conflicts in the Great Lakes Area and the International Community. London: IPPR Conference-European Union Policy Toward Potential Regions of Migration. January 19–20.

———. 1997. The Geopolitical Situation in the Great Lakes Area in the Light of the Kivu Crisis. London: Writenet. *http://www.unhcr.ch/refworld/country/writenet/wrilakes.htm* (accessed November 9, 1997).

Putnam, Robert. 1993. *Double-edged Diplomacy: International Bargaining and Domestic Politics.* Berkeley: University of California Press.

Raddock, David M., et al. 1986. *Assessing Corporate Political Risks.* Totowa, NJ: Rowman and Littlefield.

Ramcharan, B.G. 1991. *The International Law and Practice of Early Warning and Preventive Diplomacy: The Emerging Global Watch.* Dordrecht: Martinus Nijhoff.

———. 1992. Strategies for the International Protection of Human Rights in the 1990s. In *Human Rights in the World Community. Issues and Action,* ed. Richard Pierre Claude and Burns H. Weston, 271–83. Philadelphia, PA: University of Pennsylvania Press.

Rangasami, Amrita. 1985. 'Failure of Exchange Entitlements' Theory of Famine. *Economic and Political Weekly* 20(41 and 42):1747–52, 1797–1801.

Ravallion, Martin. 1990. Market Responses to Anti-Hunger Policies: Effects on Wages, Prices and Employment. In *The Political Economy of Hunger, vol. 2: Famine Prevention,* ed. Jean Drèze and Amartya Sen, 241–78. Oxford: Clarendon Press.

Refugee Policy Group. 1994. *Challenges of Demobilization and Reintegration.* Background Paper and Conference Summary. Washington, DC: Refugee Policy Group.

Reinicke, Wolfgang H. 1996. Can International Financial Institutions Prevent Internal Violence? The Sources of Ethno-National Conflict in Transitional Societies. In *Preventing Conflict in the Post-Communist World. Mobilizing*

International and Regional Organizations, ed. Abram Chayes and Antonia Handler Chayes, 281–337. Washington, DC: The Brookings Institution.

Reno, William. 1998. *Warlord Politics and African States*. Boulder, CO: Lynne Rienner Publishers.

Reychler, Luc. 1997. Les crises et leurs fondaments. La prévention des conflits violents. In *Conflits en Afrique. Analyse des crises et pistes pour une prévention*, 39–66. Brussels: GRIP.

Reyntjens, Filip. 1993. The Proof of the Pudding Is in the Eating: The June 1993 Elections in Burundi. *Journal of Modern African Studies* 31(4): 563–83.

———. 1994. *L'Afrique des grands lacs en crise: Rwanda, Burundi: 1988–1994*. Paris: Karthala.

———. 1995. *Burundi: Breaking the Cycle of Violence*. London: Minority Rights Group.

Richards, Audrey I. 1959. *East African Chiefs: A Study of Political Development in Some Uganda and Tanganyika Tribes*. London: Faber and Faber.

Risse-Kappen, Thomas. 1995. Structures of Governance and Transnational Relations: What Have We Learned? In *Bringing Transnational Relations Back In: Non-State Actors, Domestic Structures and International Institutions*, ed. Risse-Kappen, 280–313. New York: Cambridge University Press.

Rodman, Kenneth. 1994. Public and Private Sanctions Against South Africa. *Political Science Quarterly* 109(2): 313–34.

Rogers, Elizabeth. 1996. Economic Sanctions and Internal Conflict. In *The International Dimensions of Internal Conflict*, ed. Michael E. Brown, 411–34. Cambridge, MA: The MIT Press.

Ronfeldt, David and Cathryn L. Thorup. 1995. North America in the Era of Citizen Networks: State, Society, and Security. Santa Monica, Calif.: RAND.

Rosas, Allan. 1995. *OSCE Long-Term Missions*. Paper prepared for the Workshop on 'The OSCE in the Maintenance of International Peace and Security.' Turku, Finland: Åbo Akademi University.

Rosenau, James. 1990. *Turbulence in World Politics*. Princeton, NJ: Princeton University Press.

Ross, Jeffrey Ian. 1993. Structural Causes of Oppositional Political Terrorism: Towards a Causal Model. *Journal of Peace Research* 30(3): 317–29.

Ross, Marc Howard. 1993. *The Culture of Conflict. Interpretations and Interests in Comparative Perspective*. New Haven, CT: Yale University Press.

Rossel, Hubert. 1992. Le Rwanda et le Burundi à la veille de leur 30e anniversaire d'indépendance. *Genève-Afrique* 30 (2): 9–74.

Rothgeb, John M., Jr. 1993. *Defining Power. Influence and Force in the Contemporary International System*. New York: St. Martin's Press.

Roy, Olivier. 1995. The Role of the OSCE in the Peace Process in Tajikistan. In *Central Asia: Conflict, Resolution, and Change*, ed. Roald Sagdeev and Susan Eisenhower, 311–19. Chevy Chase, MD: CPSS Press.

Rozier, Raymond. 1973. Structures Socials et Politiques du Burundi. *Revue Francaise d'Études Politiques Africaines* 91: 70–87.

Ruanda. 1994. Söhne ohne Land. Der Bürgerkrieg in Zentralafrika — eine Folge der Bevölkerungsexplosion. *Der Spiegel* 21: 146–48.

Rubin, Jeffrey A., Dean G. Pruitt, and Sung Hee Kim. 1994. *Social Conflict: Escalation, Stalemate and Settlement.* 2nd ed. New York: McGraw-Hill.

Ruggie, John Gerard. 1994. Peacekeeping and U.S. Interests. *The Washington Quarterly* 17(4): 175–184.

———. 1993. Territoriality and Beyond. *International Organization* 47(1): 139–74.

Rummel, Rudolph J. 1994. Power, Genocide and Mass Murders. *Journal of Peace Research* 31(1): 1–10.

Rupesinghe, Kumar and Michiko Kuroda, eds. 1992. *Early Warning and Conflict Resolution.* London: Macmillan.

Ryan, Stephen. 1996. 'The Voice of Sanity Getting Hoarse': Destructive Processes in Violent Ethnic Conflict. In *The Politics of Difference: Ethnic Premises in a World of Power*, ed. Edwin N. Wemsen and Patrick McAllister, 144–61. Chicago: University of Chicago Press.

Sahnoun, Mohamed. 1995. Managing Conflict after the Cold War. Catholic Institute for International Relations. Text of Talk by Ambassador Mohamed Sahnoun to CIIR's Annual General Meeting, 13 October.

———. 1994. An Interview with Muhammad Sahnoun. *Middle East Report* 24(2–3): 28–33.

Salim Salim Ahmed. 1996. Localizing Outbreaks: The Role of Regional Organization in Preventive Action. In *Preventive Diplomacy: Stopping Wars Before They Start*, ed. Kevin M. Cahill, 100–120. New York: Basic Books.

Samuels, D. 1995. At Play in the Fields of Oppression. *Harper's Magazine*, May: 47–54.

Schelling, Thomas C. 1980. *The Strategy of Conflict.* 2nd ed. Cambridge, MA: Harvard University Press.

Sen, Amartya. 1990. Food, Economics and Entitlements. In *The Political Economy of Hunger, Vol. I. An Essay on Entitlement and Well-Being*, ed. Jean Dréze and Amartya Sen, 34–52. Oxford: Clarendon Press.

———. 1981. *Poverty and Famines. An Essay on Entitlement and Deprivation.* Oxford: Clarendon Press.

Shattuck, John. 1995. U.S. Commitment to Restoring Justice in Rwanda. State Department Press Briefing, Washington, DC, May 25, 1995. *Dispatch* 6(24): 499–500.

Shawcross, William. 1995. A Hero of Our Time. *New York Review of Books.* 42(19): 35–39.

Shinn, James. 1996. Conditional Engagement with China. In *Weaving the Net. Conditional Engagement with China*, ed. James Shinn, 3–95. New York: Council on Foreign Relations Press.

Shoumahoff, Alex. 1994. Flight from Death. *The New Yorker*, June 20: 44–55.

Simoska, Emilija. 1993. Macedonia and the Myths of the 'Muslim Conspiracy' and 'Endangered Orthodoxy.' In *The Social, Political and Cultural Role of the Muslim Communities in Post Bipolar Europe*, 95–101. Skopje, Macedonia: Center for Ethnic Relations, University of Exeter.

Singer, J. David and Michael D. Wallace, eds. 1979. *To Augur Well. Early Warning Indicators in World Politics*. Beverly Hills, CA: Sage.

Singer, Max and Aaron Wildawsky. 1993. *The Real World Order. Zones of Peace/ Zones of Turmoil*. Chatham, NJ: Chatham House Publishers.

Sislin, John. 1994. Arms as Influence: The Determinants of Successful Influence. *Journal of Conflict Resolution* 38(4): 665–89.

Smoke, Richard. 1977. *War: Controlling Escalation*. Cambridge, MA: Harvard University Press.

Smyth, Leo F. 1994. Intractable Conflicts and the Role of Identity. *Negotiation Journal* 10 (4): 311–21.

Soros, George. 1996. Conflict Prevention: Can We Meet the Challenge? Conflict Prevention Strategies to Sustain Peace in the Post–Cold War World. Washington, DC: The Aspen Institute.

Spencer, William J. 1994. Implications for Policy Use: Policy Uses of Early Warning Models and Data for Monitoring and Responding to Humanitarian Crises. *Journal of Ethno Development* 4(1): 111–15.

Stanley, Alessandra. 1995. Moscow Accused in Aid Worker's Killing. *The New York Times*, August 18.

Stapenhurst, Frederick. 1992. *Political Risk Analysis Around the North Atlantic*. New York: St. Martin's Press.

Statistical Office of Macedonia. 1994. *Data for the Present and the Future. First Results*. Communication 1, Skopje, Republic of Macedonia, November 14.

Stedman, Stephen John. 1996. Negotiation and Mediation in Internal Conflict. In *The International Dimensions of Internal Conflict*, ed. Michael E. Brown, 341–76. Cambridge, MA: The MIT Press.

Stein, Janice Gross. 1992. Deterrence and Compellence in the Gulf, 1990–91: A Failed or Impossible Task? *International Security* 17(2): 147–79.

Stokes, Gale. 1993. *The Walls Came Tumbling Down*. New York: Oxford University Press.

Therborn, Göran. 1991. Cultural Belonging, Structural Location and Human Action: Explanation in Sociology and Social Science. *Acta Sociologica* 34(3): 177–91.

Thibon, Christian. 1995. Les origines historiques de la violence politique au Burundi. In *Les Crises politiques au Burundi et au Rwanda (1993–1994)*, ed. André Guichaoua, 55–76. Paris: Karthala.

Thoolen, Hans. 1992. Information Aspects of Humanitarian Early Warning. In

Early Warning and Conflict Resolution, ed. Kumar Rupesinghe and Michiko Kuroda, 166–79. New York: St. Martin's Press.

Tomlinson, Rodney G. 1994. Converting Hindsight to Foresight, Building Theoretical Models of Genocides and Politicides: Some Ideas From the World Events/ Interaction Survey (WEIS). *Journal of Ethno Development* 4(1): 44–55.

Turnbridge, Louise. 1996. Burundi's 3-Year 'Campaign of Terror' Leaves a Bloody Trail on Its Campuses. *Chronicle of Higher Education* (42)49: A39.

United States Agency for International Development (USAID) 1995. Development Strategy for Macedonia, 1995–1997. Draft. Photocopy.

van der Donckt, Charles. 1995. The OAU's Conflict Management Mechanism Two Years On. *Pacific Research* 8(3): 42–45.

van der Stoel, Max. 1994. Plenary Meeting—Keynote Speech by Ambassador Max van der Stoel, CSCE High Commissioner on National Minorities. Seminar on Early Warning and Preventive Diplomacy. Consolidated Summary. 12–21 January 1994. Warsaw.

———. 1994a. Preventing Conflict and Building Peace: A Challenge for the CSCE. *NATO Review* 4.

Van Eck, Jan. 1996. The Role That Civil Society Initiatives Can Play in Strengthening the Process Leading to All-Inclusive Negotiations Through the Promotion of Conflict Resolution and Human Rights. United States Institute of Peace. Conference on Burundi. September 12. *http://www.usip.org/grants/burundi/bureck.htm* (accessed November 9, 1997).

Vansina, Jan. 1965. *Oral Tradition: A Study in Historical Methodology.* Chicago: Aldine Publishing Co.

———. 1998. The Politics of History and the Crisis in the Great Lakes. *Africa Today* 45(1): 37–44.

Vasquez, John A. 1993. *The War Puzzle.* Cambridge: Cambridge University Press.

Väyrynen, Raimo. 1993. Territory, Nation State and Nationalism. In *The Future of the Nation State in Europe*, ed. Jyrki Iivonen, 159–78. Aldershot: Edward Elgar.

———. 1994. Towards a Theory of Ethnic Conflicts and Their Resolution. Occasional Paper 6:OP:4. The Kroc Institute for International Peace Studies, University of Notre Dame.

———. 1995. Bipolarity, Multipolarity and Domestic Political Systems. *Journal of Peace Research* 32(3): 361–72.

———. 1996. Preventive Action: Failure in Yugoslavia. *International Peacekeeping* 3(4): 21–42.

———. 1997. Economic Incentives and the Bosnian Peace Process. In *The Price of Peace. Incentives and International Conflict Prevention*, ed. David Cortright, 155–79. Lanham, MD: Rowman and Littlefield.

Vilén, Heikki. 1996. Planning a Peace-keeping Mission for Nagorno Karabkh Conflict. *Security Dialogue* 27(1): 91–94.

Wagner, Michele Diane. 1991. *Whose History is History?: History of the Baragane People of Buragane, Southern Burundi, 1850–1932.* Ph.D. dissertation, University of Wisconsin.

Walker, Peter J.C. 1992. Famine Early Warning and Local Knowledge and the Resolution of Ethnic Conflict. In *Early Warning and Conflict Resolution,* ed. Kumar Rupensinghe and Michiko Kuroda, 87–103. New York: St. Martin's Press.

Wallensteen, Peter and Margareta Sollenberg. 1995. After the Cold War: Emerging Patterns of Armed Conflict 1989–94. *Journal of Peace Research* 32(3): 345–60.

Watson, Adam. 1982. *Diplomacy. The Dialogue between States.* London: Methuen.

Weinstein, Warren. 1975. Burundi, In *Civil Wars and the Politics of International Relief: Africa, South Asia and the Caribbean,* ed. Morris Davis. New York: Praeger Publishers.

———— and Robert Schrire. 1976. *Ethnical Conflict and Ethnic Strategies: A Case Study of Burundi.* Syracuse: Maxwell School of Citizenship and Public Affairs at Syracuse University.

Weiss, Thomas G. 1995. Overcoming the Somalia Syndrome — 'Operation Rekindle Hope?' *Global Governance* 1(2): 171–87.

Welsh, David. 1993. Domestic Politics and Ethnic Conflict. In *Ethnic Conflict and International Security,* ed. Michael Brown, 43–60. Princeton, NJ: Princeton University Press.

Wendt, Alexander E. 1987. The Agent-Structure Problem in International Relations Theory. *International Organization* 41(3): 335–70.

———— and Michael Barnett. 1993. Dependent State Formation and Third World Militarization. *Review of International Studies* 19: 321–347.

White, N.D. 1993. *Keeping Peace. The United Nations and the Maintenance of Peace and Security.* Manchester, IN: Manchester University Press.

Winnefeld, James and Mary E. Morris. 1994. *Where Environmental Concerns and Security Strategies Meet: Green Conflict in Asia and the Middle East.* Santa Monica, CA: Rand.

Woodward, Susan. 1995. Redrawing Borders in a Period of Systemic Transition. In *International Organizations and Ethnic Conflicts,* ed. Milton J. Esman and Shibley Telhami, 198–234. Ithaca, NY: Cornell University Press.

————. 1995a. *Balkan Tragedy: Chaos and Dissolution After the Cold War.* Washington, DC: Brookings Institution.

World Development Report 1995. Workers in an Integrating World. New York: The World Bank/Oxford University Press.

Zaagman, Rob. 1994. The CSCE High Commissioner on National Minorities: An Analysis of the Mandate and the Institutional Context. In *The Challenge of Change: The Helsinki Summit of the CSCE and its Aftermath,* ed. Arie Bloed, 113–75. Dordrecht: Martinus Nijhoff.

Zartman, I. William. 1991. Negotiations and Prenegotiations in Ethnic Conflict:

The Beginning, the Middle, and the Ends. In *Conflict and Peacemaking in Multiethnic Societies*, ed. Joseph Montville, 511–34. New York: D.C. Heath.

———, ed. 1995. *Collapsed States: The Disintegration and Restoration of Legitimate Authority.* Boulder, CO: Lynne Rienner.

———. 1997. Introduction: Toward the Resolution of International Conflicts. In *Peacemaking in International Conflict: Methods and Techniques*, ed. I. William Zartman and J. Lewis Rasmussen, 3–22. Washington, DC: United States Institute of Peace.

——— and Saadia Touval. 1992. Mediation: The Role of Third Party Diplomacy and Informal Peacemaking. In *Resolving Third World Conflict: Challenges for a New Era*, ed. Sheryl J. Brown and Kimber M. Schraub, 239–62. Washington, DC: United States Institute of Peace Press.

INDEX

Abdallah, Ahmedou Ould, 128, 143, 145, 190

Abiru, 137

Abrams, Jason S., 145

Accelerators, 74, 83

Afghanistan: as collapsed state, 82–83; institutional legitimacy, 70; and intervention costs, 16; Soviet policy in, 14, 111; U.S. sanctions against, 121*n*2; wealth per capita, 134

Africa: civilian armies in, 80; democratic socialization in, 187; and early warning, 4; and extremist youth groups, 143; and land scarcity, 54; legacy of colonialism, 185; negative effects of intervention in, 15; and positive incentives, 209; and strong civil societies, 23. *See also* specific countries

Africa Confidential, 144

Africa Watch, 209

African National Conference, 13

Agenda for Peace (Boutros-Ghali), 18, 37, 96

Agnew, John, 57, 61

Ahrens, Ambassador, 166, 170

Aideed, General, 214

Akashi, Yarushi, 165, 169

Albania: destabilization of, 174; factionalization of power in, 83; and Kosovo refugees, 169; and military coercion, 108; relationship with Macedonia, 153, 157; and UN troops, 165

Albanians: education of women, 152; in Kosovo, 62, 78; as minority in Macedonia, 149, 150–151, 154, 159–164, 176; and nationalism, 154–155; territorialism of, 57

Albert, Ethel, 137, 139

Alden, Chris, 114

Algeria, 190

Alker, Hayward R., 35

Alliance for Macedonia, 157

American Friends Service Committee, 193

Amisi, Bertha, 200

Amnesty International, 127

Amoo, Sam G., 190

Anderson, May B., 41

Anglo-Irish Agreement, 113

Angola, 14, 21, 56, 191

Anson, Hugo, 165, 169

Apartheid, 13, 81, 112. *See also* Black Apartheid

Arabism, 13

Archer, Clive, 165

Argentina, 197

Aristide, Jean Bertrande, 211, 213

Armenians, 61

Arusha Accords, 196, 205

ASEAN Regional Forum, 118

Atanasov, Peter, 168, 169, 177*n*6

Australia, 112

Auvinen, Juha, 66

Ayissi, Anatole, 118

Azar, Edward, 81

Background factors: and conflict indicators, 9; and early warning, 51–70; entitlements, 52–56; and escalation, 77–78; structural perspectives, 51–52, 68

Bagaza, Jean-Baptiste, 126, 142

Baldwin, David, 110, 111, 121n2

Balkans, 24, 62

Ball, Nicole, 114

Barnabé, Jean François, 137

ABOUT THE AUTHORS

JANIE LEATHERMAN is Assistant Professor of International Relations at Illinois State University. She has received numerous grants and published on international mediation and conflict early warning and prevention. Professor Leatherman has served as a consultant on these matters, including for the Council on Foreign Relations, the United Nations University, the United States Institute of Peace, and Catholic Relief Services. She is currently a member of the Helsinki for Africa international advisory committee at the Brookings Institution. She was previously a visiting Fellow and Visiting Assistant Professor at the University of Notre Dame and Macalester College.

WILLIAM DEMARS is Assistant Professor of Political Science at the American University in Cairo. He is writing a book, *Metamorphic Encounter: Warriors and Humanitarians in Africa,* that uses internal war in Ethiopia as a point of departure for analyzing how humanitarian NGOs make states, and how warriors transform international humanitarianism. His essays on changing roles of humanitarian NGOs have appeared in *Journal of Refugee Studies* and *Mershon International Studies Review.*

PATRICK D. GAFFNEY is Associate Professor and Chair of the Department of Anthropology and a Fellow of the Joan B. Kroc Institute of International Peace Studies at the University of Notre Dame. He has done extensive research on questions of religion and politics, social movements, and ritual authority in the Middle East with special attention to Egypt. More recently he has concentrated on issues of conflict resolution and human rights in Central Africa. From 1992 to 1994, he taught at a college in Jinja, Uganda, and he has continued to pursue these interests in subsequent field trips. In 1996 he was an Investigator with the United Nations Commission of Inquiry for Burundi and in 1997 he wrote the study of Burundi for the project of Humanitarian Emergencies sponsored by WIDER, the United Nations University in Helsinki. He has written a number of articles and reports and the book, *The Prophet's Pulpit, Islamic Preaching in Contemporary Egypt* (University of California Press, 1994).

RAIMO VÄYRYNEN is Professor of Government and International Studies at the University of Notre Dame and Senior Fellow of its Joan B. Kroc

Institute for International Peace Studies. From 1993 to 1998 he served as the Regan Director of the Institute. Since 1978 he has been Professor of International Relations at the University of Helsinki and from 1990 to 1993 served as Dean of the Faculty for Social Sciences. He has chaired the Finnish Political Science Association, Finnish Social Science Research Council, and the Nordic Committee on International Relations and has been a member of the Council of the United Nations University, the Nordic Council of Social Sciences, and the Committee for Social Sciences of the European Science Foundation. He has held visiting positions at Princeton University, Harvard University, MIT, and the University of Minnesota. Väyrynen has published extensively on the theory of international relations, international security and disarmament, international political economy, and peace and conflict studies. His most recent books are *New Directions in Conflict Theory: Conflict Resolution and Conflict Transformation* (Sage, 1991), *Military Industrialization and Economic Development* (Dartmouth Publishing, 1992), a biography of Urho Kekkonen (1994), and *Global Transformation: Economics, Politics, and Culture* (Finnish National Fund for Research and Development, 1997).